8/09

Newcastle
City Council

Newcastle Libraries and Information Service

☎ 0845 002 0336

Due for return	Due for return	Due for return
2 5 SEP 2009	0 8 OCT 2010	
	F24	
- 6 OCT 2009	H.3.6	
1 7 NOV 2009		
- 3 JUN 2010		
2 0 JUN 2010		
2 7 AUG 2010		
1 1 SEP 2010		

Please return this item to any of Newcastle's Libraries by the last
date shown above. If not requested by another customer the loan
can be renewed, you can do this by phone, post or in person.
Charges may be made for late returns.

MURDER
MOST FOUL

MURDER MOST FOUL

THE ROAD HILL HOUSE MYSTERY OF 1860

PAUL CHAMBERS

To John, Elizabeth and Sarah Baxter

First published 2009

The History Press
The Mill, Brimscombe Port
Stroud, Gloucestershire, GL5 2QG
www.thehistorypress.co.uk

British Library Cataloguing in Publication Data.
A catalogue record for this book is available from the British Library.

ISBN 978 0 7524 4873 2

Typesetting and origination by The History Press
Printed in Great Britain

CONTENTS

INTRODUCTION

'A crime has just been committed which for mystery, complication of probabilities and hideous wickedness is without parallel in our criminal records.' These were the words of a journalist who, in July 1860, had just been confronted with the bizarre and tragic circumstances surrounding the disappearance and murder of three-year-old Francis Kent from Road Hill House, a grand but lonely building situated in rural Wiltshire.

The Road Hill House mystery, as the case quickly became known, was one of the most perplexing enigmas in Victorian Britain. The known facts of the murder read like the plot from an Agatha Christie novel. The child had been taken from a room where two other people were sleeping, within a house that was shuttered and barred from the inside. It was evident that this must have been an inside job, and just three of the nine adults asleep in the house that night did not have an alibi. Each of these three suspects had an apparent motive and the means to commit the crime; but which was the murderer?

The case appeared straightforward, but within days the police found themselves tied in knots with contradictory evidence from the mysterious Kent family, who appeared to be covering up a dark secret from their past. The ensuing police investigation became legendary for its mismanagement, incompetence, infighting and corruption. No fewer than three police forces, including Scotland Yard's Detective Department, became involved, as well as various government ministers, magistrates, amateur detectives and interfering lawyers. All were defeated by the continual twists and turns that afflicted the case as it progressed, ensuring that, as the spotlight shifted from one suspect to another, so some new piece of evidence would emerge to steer the investigation in a different direction.

It is little surprise that the public's interest in the Road Hill House mystery became frenzied, with acres of newsprint being devoted to the latest developments and to the publication of theories as who murdered little Francis and what their motives may have been. It was *the* conundrum of its time, and the murder went on to influence the writings of several authors, including Charles Dickens and Wilkie Collins. The police were forced to admit defeat, but the case was eventually solved, and in a most surprising and unexpected way. The Road Hill House mystery was, and remains, a very real tragedy, and it is in every sense larger than life and stranger than fiction.

I first encountered the Road Hill House mystery while reading Wilkie Collin's *The Moonstone*, a novel whose core is built around the events associated with the murder and its subsequent investigation. Out of curiosity I obtained copies of the police notes, court transcripts, newspaper articles and other documents associated with the case and started to assemble the information they contained into chronological order. I ended up with a written calendar of events which offered a day-by-day (and often minute-by-minute) account of the movements and actions of everybody associated with the case over a period of several months. The level of available detail from these contemporary documents means that it is possible to read actual spoken dialogue and even descriptions of people's thoughts and emotions. This is quite remarkable, especially considering that nearly a century and half has passed since the murder took place.

I was transfixed by the story and wanted to write about it, but rather than provide a straightforward commentary on the case, as has been done in the past, I wanted to impart a sense of the drama and mystery that would have titillated Victorian bystanders at the time. To accomplish this, I decided to tell the story of the Road Hill House murder in chronological order and from the standpoint of somebody who would have had knowledge of the investigation and its associated events but who would not have known its solution. In structuring the book this way I hope that it has been possible to instil the sense of mystery, bewilderment and frustration felt by many at the time (but especially the police), while at the same time offering the reader an opportunity to solve the crime for themselves before the solution is given at the end of the book.

Those who have been kind enough to read through the draft manuscript have commented that it reads like a novel. In fact, the vivid descriptions and dialogue are not the result of novelisation, but instead reflect the detailed nature of the documentary evidence associated with the case. I have taken no liberties with the source material: all the dialogue, descriptions, emotional outbursts and other events originate from first-hand testimony and are fully referenced. It is my greatest desire that whoever picks this book up should enjoy reading it as much as I have enjoyed researching and writing it.[1]

ACKNOWLEDGEMENTS

My profound thanks go to all those people who were kind enough to offer me their time, advice and knowledge during the time it took to research and write this book. In particular I should like to thank the staff at the following institutions for allowing me access to their records and for their patience when answering my many questions: The British Library; British Newspaper Library; Cambridge University Library; Family Records Centre (The National Archives); Guildhall Library, London; The National Archives; Institute of Historical Research; Royal Historical Society; Society of Genealogists; and University College London, the Wellcome Library.

A big thank-you must go to my agents, Sugra Zaman, Isabel Atherton and Mandy Little of Watson, Little for their sound advice and for their continued nurturing of my career. I should also like to offer my thanks to Christopher Feeney of Sutton Publishing and Simon Hamlet and the other staff at The History Press for their help and advice during the production process.

Finally, I could not have undertaken this project without the support of my immediate and extended family, but especially my father, Martyn Chambers, and my parents-in-law, John and Elizabeth Baxter. However, my greatest debt is to my wife Rachel and daughter Eleanor, whose humour and sense of fun soon remove the mental strains that come from sitting in front of computer all day: my love for you is without end.

SATURDAY 30 JUNE 1860

It was the sight of a breathless teenage boy running at full speed down the road that caught Thomas Benger's attention. He knew the lad to be John Alloway, a local gardener's boy, but Benger had never seen him move so fast, nor with such a look of concern upon his face. Benger watched as Alloway ran past his cottage and, as his footsteps faded, returned to work on his smallholding. A few minutes later there was another commotion in the road, this time caused by a clattering of hooves coming down the hill leading into the small village of Road where Benger lived.

Looking up, Benger saw a four-wheeled Brougham carriage being pulled along by a ready horse. At the reigns was the stout, whiskered figure of Samuel Kent, the occupant of Road Hill House, a large manorial-looking building located a few hundred yards uphill from the village. It had been his gardener's boy that Benger had seen running past and, like him, Mr Kent wore the same look of concern upon his face. Walking in the opposite direction were the village's two policemen, James Morgan and Alfred Urch; on seeing them Mr Kent drew his carriage to a halt.

'What do you want with us?' asked constable Morgan, whom Mr Kent's gardener's boy had roused a few minutes earlier.

'I have had my little boy stolen,' said Mr Kent. 'I am on my way to Trowbridge to fetch a senior policeman.'

'You need go no further than Southwick,' said Morgan, 'as the policeman there will forward the news to the Trowbridge station, and you may return back here as soon as possible.'

'I shall go on,' said Kent, 'I will not begrudge ten pounds if the child can be found.' With this the carriage set off into the village, leaving the two policemen to trudge the short distance uphill to Mr Kent's residence.

It was just before eight o'clock in the morning, and even though Benger had only been at work for a short while, he was attracted by the idea of the ten pounds reward, and so, dropping his tools, he started to follow the two constables uphill. Benger had not travelled far before he met with William Nutt, a cobbler who lived by the village church. Nutt had also heard of the missing child and, although he was not overly fond of Samuel Kent, had decided to put aside his personal feelings and join with the search. The men exchanged pleasantries before making their way towards Road Hill House, checking the roadside verges for any sign of the missing boy as they did so.

Other villagers had also noticed the commotion and were looking out from their windows or chatting to one another across their front gates and hedges. The news was travelling fast and it was soon common knowledge that the missing child was Mr Kent's three-year-old son Francis, who had not been seen since the previous evening.

Thomas Benger and William Nutt were among the first to arrive at the large iron gates that guarded the driveway to Road Hill House. Ahead of them they could see constables Morgan and Urch who, with various members of the Kent household, were engaged in the search for young Francis. Benger and Nutt assumed that the boy must have escaped from his nursery during the night and hidden himself somewhere in the landscaped grounds that were attached to the property.

Road Hill House was a familiar sight to the residents of Road village. It was a large residence set in its own grounds on top of a low hill that overlooked the small hamlet of around a hundred people, including Benger, Nutt and Morgan. The main house was separated from the highway by an area of lawn and a semi-circular driveway that led from the road past the ornate front door. The house was three storeys high with tall, semi-circular windows, a portico and a host of outbuildings, including a stable, coach house, sheds and a walled yard. Being only sixty years old and dressed with classic ashlar Georgian stonework, Road Hill House was considered to be a modern and imposing building by the villagers, most of who could see it from their windows or gardens.

Since the arrival of Samuel Kent and his family in 1855, Road Hill House had picked up something of a poor reputation locally. It was quickly observed that the Kent family enjoyed a high turnover of servants, with some estimating that nearly a hundred cooks, housemaids, gardeners and nursemaids had come and gone in only five years. More unnerving was Samuel Kent's obvious dislike for his neighbours and the unusual behaviour exhibited by some of his elder children. The Kent family were often the subject of gossip, and Road Hill House was generally a place to be avoided, but as news of the missing boy spread, so people put their prejudices aside and started to make their way up the hill.

Standing at the gates, William Nutt expressed reservations to Benger about setting foot on the property. He was mindful that his father had been prosecuted for trespass by Mr Kent only a couple of years previously.

'No-one could be angry with us for looking for the lost child,' said Benger, who suggested that they begin by searching the patch of garden to the left of the driveway. This was a broad, curving area of recently mown grass that played host to several mature trees, and which was separated from the road by a thick hedge. To Benger's way of thinking it was an ideal place for a young boy to hide and so he, with the still-reluctant Nutt, began to search among the shrubs in the area furthest from the house.

After only a few minutes Nutt paused and, filled with a sudden feeling of dread, said to Benger, 'If we can't find a living child, then I think we should be looking for a dead one.' Benger dismissed this idea but his friend continued on: 'If the child was taken from the house, it was taken for some unfair play. I think we should search inside the water closet.'

Benger was bemused, especially as Nutt had earlier expressed reservations about setting foot inside the grounds at all, but he agreed to move their search to the Kent's outside lavatory, which was located a short distance away, immediately opposite the right-hand side of the house. The privy closet was small and set into a tall wall that enclosed an adjoining yard. It was Nutt who, on opening the door, noticed the large pool of blood that lay on the bare earth floor in the closet's left-hand corner.

'Oh Benger, it is as I predicted,' said Nutt, stepping back from the privy door. His friend, however, was concentrating on the lavatory itself: 'I think there is something in there,' he said. 'William, fetch me a light.'

Nutt made his way across the yard to the kitchen, where his pallid complexion gave him away. 'For God's sake whatever is the matter?' asked the charwoman, before directing him to the cook for a candle. Nutt returned to the privy and held the light above the seat, while Benger reached his arm into the pit below. His hand closed on something.

'Oh William, here it is,' he said, pulling the object into the light. It was a blanket, small, rectangular and covered in blood. Benger put his hand back into the toilet and grasped a much larger object. 'Here is the dear little thing,' he said, gently withdrawing a young boy's body feet-first from the hole. Benger handled the body delicately, but as the child's head emerged it flopped first sideways then backwards, revealing a deep cut to the throat. The child had been murdered: it was an horrific fulfilment of Nutt's earlier prediction of foul play.

Too shocked to say anything, Nutt spread the blanket onto the floor. Benger lowered little Francis's body to the ground, gently wrapping it inside the blanket. He noticed that the eyes were shut and that, to his surprise, the child looked peaceful and 'quite pleasant'. The little bundle was lifted into Benger's arms and carried silently around the back of the house and into the kitchen, where some of the household were gathered awaiting news. To the disbelief of all, the body was placed on the kitchen table, where the staff were able to confirm that this was indeed Francis Kent, the missing boy. This revelation alone was shocking, but the obvious violent manner of the boy's death raised a frightening possibility: that somebody in the village, and maybe within the Kents' own household, had kidnapped and murdered a helpless three-year-old child.[2]

At the exact time of Benger and Nutt's horrific discovery Samuel Kent was travelling at speed along the turnpike road towards Trowbridge, the closest large town to Road.

At the village of Southwick he reached the tollbooth, which was manned by an ageing lady named Ann Hall. As he paid his toll Mr Kent asked her where the nearest policeman was located; she told him that he needed Henry Heritage, the Southwick village constable, but Hall was a curious sort and asked Kent what the trouble was.

'I have had a child stolen and carried off in a blanket,' replied Kent.

'When did you lose it?' enquired Hall.

'This morning, and if you see anyone coming you are to stop them!' With that he carried on into Southwick in search of the policeman's house, but the woman's directions proved difficult to follow and so Mr Kent resorted to paying a local lad to show him the way. On reaching the policeman's house Kent was greeted by the constable's wife, Ann Heritage, who had watched him draw up outside.

'Is your husband at home?' demanded Kent.

'He is in bed.'

'You must call him up. I have had a child stolen out of my house tonight, or rather, we missed him at five o'clock this morning. He is a little boy aged three years and ten months, supposedly taken out of the drawing room window.'

On hearing this Mrs Heritage showed more interest. 'Have they taken any clothes, sir?'

'No, wrapped up in a blanket. Tell your husband that he must get up immediately and make every enquiry. I am going to Trowbridge to give information to Superintendent Foley.' With that, and without having ever left his carriage, Kent set off again.

It took him a further fifteen minutes to reach Trowbridge, and thereafter a little more time to find John Foley, who, as a superintendent in the Wiltshire County Constabulary, was the most senior officer in the district. Foley understood the urgency of the situation and agreed to come as soon as possible; he instructed Mr Kent to return home immediately to help direct the search for his son.

Kent set off back towards Road, but did not get far before a carriage travelling in the opposite direction waved him down. Inside was the Reverend Edward Peacock, the clergyman from Road village and a personal friend of Mr Kent. Peacock had heard about the missing child and had gone directly to Road Hill House, only to discover that the boy's body had been found. He then set off in pursuit of Mr Kent and, on finding him, decided to break the painful news about his son's fate.

'I have bad news for you,' said Peacock. 'The little boy has been found murdered.'

There was little more to be said and so, at Mr Kent's insistence, the friends parted company. Kent continued on to Road Hill, while Peacock travelled to Trowbridge to find Superintendent Foley. On reaching the Southwick toll gate Mrs Hall greeted him cheerfully.

'Then, sir, the child is found?'

Kent did not even slow his carriage, but shouted to her, 'Yes, and murdered.'[3]

In Samuel Kent's absence, and in the light of the discovery of Francis's body, Road Hill House had descended into a state of mild panic. The terrible news had travelled widely and attracted a couple of dozen villagers to the house, some of whom were wandering the grounds in search of clues, while others tried to elucidate information from the staff.

In the absence of a senior police officer, the village constables, Alfred Urch and James Morgan, had taken charge as best they could. On seeing the small boy's body laid out in the kitchen they immediately despatched Mr Kent's fourteen-year-old son William to fetch a surgeon from the neighbouring village of Beckington. They then attempted to make sense of the novel situation in which they had unwittingly found themselves.

Constables Morgan and Urch had arrived at Road Hill House before the boy's body had been discovered, and had started to make their enquiries into what was then simply a missing person case. They questioned the household servants but none had the faintest idea where the boy had gone or who might have kidnapped him, if anyone. When asked how the child might have been removed from the building, Sarah Cox, the Kents' housemaid, was more forthcoming, and insisted that the two constables accompany her to the drawing room, located at the rear of the house.

The room was rectangular with a large semi-circular bay window, but its dominant feature was a row of three full-length windows which looked out across the manicured lawns that ran downhill towards a small river. The windows were of a heavy sash type and had shutters that could be secured from the inside with a broad bar that went across their width. Both men observed that, while two of the windows were closed and had their shutters fastened, the left-hand window had been opened to leave a gap of a few inches, and that the bar that kept its shutters closed had been removed. Sarah Cox explained that she had closed the windows and fastened the shutters herself the previous evening and was certain that they were secure when she went to bed.

'When I came down the next morning,' said Cox to the constables, 'I went to the drawing room, as I always did, and found the door, which I had left fastened the previous night, opened. I went into the room and found the upper shutter closed, but not fastened, and the window opened a little bit.'

As she had discovered this scene before learning that little Francis was missing, Cox thought little of it. However, when the alarm was raised Cox showed Mr Kent the open window; he immediately assumed that this was evidence of a break-in and that it must have been an intruder that had taken his son, but Cox was not so sure.

'No-one could come into the house through the drawing room window without breaking the glass, making a hole in the shutters, and bursting open the door,' she explained to the policemen. 'The bolt was back and the lock turned. The furniture was not displaced and there were no marks of force, as if anyone had broken in.'

Cox insisted that the entire house had been securely locked and bolted the night before and that there was no sign of forced entry anywhere. The implication was obvious: if the house had been locked up, and the drawing room door and shutters could only be opened from the inside, then whoever had opened the window must have been inside the house before it was locked up. This meant that the windows could only have been opened by an intruder if they had first hidden themselves in the house or, more disturbingly, that they were opened by a member of the Kent household.

The thought that someone inside the house might have broken out of the building led Morgan and Urch to ask whether they could be shown the nursery from where Francis had been taken. Cox led them into the hallway and up the stairs to the first floor where, across a landing, they were greeted by a young, attractive woman with long jet-black hair. She introduced herself as Elizabeth Gough, the family's nursemaid. It had been Gough's job to care for the Kents' two youngest children: Francis, the missing three-year-old boy, and his twenty-month-old sister Eveline. It was from her bedroom that Francis had been taken, while she lay sleeping only a few feet away.

'Can you show us the child's bed?' asked constable Urch. Gough pointed through the doorway behind her and into the nursery. At the far end of the room, to the right of the single window and pushed up against the wall, was a small cot. Gough led Morgan and Urch over to the cot; the two men spent a few moments studying it, aware that something was not quite right.

'Do you mean to say that this is where he was?' asked Morgan.

'Yes,' replied Gough.

The cot looked pristine. The counterpane and upper sheet were pulled close to the pillow and had been turned down neatly towards the foot of the bed. They were smooth and looked unslept in, as though someone had just made the bedclothes afresh. Gough reached across and turned back the top sheets to reveal where the boy had lain; there was a depression where the boy's head had rested on the pillow and, further down the bed, signs of where his body had been. Both men thought that the bed looked far too neat and suspected that somebody had re-made it following the boy's disappearance, but Gough denied that this was the case. She claimed that the bed was in that state when she awoke and that no-one had interfered with it since.

'At what time did you miss the child?' asked Urch, who was the more experienced of the two policemen.

'I saw he was gone at five o'clock, but I did not make any enquiries for him till seven,' replied the nurse.

'Why ever not?'

'I thought that Mrs Kent had heard the child cry during the night and had come and taken him away.'

'Has Mrs Kent done this before?'

'No,' replied Gough, 'not in my time here, but I heard that Mrs Kent had done so when the other nurse was here.'

Satisfied with this, the two men left Gough in the nursery and went downstairs to search for any signs of an intruder. They examined the drawing room again, but, as the housekeeper had predicted, could find no signs of violent entry. They moved outside and examined the section of lawn that led away from the opened window; they were looking for footprints, but the ground was dry and none could be seen. It was while he was at the back of the house that Urch spotted Thomas Benger walking solemnly towards the kitchen door. In his hands was the bloodied blanket containing Francis Kent's body.[4]

By nine o'clock in the morning the body of young Francis Kent had lain on the kitchen table for just over half an hour. News of his horrific death had reached all members of the Kent household, with the exception of Samuel Kent's wife Mary, the mistress of the house, who was eight months pregnant and as such was considered too fragile to handle the news. It had been decided that it should be up to Mr Kent to break the news of Francis's murder to his wife on his return from Trowbridge. Meanwhile, Elizabeth Gough had been despatched to Mary Kent's bedroom to keep her company; while there she dressed her mistress's hair, but the conversation was dominated by the subject of Francis.

'I hope that the child has merely been stolen and has not been harmed,' said Mrs Kent to the nursemaid. On hearing this Gough could contain herself no longer and in a fit of emotion cried out: 'Oh, ma'am, it's revenge!'

Downstairs other members of staff, and some of that morning's visitors, had gathered in the kitchen. Occasionally one of the female servants would approach Francis's body, lean over it and gently kiss the forehead. The menfolk would occasionally and briefly enter the kitchen to check on the situation before leaving to go outside again: most of them continued to search the grounds for any further evidence. Of especial interest was the area surrounding the water closet where it was presumed that the murder must have taken place.

John Alloway, the gardener's boy who had earlier run into the village to alert Morgan, was engaged in searching around the bushes to the left of the lavatory door when he spotted a scrap of paper lying on the ground. Looking closer, he saw what he thought was blood and, nervous of touching it, drew the attention of Edward West, an aged gentleman who lived in one the cottages opposite Road Hill House.

'Don't destroy the paper,' said West to the boy. 'Pick it up and take care of it. It will be the means of bringing about a discovery.'

The boy did as he was told and reached down: it was a torn piece of newspaper, about five inches square, that had been folded in two. On opening it out Alloway saw a smeared bloody impression that went along the entire length of the paper; the blood pattern on either side of the fold was symmetrical, exactly as if somebody had wiped a knife clean with it. There could be little doubt that this horrific object was connected with the boy's murder. Young John Alloway felt uneasy and handed the bloodied paper to the person next to him, a butcher named Stephen Millett.

Presently, Samuel Kent's carriage drew up in the stable yard behind the house. He entered the house via the rear entrance and was concerned to discover that his dead son had been laid out on the kitchen table in full view of staff and visitors; he ordered that the body be removed to the laundry room. This having been done, Mr Kent locked the door and placed the key in his pocket for safe keeping. Almost immediately his son William entered the house in the company of Joshua Parsons, the family surgeon; William did not know whether his mother had been told of Francis's death and so he took Parsons into the back of the house via the kitchen and asked him to wait inside the library. A short while later Parsons was joined by Mr Kent and, following an exchange of condolences, it was agreed that Parsons should examine Francis's body. Mr Kent could not face looking at his son's injured remains and, after taking the surgeon to the laundry room door, gave him the key and asked him to proceed alone.

Parsons entered the laundry room, where he was confronted with Francis's body stretched out on a table and bathed in the light from a single window. Parsons knew that he could not at that stage touch the body or its clothing without the express consent of a coroner, but, as the only doctor on the scene, his task was to confirm that Francis was dead. Only after death had been established could a coroner be informed and thereafter a post mortem examination (sometimes called an autopsy) ordered. Parsons was the Kents' family doctor and had last seen the boy alive only a few days previously; the sight that greeted him in the laundry was distressing and the memories remained with him for some time afterwards. Parsons recalled:

I found the body of the child wrapped in a blanket. The blanket was covered with stains of blood and with old soil from the place it had been taken from. There were considerable stains, but not a large quantity of blood on the blanket itself. The child had a nightgown and flannel shirt on. They were both much soiled with blood and soil from the privy – not from the child. I found some wounds upon the child. The first I observed was upon the throat. It was a clean incision, which severed the whole of the structures down to the bone, the skin, muscles, etc., all being severed. The wound was from the left to the right. It must have been a very sharp knife with a long blade to produce such a cut. It appeared to be one cut. A considerable amount of blood had flowed from the left angle of the wound down the arm to the elbow. I observed black marks near the mouth. The tongue protruded between the teeth, so as to be visible between the lips, and it appeared to be of a dark colour and livid. It was just visible between the lips.

There was little doubt that the boy had met his end in an unnecessarily violent manner. Parsons estimated that at least five or six hours had passed since the point of death which made the time of the murder at around two or three o'clock that morning. Parsons withdrew from the laundry, ordered that the room be kept locked, and then spoke with Mr Kent. It was imperative, said Parsons, that the coroner be informed of the situation so that a post mortem examination could be started as soon as possible; until such time the body must not be touched by anybody, including the police and any members of the family.

Accordingly a rider was sent to Trowbridge to speak with George Sylvester, a retired surgeon who acted as the coroner for the Bradford-upon-Avon district, in whose jurisdiction Road village lay. Parsons suspected that the seventy-four-year-old Sylvester would not journey out to witness the examination of the body for himself, and so he requested that another surgeon be summoned to act as his assistant. While he awaited news from the coroner, Parsons headed off into the main part of the house, where he wanted to make some enquiries of his own.[5]

By ten o'clock Road Hill House contained four policemen: constables Morgan and Urch, who had been first to arrive; Henry Heritage, the constable from Southwick village; and Superintendent John Foley of the Wiltshire County Constabulary, who had been summoned by Mr Kent and was by far the most senior officer present.

Morgan and Urch had been on the scene for over an hour by the time Heritage and Foley arrived, and so were able to divulge a certain amount of information to the officers. As a consequence both Foley and Heritage went to the laundry to view the boy's body for themselves and afterwards agreed that they should split up in order to pursue different lines of enquiry. Constable Heritage was to search for the murder weapon, and so he went directly into the garden to examine the garden tools and knives, while Foley went upstairs to interview Elizabeth Gough, who had returned to the nursery. There Foley was shown Francis's cot and, like his colleagues, was struck by the neatness of the bedclothes. He began to question Gough intensely on the matter.

'I covered the child with a quilt, blanket and sheet,' said the nurse, explaining that when putting Francis to bed the night before she had tucked the quilt and sheet into the sides, but that the smaller blanket had been placed between the sheet and quilt, where it would have been entirely hidden from sight. 'When I woke I found the quilt and sheet turned back and the child and blanket taken up.'

In response to further questions, Gough recounted again how she had first missed the child at five in the morning, but had thought that Mrs Kent had taken him. She showed Foley where she and the young girl Eveline had slept the night before. Foley noticed that Gough's bed was pushed up against the wall opposite the door with the little girl's bed directly alongside it. To have reached Francis, the murderer would have had to open the door, walk past Gough's bed and then cross the length of the nursery to the cot without making a noise. They would then have had to remove the boy, smoothing the sheets afterwards, and then get him from the room, all without waking either the nurse or Eveline. It seemed a near-impossible feat and immediately led Foley to place the nursemaid on his list of suspects.

When asked if she had noticed anything odd during the night, Gough insisted that she had not woken until five o'clock. This seemed a little far-fetched to Foley, but he decided to leave the matter for the time being and went downstairs, where Sarah Cox showed him the open drawing room window and shutter.

The housemaid once again explained the open window's significance, alerting Foley to the possibility that the murder had been committed by someone inside the house. With this in mind he went through to the kitchen and asked to see the cook's knives, of which there were nearly two dozen. Foley examined each blade and handle carefully, but could find nothing incriminating, such as blood, upon them. He was then told that the knives had been cleaned and sharpened first thing that morning by John Alloway, the gardener's boy. There was nothing suspicious in this: the knives were cleaned and sharpened every morning, but it meant that any trace of blood would have been removed in the process.

With his preliminary examination of the inside of the house finished, Foley turned his attention to the probable murder scene. He walked through the stable yard to the water closet, which had remained out of bounds on the instructions of Morgan and Urch. Peering inside, Foley could see little apart from the bloodstain that had first attracted the attention of Benger and Nutt. He got onto his knees and placed his head close to the lavatory seat in an attempt to see into the gloomy cesspit below; in doing so he found that his view was partially obscured by a short wooden plank that had been fixed beneath the seat in a slanting direction, so that its free edge came within six inches of the back wall of the privy. The plank evidently acted as a splashboard, but the constriction it created had trapped Francis's body, preventing it from falling directly into the pool of sewage below. Had the splashboard not been there, then the body would have sunk into the waste material, where it could have remained hidden for hours or even days before being found.

No further evidence could be discerned from the splashboard itself, but in the half-light Foley fancied that he could see an object resting on the semi-liquid surface of the cesspit, about three feet below the seat. He left the privy and grabbed the attention of a passing servant: 'Fetch me a crook,' he demanded.

A few minutes later saw Foley enter the water closet with a long stick to which he had fixed a hook. He carefully inserted the stick into the cesspit, angling it into the narrow gap between the splashboard and the base. With great skill the superintendent was able to manoeuvre his makeshift crook so that it first hooked the object and then gently lifted it away from the surface and back into the closet.

Foley unhooked it and, with the aid of sunlight, was able to see that it was a piece of flannel about ten inches square. Turning it over in his hands, he was able to observe that there was a good quantity of blood on it.

'The piece of flannel appeared to have been very recently there,' recalled Foley later. 'There was no soil [i.e. sewage] upon it. The blood had penetrated the flannel, but it appeared to have dropped so gently that it had congealed drop by drop as it fell. It was still fluid. The blood was principally in the centre, as though it had dropped on it.' The presence of blood made the flannel of interest, but whether it was relevant to the murder could not yet be determined. There was, after all, the possibility that the cloth had been in there for some time before the boy's death, with the blood having dripped on to it from above. It occurred to Foley that the cesspit might contain further evidence and that it would have to be drained and searched. This was not the sort of a task he wanted to trouble himself with, so he decided to await the arrival of a junior officer into whose hands this smelly operation could be passed.[6]

Since his arrival at Road Hill House Superintendent Foley had made a strenuous effort to stamp his authority on what had hitherto been a chaotic and disjointed crime scene. Alarmed at the number of bystanders who had been attracted to the house, Foley ordered that a cordon to be placed around the whole of the estate with only essential personnel being allowed through. On learning this, Mr Kent suggested to Foley that he might want to extend the cordon to include a ramshackle group of dwellings directly opposite his house which was known locally as 'the Rookery.' The relationship between Mr Kent and his immediate neighbours was not good, and he had already been heard to suggest that one of the Rookery's residents might be the person who had murdered his son.

'That is where the murderer will be found,' Mr Kent said to the superintendent, 'or at least some clue to his discovery.'

Superintendent Foley declined Mr Kent's advice; despite having been on the scene for only a few hours, Foley was certain that the killer had not broken into the house from the outside but had originated from within. To this end he had begun to conduct interviews with the staff and family members, but thus far they had resulted in little useful information. The interviewees were for the most part shocked and emotional, as might be expected, but they also seemed to be on their guard and gave every impression of being wary of the police. Despite repeated questioning, Foley could not persuade any of the household to accept that the murder could have been committed by anyone other than an intruder. The family gave the names of neighbours and former employees whose dealings with Mr Kent might have caused them to seek retribution on his youngest son, but would not for a moment consider that someone from within the house could be responsible.

By midday there was a clear difference of opinion operating between the police and the Kent family, the effect of which was to make the attending policemen feel wholly unwelcome at Road Hill House, even though they were investigating the brutal murder of one of the Kents' own children.

The atmosphere became even more tense when, just before lunch, Mr Kent's solicitor, Rowland Rodway, arrived from Trowbridge. A short while earlier he had received word that his services might be required and had travelled immediately to Road. Superintendent Foley was not happy to learn that Mr Kent had an attorney present, but rather than take Mr Rodway directly to see his client, Foley took him to one side to complain about the family's behaviour.

'I do not feel as though we have the full range of the house,' said Foley, complaining that thus far Mr Kent had neglected to give him or his men permission to go about their business as they saw fit. This made the task of searching the house and interviewing the staff very difficult: Mr Kent had even stopped the police from drawing up a plan of the house, saying that it was an intrusion into his privacy. Rodway promised to rectify the situation and left Foley to find Mr Kent; a few minutes later the solicitor returned with the news that Mr Kent had surrendered 'himself and everything in the house, together with every member of his family and household, to the control of the police'. Rodway also promised that Mr Kent would instruct his friends to help the police in any way they could. With this matter resolved to his satisfaction, Foley began to act more assertively and immediately embarked on a detailed examination of the property.

By lunchtime Superintendent Foley was certain that the murderer was not an intruder, or indeed even a stranger, but was most probably a member of the Kent family or one of their servants. Shortly afterwards the surgeon Joshua Parsons observed that, given the nature of the wound to the neck, whoever had committed the crime ought to have been drenched in arterial blood. Foley suspected that the bloodstained clothing worn by the assailant would still be on the premises and so he asked Parsons to accompany him while he examined all the wardrobes and chest of draws in the house. The search was systematic, going from bedroom to bedroom with one or both men checking through the various chests of draws, cupboards and linen baskets. Every garment was examined for signs of fresh or dried blood and each person was asked to point out the bedclothes they had worn the previous night.

The search began on the first floor with Mr and Mrs Kent's bedroom, which they shared with their five-year-old daughter Mary Amelia. It then moved on to the nursery, which had been occupied by Elizabeth Gough, the murdered boy and twenty-month-old Eveline. In neither room was anything suspicious found. On the second floor they searched five more bedrooms, including one shared by Mr Kent's two eldest daughters, Elizabeth (aged twenty-eight) and Mary Ann (aged twenty-seven), and another shared by the cook, Sarah Kerslake, and the housekeeper, Sarah Cox. There was a spare room and, finally, two smaller, single rooms used by Mr Kent's eldest son William (aged fifteen) and his daughter Constance (aged sixteen), both of whom had slept alone and claimed to have heard nothing unusual during the night.

In none of these rooms was there any evidence that could be related to the boy's murder, but the exercise was not a total failure: during his tour of the house Foley had been able to narrow down his list of likely suspects to just three. He did so by excluding the two youngest children (Eveline and Mary Amelia) and those sharing a bedroom, all of whom vouched for their roommate's whereabouts during the night. This left just the nursemaid Gough, from whose room Francis had been taken, and William and Constance Kent, both of whom had returned to the house from boarding school two weeks previously. Gough, William and Constance were the only adults to have occupied rooms on their own and all were without an alibi: they were immediately placed at the top of Foley's list of suspects.[7]

It was gone midday when further police reinforcements started to arrive and a more thorough examination of Road Hill House could begin. The tedious task of searching the cesspit beneath the water closet had been handed to Constable William Dallimore who had arrived from the Trowbridge constabulary. He quickly delegated this job to Benjamin Fricker, a local handyman and sometime plumber who had come to Road Hill House offering his help after lunch. Fricker started to dismantle the water closet, but he was having trouble seeing anything in the gloom and, desiring a light, went to the kitchen, where he found Elizabeth Gough standing with Constable Dallimore's wife Eliza. Fricker asked Gough to provide him with a candle.

'What have you been doing, Fricker?' demanded Gough sharply.

'I've been opening the water closet,' he replied.

'And have you found anything?'

'No.'

'Then you won't!' said Gough roughly, before handing him a candle.

Fricker, together with another man, successfully opened the water closet, but was dismayed to see that the pit was disproportionately large for a domestic privy, it being about seven feet square and around ten feet deep. It was also quite full. The level of effluvia was measured at around six feet, all of which had to be removed manually and then sieved for any physical evidence. This was not an easy nor a pleasant task, and it took Fricker the best part of the afternoon to complete. It had been Foley's hope that the murder weapon would be found at the bottom of the cesspit, but as the last buckets of sewage were lifted away, it was evident that the murderer had not seen fit to throw anything of use down the lavatory other than the boy's body, the blanket and possibly a piece of flannel. It was a dead end, but the search of Road Hill House had only just begun.

Around mid-afternoon Constable Dallimore was asked to summon his wife Eliza from Trowbridge to assist in the investigation. The request came from Foley who, having found nothing incriminating on the clothing of the staff and family, wanted someone to make a personal examination of all those resident the night before. Foley reckoned that, while the killer could have already hidden or destroyed their bloodied clothing, they might not have had a chance to wash any incriminating evidence from themselves. He wanted the house servants, but not any members of the Kent family, to be examined for any spots of blood that might have splashed onto their hair or exposed areas of skin, such as the face, or had soaked through their clothing onto the body. This meant performing a strip-search which, in the absence of any women police officers (the first would not appear in Britain until 1916), had to be performed on the female residents by a serving policeman's wife.

Eliza Dallimore arrived at Road Hill House at around four o'clock and was only too glad to help. She took a keen interest in her husband's work and, to judge by her behaviour, already had some experience of searching and interviewing suspects in criminal cases. On arrival she was asked not only to examine the servants, but also to re-check their nightclothes both for signs of blood, and also to see if they had recently been changed. She was told to begin with Elizabeth Gough, who was waiting in the first-floor nursery.

Before reaching the nursery Mrs Dallimore had already been briefed about the nature of the crime and was primed to be on the look-out for anything suspicious. She was an observant woman and on entering the nursery she noticed that the door made a creaking noise when opened. Given that the killer was meant to have opened the door and crept past the sleeping Elizabeth Gough without waking her, this seemed odd. 'Perhaps anyone accustomed to the door might with care have opened it without making a noise,' she later told her husband, 'but a stranger could not.'

Inside the nursery, Mrs Dallimore encountered Elizabeth Gough, who was less than pleased to be bothered by the policeman's wife. 'What do you want with me?' she snapped.

'You must undress yourself,' replied Dallimore.

'I cannot,' said Gough, refusing the order point blank. Mrs Dallimore did not argue the issue but led Gough to the small dressing room located in the far corner of the nursery and started to conduct an impromptu interview.

'Well, nurse, this is a very shocking thing about the murder.'

'Yes, it is.'

'Can you give any account of it, do you think?'

'I got up at five o'clock,' replied Gough, 'and missed the child from the cot. I then lay down again.'

'Why did you lie down again after you missed the little boy?'

'I thought he was with his mamma because he generally goes in there of a morning. This is done through jealousy. The little boy goes into his mother's room and tells everything.'

'No one would murder the child for doing such a thing as that. Who do you think would do it?'

'I cannot tell,' said Gough who ended the conversation by starting to undress, forcing Mrs Dallimore to leave the closet while she did so.

No blood or other incriminating evidence could be found on Gough's body or her clothing; Mrs Dallimore left the nursery and made similar examinations of the other women in the household. Nothing suspicious was discovered, with the exception of a nightdress belonging to one of the elder Kent daughters, who shared a room on the second floor. The nightdress had a small amount of blood upon it and was immediately taken down to Superintendent Foley, who was on the ground floor. On seeing the stains, Foley thought that the nightdress should be looked at by a surgeon.

As luck would have it, Joseph Stapleton, a surgeon who knew Mr Kent professionally, had taken it upon himself to travel to Road Hill House in the hope of offering some assistance. In the absence of Mr Parsons, who was nowhere to be found, Stapleton was called upon to examine at the nightdress; he was only too pleased to help and made a close study of the garment, eventually declaring that the shape and location of the stains were indicative of menstrual blood.

'The marks upon it,' wrote Stapleton later, 'and all the circumstances connected with them, and the history of the garment itself, furnished unequivocal evidences as to their nature, and refuted the possibility of their being associated with the murder.' Foley was disappointed and ordered his men to continue their search of the house in hope of finding either the murder weapon or the bloodied clothing worn by the killer.[8]

It was late in the afternoon when Superintendent Foley called a meeting to make an assessment of the day's events. In the dining room he gathered together his policemen plus the two surgeons, Stapleton and Parsons, and asked them about what had been discovered so far. After hearing from his officers, Foley adjudged that they were still a long way from discovering the killer's identity, especially as the murder weapon remained unfound, and because the staff and family had proved unwilling to speculate about who might have wielded the knife. The behaviour of Mr Kent had proved to be especially puzzling: he had been interviewed during the course of the afternoon, but the experience had been frustrating.

'His mind seemed to wander irregularly, discursively, and unsteadily, over a wide field,' recalled one of his interviewers. 'He suggested a succession of suppositions, all equally vague and improbable, and unsupported by any testimony or by the evidence of a single fact.'

Mr Kent held an apparently unshakable belief that the murderer had come from outside his household, and throughout the day had asked Foley to extend his investigation across the road into the Rookery. He gave the names of several people who might bear him ill will (mostly neighbours and ex-servants), but Foley would not be diverted from his theory that the murderer had been inside Road Hill House the previous night. To some of those present, Mr Kent appeared to be in a state of denial, a situation which led one person to remark that he had 'failed to find in his heart the Brutus-courage to grapple with the thought that lurked there and stung him'.

When asked about the trustworthiness of his current servants, Mr Kent praised them roundly, especially Elizabeth Gough, who throughout the day had remained in charge of his two youngest children. Foley noticed that Mr Kent would shrink 'instantly and sensitively, from every suggestion that the murderer had slept in his house, and was still there'. It did not take Mr Kent long to tire of Foley's apparent intransigence and so he pleaded with him to send for a detective from London's Metropolitan Police. The Wiltshire policeman took offence at the suggestion, seeing it as a slight against his ability to conduct a thorough investigation into the murder.

'That is unnecessary,' Foley replied, 'and it might be productive of difficulty and disappointment.' Mr Kent backed down and the interview progressed onto the events of the previous night. This proved to be more fruitful and allowed Mr Kent to give an account of his actions in the hours prior to his son's death:

> I was the last person downstairs that night. I was in the habit of going round every night to see all was safe. I went about the house that night, and found all the doors and windows fastened. I went into the drawing room to see if the windows were fastened, it was about half past eleven or twenty-five minutes to midnight. When I left the drawing room I locked and bolted the door, leaving the key in the door. I then went upstairs to bed and fell asleep soon afterwards and did not wake during the night.

The policeman went on to ask Mr Kent about his actions from first thing that morning:

> I awoke about half-past seven in the morning. I was awoken by the nurse knocking on the door and asking for the children. Mrs Kent got out of bed when we heard a knock at the door, I then learned that the child was missing from its bed. Ultimately I went to Trowbridge for the police but before I returned I learned that the body of the child had been found.

Although Foley had found Mr Kent to be highly strung and unco-operative, there was nothing about his testimony to arouse undue suspicion and much of its detail could be confirmed by Mrs Kent, with whom he had shared a bedroom. Of more concern was the nurse Elizabeth Gough, whose insistence that she had slept through the boy's kidnap remained unconvincing. Foley asked that Gough be brought to him in the dining room so that she could be 'closely and verbally examined'.

The nurse had already been interviewed several times and must have known that the police investigation was focused upon her. If she did not, then Superintendent Foley left her in no doubt as to the seriousness of her position.

'Might I remind you that the child was in your custody and that its removal from your charge under such extraordinary circumstances makes you subject to suspicion?' he said.

Gough readily admitted that she knew this and was worried by it. This concern had taken a physical toll, for although Gough was only twenty-two years old, she was described as wearing 'a look of fatigue and gave the impression that she had passed a restless night'. Mr Stapleton, who was present during the interview, believed that the nursemaid's haggard expression could be explained by 'the shock to her feelings, her sense of isolation and subjection to a charge of neglect, her near relation to the deceased and the effects of weeping'. He was impressed by her conduct during the interview and especially at her ability to keep her answers simple and consistent.

In response to Foley's questions, Gough once more outlined her movements, explaining that she had put Francis to bed at eight o'clock the night before, at which time he was sleeping soundly, facing the wall. She then checked on the boy a couple of times before, at around ten o'clock, she headed upstairs with Mrs Kent to look at a large comet that had been prominent in the sky for several days. Gough went to bed in the nursery at eleven o'clock and was awake when, half an hour later, Mrs Kent came in to say goodnight to her children. After that the nurse remembered nothing until five o'clock the next morning, when she saw that Francis was missing, but assumed that his mother had taken him.

On several occasions Foley interrupted her to ask the same question: 'Do you have any suspicion of the motive or person of the murderer?' Each time Gough insisted that she had no idea who could have committed such a crime, but was certain that it was not a member of the family or any of the servants.

Mr Stapleton was impressed with Gough's performance and believed her to be 'a person of considerable intelligence, and perfectly free from all guilt or complicity.' Others were not so sure and voiced their belief either that she herself was guilty or, if not, then she had an idea as to the murderer's identity. Foley released Gough but he did not leave the matter of her supposed guilt alone and began to ask other members of the household about their opinion of the nursemaid. All gave Gough their unflinching support, including Mrs Kent who, having lost her son, had the best reason of all to distrust her. Foley faced an apparent wall of silence and had become exasperated by the situation. Only Mr Kent had dared to suggest who might be responsible, but all his suspects lived outside the boundaries of Road Hill House, and if Foley was sure of only one thing, it was that the murderer had been inside the house the previous night.[9]

At five o'clock Mr Kent was in the drawing room talking with Joshua Parsons, the family surgeon, and Joseph Stapleton, who had continued to offer his help, when a messenger arrived from Trowbridge. He brought with him a warrant from the coroner giving Mr Parsons the authority to carry out a post-mortem examination of the dead boy. Stapleton immediately asked if he could act as Parsons's assistant during the procedure. Aware that time was of the essence, the offer was gratefully received. Both men went immediately to the laundry room to perform their unfortunate duty.

Inside the laundry room the surgeons started their autopsy by examining the blanket in which the body had been carefully wrapped. The outside of the blanket was relatively clean and free from staining, but the same could be not said of the inside, which was covered in large, irregular patches of stiffened blood. Judging by its pattern, the surgeons deduced that most of the blood had flowed across the blanket's surface in an uninterrupted stream; there were, however, a few places where the blood had spurted on to the material, probably as a result of the murderer having cut through the powerful arterial veins in the neck. When compared with the child's body, it could be seen that the bloody patches of blanket had lain next to the upper-left part of the body. A check of Francis's body revealed that almost all the blood staining on his clothes was on the left side of the body, with a stream of blood having trickled over the left temple and into the child's hair. This, together with the staining on the blanket, led to the deduction that the body had been lying on its left side with its head downhill when placed in the water closet (this was something that Thomas Benger had already mentioned to the police). The surgeons estimated that eight to ten fluid ounces (half a pint) of blood had flowed on to the blanket, which, they noted, contained no cuts or tears and showed no finger marks or stray hairs, nor had the murder weapon been wiped upon it.

Moving onto the boy's body, which they gently undressed, the medics were able to observe the horrific neck wound which, as Parsons had already noted, was a single, clean, very deep cut starting on the left side. Given the severity and instant fatality of this dreadful cut, neither man could have expected to see further wounds on the body, but this was not the case. On the left side of the boy's chest, just below the nipple, was a single deep stab wound that had gone straight through the ribs and had narrowly grazed the heart and stomach. The weapon used must have been a sharp, pointed knife and, to judge by the ragged marks left on the ribs and muscles, the assailant had violently twisted and wrenched the knife while it was still in the body. There was little blood from this wound, although the surgeons could not agree as to whether this meant the boy was dead when stabbed.

More perplexing were two small cuts that had been made on the forefinger of the left hand. Both cuts were on the knuckle, the first down to the bone, the second just a mere scratch. It was impossible to discern whether they had been made before or after death, although Stapleton rather fancied that they might be wounds caused by the boy holding up his hands to fend off his assailant.

It was then that the gentlemen turned their attention to some discolouration on the skin surrounding the boy's mouth and eyes. Both surgeons agreed that the skin was distinctly blackened, but they disagreed about its significance, Stapleton believing it merely to be an artefact of the throat being cut while Parsons thought that it might have more significance to the case. With time pushing on, there was little debate on the matter, a situation that may have led Stapleton to believe his viewpoint had prevailed over that of his colleague.

With the external examination complete, the internal one proceeded. This was not very revelatory, with the heart, lungs and other organs being in perfect health, and there was no evidence of any drugs or narcotics having been administered. Inside the stomach was a small amount of food and, more significantly, the remains of a pill, which Parsons immediately recognised: it was a laxative that he had personally made up and delivered to the family the week before. Parsons was aware that the pill needed at least six hours to dissolve and possibly as much as ten. If he could discover when the pill was administered then this might be used to narrow down the time of death.

With the autopsy complete, the surgeons closed up their incisions and tidied the body so that it could be laid out, a job that would be carried out almost immediately by two women from the village. After cleaning themselves, both men left the laundry and went to find Mr Kent, who was anxious to know what they had discovered. The truth horrified him and he sought assurance from the surgeons that his little boy had not suffered unduly.

'The child died an instant and comparatively painless death,' they said, trying to offer some crumbs of comfort. The day had been a harrowing one and, with the arduous task of examining poor Francis finished, Joshua Parsons took his leave of Road Hill House, although his colleague Mr Stapleton chose to linger for a short while longer.[10]

It was just after seven o'clock, with the light beginning to fade, when the police search was scaled down. Foley ordered that the few objects of interest recovered during the day should be loaded into a cart and taken to Trowbridge police headquarters for further examination.

It was around this time that Mr Stapleton, who lived five miles away from Road Hill House, decided to head for home. He was in the process of retrieving his carriage from the stable yard when he spotted the police cart which was in the process of being loaded with the physical evidence gathered during the day. He wandered over to take a look and, in doing so, caught sight of the blood-stained nightdress which he had examined and dismissed earlier in the day. This was somewhat of a relief to Stapleton, who was concerned that the nightdress might have been disregarded as evidence purely on his say so; he thought it only right that another surgeon should examine it as well, just to be certain.

'Under the circumstances, it would be proper to mention this to the authorities,' he said to the duty policeman who was stood by the cart. His advice was heeded and within forty-eight hours the nightdress was returned to its owner, but only after having been examined by two further surgeons, one of them Mr Parsons, the other probably George Sylvester, the Trowbridge coroner. They concurred with Mr Stapleton's belief that the bloodstains were natural in origin and that the nightdress need play no further role in the case.

As the evening drew on, the police prepared to leave Road Hill House for the night. Superintendent Foley was keen that some of his men should remain on the premises, not least because he suspected that the murderer was still resident in the house. He reasoned that the guilty person may have hidden the knife and/or their bloodied clothing somewhere on the premises and therefore might have to emerge that night to reclaim them. If anyone should choose to wander about the house then Foley wanted his men to be there to observe them.

At nine o'clock Foley took Mr Kent to one side and asked his permission to station two policemen inside the house. Mr Kent was not keen on the idea but, with some reluctance, acceded to Foley's request. However, he asked that the policemen delay their arrival until after his family had gone to bed, that they come under the cover of darkness and that they take especial care not to be seen, as he did not want to cause undue alarm. With Kent's consent having been obtained, Foley asked Sergeant James Watts, who had recently arrived from the neighbouring Somerset Constabulary, if he could spare Constable Urch for the night; he then instructed Constable Heritage to accompany him. With this sorted, Watts took Urch to one side so that he could issue him with some 'secret orders.'

'Go home and get some supper,' said Watts, 'then trim your lamp well. Bring it with you but keep it turned off when you reach the house. I want you to remain in the drawing room, at the bottom of the stairs, and if anybody goes about during the night, turn on your light and see who it is.' With these instructions understood, Watts and Urch left Road Hill House, followed shortly afterwards by Foley and Heritage. His role as senior officer was taken by Superintendent George William Summers of the Somerset County Constabulary, who arrived shortly after nine o'clock and remained in the house until the return of Urch and Heritage.

Mr Kent was also determined to stay up all night, but this necessitated some changes to the sleeping arrangements at Road Hill House. Rather than leave his wife alone he arranged for one of his older daughters, Elizabeth, to spend the night with Mrs Kent, while the younger daughter, Constance, would move from her single room to that of her sister Mary Ann. Only the son, William, and the nurse, Elizabeth Gough, would be left to sleep on their own, presumably by their choice.

At eleven o'clock Constables Heritage and Urch walked up the road from Road village and, on reaching the gates to Mr Kent's property, extinguished their lamps. The moon was almost full and allowed them to pick their path up to the house with relative ease. Once there they tapped lightly on the dining room window, as had been agreed, and were let into the house by Mr Kent, who confirmed that his family and servants were all in bed.

Instead of leading the policemen to the drawing room, where Watts had asked Urch to remain, Mr Kent took them through the hallway to the kitchen where a supper of cheese, bread and beer had been prepared. Mr Kent asked if their night-long vigil could be conducted from the kitchen area, explaining that he would be in the library all night. This was contrary to Urch's orders, which were to stay in the drawing room, but not to those of Heritage, who had been told by Foley to follow Mr Kent's orders. Both men agreed to remain in the kitchen and were left alone by Mr Kent, who pulled the door firmly shut behind them.[11]

Urch and Heritage sat in the kitchen for some hours, chatting and eating their meal. Heritage had agreed with Foley that he would stay until two o'clock in the morning, and at this time he rose and went to the kitchen door, but on trying the handle, he found that it appeared to be stuck. After several more attempts Heritage realised that the door had been bolted from the other side: it appeared that he and Urch had been deliberately locked in the kitchen by Mr Kent. They tried the back door, which proved to be unlocked but it opened onto the stable yard into which the Kents' large guard dog had been released. Neither man fancied their chances with the dog and so Constable Heritage, who was outraged that he had been imprisoned, started to hammer on the kitchen door loudly.

'You're making enough noise to wake all the people in the house,' scolded Urch.

'I am locked in and I must get out!' replied his annoyed colleague.

After twenty minutes Mr Kent arrived and unbolted the door. A minor altercation followed, in which Heritage demanded to know why the door had been bolted.

'I did not know I was to be bolted in,' the policeman complained.

'I did it so that if anybody came down the stairs they would find everything as usual. I did not want anyone in the house to suspect that you are on the premises.'

'Did you not hear us knocking?'

'No. I was walking about.'

31

The policemen were not happy with this explanation, but Mr Kent would say no more on the matter. There was little they could do and so Heritage went home, leaving Urch alone in the house. Bizarrely, Urch chose to remain in the kitchen for the remainder of his shift, only to discover that he had once again been locked inside. Just before six o'clock Mr Kent came to the door and told Urch that the servants were getting up and that he should go. Urch did as he was told, but remained perplexed at Mr Kent's behaviour.

When Superintendent Foley was later told what had happened, he exploded with rage and for a while considered having both officers sacked for allowing themselves to be locked up. 'I was very much surprised when I heard of it;' he commented afterwards. 'I have never been able to find Mr Kent's reason for locking the men up.'

'That was the first time I was ever locked up in that way,' said Heritage. 'I suppose he wanted to prevent us from wandering about.'[12]

SUNDAY 1 JULY 1860

The occupants of Road Hill House had been traumatised by Francis's murder, but Mr Kent paid little regard to their feelings: he was determined that family life should proceed as usual. On Saturday evening he had instructed the servants to keep to their routine and so, at six o'clock on Sunday morning, just as Constable Urch was leaving the house, the housemaid and cook emerged from their rooms to start their domestic duties. They may have been surprised to find Mr Kent already awake and dressed but, of course, did not know that he had been up all night or that there had been two policemen in the house. Only Mr Kent and his wife were privileged to that information.

The rest of the Kent family and the nursemaid Elizabeth Gough remained in their rooms for another hour or so before they too started to make their way downstairs in dribs and drabs. The fact that this was anything other than a normal day was soon underlined by the return of the police, albeit in fewer numbers than the day before. Superintendent John Foley, who had coordinated the previous day's investigation, was initially absent; his role was taken by Superintendent George Summers of the Somerset Constabulary, who had hitherto made only a fleeting appearance the previous evening. Even though just twenty-four hours had passed since the awful discovery of Francis's body, the police investigation was already becoming low-key. The servants and family were for the most part left to their own devices, while the policemen undertook a closer examination of the house and its grounds.

On the second floor Sarah Cox, the housemaid, began making the beds and gathering together the family's dirty clothing ready for the next day's laundry. On entering Constance's room Cox was surprised at how disorganised it was, especially her used clothing and linen, which was strewn about the floor. She tidied up and made the bed before taking some of the garments downstairs to the laundry baskets.

Elsewhere in the house Mr Kent learned from Superintendent Summers that the coroner's inquest into his son's death was to be held the following day at the Red Lion, a local public house. The inquest was to be chaired by George Sylvester, the Trowbridge coroner, in front of a jury made up of men from the parish. The involvement of local jurors did not altogether please Mr Kent, who knew that spurious rumours concerning the murder were even then gaining currency in the village. He was also aware that news of his son's death was spreading beyond Road and into the surrounding countryside. There had already been one journalist, a man named Albert Groser, on his property asking questions, and it would be only a matter of time before others arrived and the first articles appeared in print. In a rural neighbourhood the murder of a young boy was a highly newsworthy event, especially as the killer had yet to be identified.

On being told that the coroner's inquest would be held on the Monday, Mr Kent sent word to his lawyer Rowland Rodway that he was to attend the proceedings in place of the family, who would remain at the house all day unless they were specifically requested to make an appearance. Mr Rodway pointed out that it was the duty of the coroner to gather all the evidence relevant to the death of Francis Kent and so the exclusion of testimony from the dead boy's family was most irregular. However, Mr Kent explained that he, his wife and his children were too distraught to face any form of public examination. To Rodway's surprise, the coroner accepted this argument and agreed that the Kent family could be excused from attending the inquest.

The task of selecting the inquest jury was given to James Morgan, the parish constable for Road village, who was instructed to gather together twelve trustworthy tradesmen from the village. This task took much of Sunday to complete, but by the evening Morgan had a list of people whom he considered to be suitable. The men he had chosen came from a mixture of backgrounds: some were wealthy and well-connected, such as Edward West, a gentleman farmer, and Thomas Langley, the local registrar; while others were skilled manual workers, including the village tailor, shoemaker and cordwainer.

Morgan was pleased with his efforts and believed that his jury bench was complete, when he received an unexpected visit from two friends, Charles Happerfield, a former parish constable, and Stephen Millett, the village butcher. Happerfield and Millett had come to enquire about Morgan's jury list and, on being shown it, expressed their surprise at some of the names he had chosen.

'This is a solemn affair,' the two men warned, 'which requires the attention of people of good judgement.' They followed this by suggesting to Morgan that he might want to remove William Nutt, the cordwainer, from the list, as his family held a grudge against Mr Kent, and, in his place, include the Reverend Edward Peacock, who, they said, was eminently more suited to the task. Happerfield and Millett also suggested finding a means of getting the victualler William Dew onto the panel, as he was thought to be 'a man of good judgement'. The fact that both Peacock and Dew had strong connections to the Kent family does not seem to have been mentioned to Morgan who, in the belief that his friends were acting 'from the best motive', agreed to make the changes.

Shortly afterwards Morgan received word from the tailor Edward Freeman, who wished to be excused from jury duty as he was due to travel to Westbury on the day of the inquest. Morgan excused Freeman and put William Dew on the jury panel in his stead. Freeing up a place on the bench for the Edward Peacock was more problematic, and required Morgan to pay a visit to William Nutt junior, the son of the man who had helped retrieve Francis's body from the water closet. The Nutt family was large, locally prominent and on very bad terms with Mr Kent following the prosecution of two their number for stealing apples and fish from the grounds of Road Hill House. Morgan knew that it did not pay to upset the Nutt family and tried to explain to William junior that the decision to remove him from the bench was routine and had not been done because of Mr Nutt senior's prosecution for trespass.

'I do not suppose your father's feelings will be hurt in consequence of this,' said Morgan to William who, like it or not, discovered that he had been stood down in favour of Peacock. It was late on Sunday evening, but Morgan, with the advice of Happerfield and Millett, had chosen his twelve men of good judgement for the jury. Or so he believed.[13]

It was no great surprise that details of Francis Kent's horrific murder were travelling through the surrounding countryside at some speed, and by Sunday had reached the city of Bristol, some thirty miles away. In most circumstances such news would have engendered feelings of sympathy or pity, but the local reaction was somewhat mixed, as the circumstances surrounding Francis's death became entwined with pre-existing rumours and stories that the Kent family had generated during their short stay in the region.

Mr Kent had taken the lease on Road Hill House in 1855, and almost since the day of his family's arrival there had been concerns about the family's behaviour. There were stories detailing the abuse of servants, few of whom had stayed with the family for any length of time. There was talk of financial problems and of certain strange incidents in Kents' recent history. Some of these stories were just gossip, but others were known to be true and reflected badly on the family.

Mr Kent was thought by many to be a proud man who had roundly ignored the inhabitants of Road village and whose wife and children were apt to put on airs and graces. The family gave every impression of being rich and had leased an expensive property which required several full- and part-time servants to run it. However, Mr Kent was employed as a government sub-inspector of factories (first class), and as such earned £350 a year (equivalent to about £23,000 in 2009). This was a good wage, but it was nowhere near enough to afford the kind of lifestyle that the Kent family had adopted, and it was known that there was little extra money available to Mr Kent in the form of investments and legacies. Quite how he could afford to live at Road Hill House was, and remains, something of a mystery.

The Kents' history prior to their taking Road Hill House was largely unknown, even to the few friends they had locally. However, in the days following Francis's murder, the privacy so jealously guarded by Mr Kent and his wife was invaded by the police, who demanded to know everything about their background and history. Mr Kent was forced to comply and reluctantly divulged details of his recent past to Superintendent Foley and possibly to Superintendent Summers as well. What Foley heard did nothing to ease his suspicion that the murderer came from within the Kent household; indeed, it served to strengthen this conviction.

Samuel Kent had been born in July 1800, the only son (although he had two sisters) of Samuel Luck Kent, a carpet manufacturer based in the City of London, and his wife Elizabeth. Samuel's parents were an unusual social mixture: his father was a tradesman while his mother came from the wealthy Savill family of Colchester, Essex, after whom the London street Savill Row is alleged to have been named. The London carpet-manufacturing business was a family-run affair, with the profits being shared between several members of the Kent and Luck families.

As soon as he was able, the young Samuel Kent joined the firm and worked alongside his relations until, in 1826, he left to become a partner in a company of dry salters. At this time he met and courted Mary Ann, the daughter of Thomas Windus, a wealthy and well-educated coach builder from Stamford Hill, Middlesex. In 1829 they were married and lived prosperously in London's fashionable Finsbury Square, and had three children; only two, Mary Ann and Elizabeth, survived childhood, both of whom were sleeping in Road Hill House on the night of Francis's murder.

In 1833 Samuel became ill and, fearing that he had contracted tuberculosis, decided to cease working in London and instead to move the family to Sidmouth in Devon. Thomas Windus arranged for his son-in-law to become a government factory sub-inspector; this was then a newly created civil service position that served to enforce the 1833 Factories Act. As one of only fifteen national sub-inspectors, the job came with a certain amount of prestige, but the hours were long and required Mr Kent to be away from home for days at a time. In his absence his wife found herself stranded in a remote seaside town, cut off from her family and friends and with two young daughters to care for. Another baby was born, Edward Windus Kent, but the strain began to take its toll on Mary Ann Kent's physical and mental health and, in 1836, she began to display signs of instability.

Few descriptions of Mrs Kent's alleged madness exist, making it difficult to diagnose its nature, but it is said to have involved delusions and paranoia. For example, Mrs Kent once took her children from the house and became entirely lost, even though she knew the neighbourhood well. She was also discovered destroying books and prints in the house and would sometimes sleep with a knife under her bed. Mr Kent was allegedly advised to get his wife committed to an asylum or at least to obtain some live-in care, but he refused and pretended that all was well. Eventually he had his wife confined to a separate apartment at the far end of the house and would only visit her to enact his marital duties.

Between 1837 and 1841 Mrs Kent produced another four children, none of whom lived for more than a few months. Pathologists claimed that this succession of deaths was a by-product of Mrs Kent's poor physical and mental health, which had adversely affected the babies' nervous systems. When news of these infant deaths became known in 1860, many villagers quickly concluded that the children had been murdered by Mr Kent, although there is no proof of this whatsoever.

Two further births followed: Constance Emily Kent in February 1844 and William Savill Kent in July 1845. This time both children lived and were present in Road Hill House on the night of Francis's murder. By the time of Constance's birth Mrs Kent's insanity had reached an advanced stage and rendered her unable to care for her own children. On the recommendation of a local surgeon, Mr Kent employed a twenty-three-year-old governess named Mary Drewe Pratt, the daughter of a yeoman farmer from the nearby town of Tiverton. She was given the task of raising and educating the youngest children in place of their mother.

In 1848, and with the aid of a modest inheritance from his father, Mr Kent moved from Sidmouth, in south Devon, to the town of Walton-in-Gordano by the Bristol Channel, where they remained until March 1852, when the family relocated to Baynton House, just outside Trowbridge. It was here, on the 2 May that same year, that Mary Ann Kent was taken suddenly and seriously ill and, three days later, died. The cause of death was given as 'obstruction of the bowels' and the surgeon who attended Mrs Kent did not suspect foul play. However, when Mr Kent married his governess, Mary Pratt, just over a year later, it was rumoured that their passion had been active for some time prior to the death of the first Mrs Kent. The accusation of infidelity was never proved, and the presence of Mr Kent's daughters as bridesmaids at his wedding was given to be proof of the family's contentment with their new stepmother.

This did not, however, stop the gossips' tongues from wagging, and before long the talk of an affair between Mr Kent and his governess had morphed into a conspiracy theory which alleged that the pair had murdered Mrs Kent. The only proof offered of this was the absence of the governess at the time of Mrs Kent's sudden illness and death; she was said to have been 'visiting friends,' which led to talk of her being offered a pre-arranged alibi by Mr Kent, who wanted her out of the house while he poisoned his wife. In fact, Miss Pratt had not been with friends but had been in Devon tending to her terminally ill father, a fact that was later established by the police. It is perhaps of little surprise to find that these rumours were revived in the light of Francis's murder, but they were strenuously denied by all, including the surgeon who had attended the first Mrs Kent during her final illness. But not all the rumours were without foundation, and the talk of Mr Kent's first marriage having been unhappy and of being beset with financial problems did have some substance.

Mr Kent told Superintendent Foley that he had received the blessing of his first wife's family with regard to her treatment following the onset of mental illness. This was not entirely true, as can be seen from the 1837 will of Mrs Kent's father, Thomas Windus, which expressed a dislike and distrust for his son-in-law. When apportioning out his estate to his children, Mr Windus left his daughter Mary Ann the grand sum of £3,600 (about £250,000 in 2009), on the strict condition that it be 'for her sole and separate use and not to be subject to the debts, control or engagements of her present husband' (i.e. Samuel Kent). He then left instructions that should Mary Ann die young then the money was to be immediately assigned to a trust for her children for the time when they reached twenty-one years of age. Should none of her children survive then the money was to be split between Mr Windus's other daughters. At all times it was made explicitly clear by Mr Windus that Samuel Kent was not to be a beneficiary of his will. The obvious implication is that Mr Windus had a loathing for his son-in-law and believed him to be untrustworthy and heavily in debt.

Thomas Windus died three years after his daughter and so his legacy of £3,600 was placed in trust for the five Kent children. However, Mary Ann and Elizabeth, who were both older than twenty-one, were immediately entitled to their share, which may have been as much as £720 each (about £45,000 in 2009). It is probably not a coincidence that immediately following the receipt of this legacy Mr Kent moved his family into Road Hill House, a large property that was considered to be well beyond any budget associated with his wages. How this move was accomplished remains a mystery, but it is not beyond the realms of reason to assume that it was financed by Mr Windus's legacy to the two eldest Kent daughters, who were perhaps asked by their father to contribute their legacy to the family's well-being.

The marriage of Mr Kent and Mary Pratt was the start of a widening rift between the father and his children. His eldest son Edward had been away at sea when the wedding took place and on his return was horrified to learn that his former governess had become his stepmother. An unpleasant scene followed in which Edward launched a verbal attack on the new Mrs Kent during which he expressed his 'dislike and resentment' of her. He argued briefly with his father before storming from the house and off to Bristol where he rejoined his ship, the *Kenilworth*, which soon afterwards departed for Balaclava, then at the heart of the Crimean War. This looked to have been a fatal mistake when, a few months later, news reached the Kent family that the *Kenilworth* had been lost with all hands. For days the family mourned Edward's death until a letter arrived that announced his 'providential escape from shipwreck': he was one of only six survivors of a hurricane that had dashed his vessel to pieces.

A truce was declared between Edward and his father, something which may have been helped by the receipt of his share of the Windus legacy. In June 1855 Mrs Kent gave birth to her first daughter, Mary Amelia Savill Kent, and it was shortly after this that Mr Kent started to make local enemies by prosecuting Abraham Nutt (the father of William, the man who had discovered Francis's body) for stealing apples.

Abraham Nutt was an inhabitant of the Rookery cottages which lay across the road from Road Hill House, and for many years he and his neighbours had been allowed to help themselves to the fruit and fish on the estate. By prosecuting Nutt, Mr Kent made it clear to all that he did not welcome trespassers: to underline the point he erected a fence along the perimeter of his property and obtained exclusive fishing rights to its streams and ponds. Signs along the fences warned outsiders that they risked prosecution should they set foot inside the grounds. Perhaps unsurprisingly, the villagers did not take kindly to this and it was considered good sport to taunt and tease the Kent family, especially the children, whenever they were abroad in the village.

The arrival of a baby (Mary Amelia) in the summer of 1855 widened the gulf between Mrs Kent and her stepchildren. It is alleged that following the birth she lost interest in her husband's children and even treated them cruelly. Mary Ann and Elizabeth, the two eldest sisters, became withdrawn and would keep out of the way of their stepmother, spending hours by themselves. William, aged ten in 1855, also became withdrawn and, in the absence of his elder brother Edward, came under the influence of his sister Constance, who was a year older than him. Of all the children, it was the pubescent Constance that was the most resourceful and it was she who provided Mrs Kent with her greatest challenge by continually defying her authority.

Constance and William had been raised almost exclusively by the new Mrs Kent who, as their governess, had wholly assumed the role of their mother. She was alleged to have been a hard task-mistress who, as well as educating the children, required them to work alongside the staff, mending and cleaning the house. This created much resentment, but while Mr Kent's other children kept their heads down, Constance chose to express her displeasure by being disruptive and inso-lent. In return, Constance found herself regularly banished from the parlour to the hallway with her ears smarting from the boxing they had received from Mrs Kent. When news of this treatment leaked out after the murder, the family denied strenuously that any of the children had been maltreated, but it was evident to the servants and visitors that there was a great deal of friction between Mr Kent's children by his first marriage and their stepmother; so much so that six months after their arrival at Road Hill House, Constance and William were packed off to a boarding school in Bath.

This arrangement appeared to suit the children well and it is said that Constance and her brother greatly enjoyed their time at school, whose social side probably made a pleasant contrast to the isolation of Baynton and Road Hill Houses. Both children settled into their studies, but it was at home, not at school, where their troubles lay, and it is said that Constance in particular did not enjoy returning to her stepmother.

Constance had only been at school for a few months when she began to complain of a pain in her legs for which no specific cause could be found. This even resulted in her being in a wheelchair for a while, but by June 1856 the symptoms had eased and she and William found themselves at home for a short break and awaiting the return of their father who had been away on business. Constance believed her life to be dull and monotonous and that she was not wanted by her father and stepmother. She had read stories about women, such as Hannah Snell (a woman who disguised herself as a soldier and fought in India), who had dressed and acted as men and had as a consequence made a great success of their lives. Constance hatched a plan to run away from home to Bristol, where she would join a ship as a cabin boy, an idea that was perhaps inspired by her brother Edward's naval career. Somehow Constance managed to strong-arm her younger brother William into joining her.

In July 1856 Constance and William crept from Road Hill House and, hiding behind a shrubbery, took a pair of scissors to Constance's long brown hair, cutting it short and urchin-like. She then changed into a set of her brother's old clothes and the siblings set off on foot towards Bath, which was some ten miles away. They did not arrive until the evening and, not knowing what to do, they turned up at the Greyhound Hotel and asked for a room. The manager was suspicious and confronted the children; William immediately burst into tears while Constance stoically refused to answer any questions put to her. The police were called but Constance still refused to co-operate and was put in a cell for the night while William, who became even more distraught at the prospect of being separated from his sister, remained at the hotel.

The next morning a sergeant arrived in Bath with news that two children had been reported missing from Road Hill; when confronted with this news Constance confessed her identity. The police took the children back to Road Hill House where Mr Kent had recently arrived back from his business. Constance was severely punished but refused to express any regret over the incident, telling her father: 'I wished to be independent.'

To the family's shame, the incident was reported in the local newspaper under the headline 'A Little Romance.' The reporters did not castigate the children for their prank, but instead seemed to praise them. 'The little girl,' wrote the paper, 'behaved like a little hero, acting the part of a boy to the admiration of all who saw her. We learn from Mr Inspector Norris that Miss Kent manifested great shrewdness and resolution. The boy's clothes she wore were too small for her, and she carried a small stick, which she used as if she had been accustomed to it.'

The affair was not forgotten by Mr and Mrs Kent, who told neighbours that the children had set off because they had a 'simple love of adventure', an excuse which was rejected by almost everybody that heard it. Rumours of abuse within the family became widespread and from then onwards the teenage daughter was rarely seen at Road Hill House: she preferred to remain at school or with friends for part of her holidays, returning home only when necessary.

The escapade with Constance and William came a matter of weeks before the birth of Francis Savill Kent in August 1856, which was seen as something of a joyous event by the whole household, including the elder Kent children. In July 1858 tragedy struck Road Hill House when news reached them of Edward Kent's death aboard a ship in Cuba. He had died aged just twenty-three of yellow fever and, unlike the earlier report of his demise, this time there was no mistake. His brothers and sisters were traumatised; even Edward's legacy from Mr Windus, which was shared equally between them, did little to ease the pain. A few weeks later saw the arrival of yet another baby, Eveline Savill, but any thoughts about family planning appear to have escaped Mr Kent and by the next winter his wife was yet again expecting a child.

By June 1860 Road Hill House was home to ten members of the Kent family, three residential members of staff and seven non-residential staff. This must have placed an excessive pressure on Mr Kent's modest salary and may even explain the high turn over of employees seen at Road Hill House. In just five years the Kents were alleged to have employed around a hundred staff and it seemed to the villagers that barely a week went past without someone being let go. In fact, only six days before the murder the gardener's boy, John Alloway, was given a week's notice after arguing with Mr Kent over his pay.

Even crucial members of staff were liable to change at short notice; just eight months before the murder the Kents had lost their nursemaid as the result of a dispute. In her place had come twenty-three-year-old Elizabeth Gough, a slim, attractive, dark-haired girl whose appearance was notable because of a missing upper front tooth. Already an experienced nursemaid, Gough came with good references and appeared to fit in well at the house. However, the financial strain may have been telling, for at the time of Francis's murder Mr Kent was engaged in putting together an 'extraordinary application for promotion' for the recently vacated position of Full Inspector of Factories; this would have seen his salary rise three-fold to a handsome £1,000. Such was Mr Kent's desire for the job that he appended the signatures of some 200 magistrates from his district to the application, a task that must have taken some time to achieve. Unfortunately, the brutal death of Francis brought the application to a juddering halt, frustrating Mr Kent's ambitions and, worse still, engendering further expenses in the form of lawyer's fees and, eventually, funeral costs.

Given this convoluted and unusual family history, it is little wonder that the Kents were viewed as being eccentric or even suspicious by their neighbours. To some the murder of little Francis was a further expression of the family's dysfunctional nature, but at this stage there were few hard facts concerning the death in general circulation. It was hoped by many that these would be provided by the coroner's inquest that was scheduled to start on the Monday morning.[14]

MONDAY 2 JULY 1860

From early in the morning journalists and curious bystanders began to gather at the gates of Road Hill House, hoping to glimpse a sight of the family or the scene of the crime. Inside the building the police had resumed their investigation and Mr Kent found himself conducting a tour of the premises for the Chief Constable of Wiltshire, Captain Samuel Meredith, and one of his juniors, Superintendent Francis Wolfe. It was unusual for the chief constable to become personally involved in a case, but he felt that the level of notoriety that Francis Kent's murder had already reached warranted attention from the highest ranks.

Captain Meredith wanted to be shown into every part of the house, but he was especially keen to see the drawing room, with its mysteriously opened window, and the dead child's nursery, with the apparently undisturbed cot. Mr Kent had volunteered to take the policemen about his premises but he soon used the opportunity to promote his idea that there had been an intruder hidden about the house on the night of the murder. As they reached the first floor the policemen were diverted away from the nursery and into a spare room that abutted Mr and Mrs Kent's bedroom.

'Here is a room that is not frequently occupied,' said Mr Kent to Wolfe. The superintendent looked inside and observed that it was sparsely furnished.

'It is not likely a person would go in there,' the policeman said. 'There is no hiding place in this room.' Mr Kent then went across the corridor to the lumber room and expressed his opinion that it would make an ideal hiding place. The room was small and barren, save for some toys and a few chairs.

'No one would surely be here,' said Wolfe, 'because they might not know that one of the servants would not be coming at any time for some of the children's playthings that are in it.'

The journey around the house continued, but the policemen could discover only one potential hiding place, and this was a small space in the attic next to the water tank. This, however, was discounted because it was only accessible from the roof via a small window which evidently had not been opened in years. The police even attempted to climb the trellising on one of the outside walls to see if a person could have made their way in through an upstairs window, but found that the task was quite impossible. To the protests of Mr Kent, the senior policemen concluded that the murderer did not break in and that, following the housemaid's description of her nightly security routine, he or she was unlikely to have been hiding in the house when it was locked up. By implication the guilty person was therefore one of the nine adult (or near adult) people who had slept in the house on that Friday night.

After being shown the shutters in the drawing room Captain Meredith concluded his tour and went outside to the gates to address the crowd of 'anxious and waiting' spectators and reporters. When asked to comment on what he had seen, Meredith replied that, in his opinion, the murder could only have been accomplished by two people working in co-operation.

This news caused much excitement and, although Meredith refused to name any suspects, it was widely speculated that he must be referring either to William and Constance Kent or, more scandalously still, Mr Kent and Elizabeth Gough. This was more than enough information to keep local tongues wagging for days to come.

Elsewhere in the house the usual weekly routines were continuing to operate as though nothing had happened. Monday was laundry day and so Sarah Cox, the housemaid, moved from room to room gathering up any loose and soiled clothing and adding them to the laundry basket. Cox was somewhat surprised to discover a pile of dirty clothing on the landing outside Constance's room, as she had already taken much of her laundry the day before. On picking up the pile Cox noticed that among Constance's linen there was a solitary nightdress.

The housemaid took the laundry basket downstairs into the first-floor lumber room (the ground floor laundry room still held Francis's body) and started to sort through it, separating the clothes into piles. Then, following her usual routine, Cox fetched Mary Ann, Elizabeth and Constance and stood by as the children identified each item of their clothing; as they did so the children marked the item in the household laundry book and then signed for it. This piece of bureaucracy was designed to keep track of the laundry so that should any pieces of clothing go missing, it would be possible to deduce when and where it had had last been seen. As the girls marked the items in the book, so Cox put them into the laundry basket; she then left the lumber room to fetch another basket that contained Mr and Mrs Kent's dirty clothes which had already been sorted and entered into the laundry book.

At around half past ten Cox was in the lumber room and on the verge of finishing with the two baskets when Constance appeared at the door. Taking a step inside, the girl asked the housemaid if she could check inside the pocket of her slip, to see if she had left a purse there. Cox rummaged about in one of the baskets, found the slip and declared the purse not to be there.

'Could you go downstairs and fetch me a glass of water?' asked Constance of the maid. Cox got up and went downstairs, brushing past a reporter named Albert Groser as she did so. As she reached the bottom of the stairs Cox turned around and was surprised to see that Constance had followed her across the landing to the top of the stairs;

when Cox returned with the water Constance was once again stood in the lumber room. She took the water, drank it and then returned to her room on the second floor. Cox finished packing the laundry and then secured the two baskets in preparation for the arrival of the laundress from the village, who was due later that morning.[15]

At around the time that Sarah Cox was finishing her laundry duty, the twelve jury members were being assembled at the Red Lion Hotel in preparation for their swearing in before the coroner, George Sylvester. With the oaths taken and the court formally in session, the aged Mr Sylvester proposed taking the jurymen directly to Road Hill House so that they might be permitted to view the dead boy's body and see the scene of the crime.

The jurymen arrived at the Kent residence sometime around eleven o'clock and were first taken to the downstairs laundry room, where little Francis's body had been laid out inside a small coffin. Superintendent Foley held the only key to the laundry room and was, under English law, the custodian of Francis's body until after the inquest, at which point the coroner could release it to the family. The small size and inconvenient situation of the laundry room probably meant that the twelve jurymen had to take it in turns to enter and see the body; after this they were taken into the drawing room to be shown the shutters and thereafter to the nursery from whence the child had been stolen.

It was after midday when the coroner's court reassembled at the Red Lion Hotel, but by this time such a sizeable crowd had gathered that people were scuffling in order to gain entry to the building. George Sylvester declared that given the large degree of public interest, the Red Lion was too small a venue and that the court should reconvene down the road at the Temperance Hall, the largest public building in Road village. The announcement initiated a rush as people ran down the road to bag a seat in the public gallery. Further scuffles ensued and it was a little while before the court could go into session. In the absence of the entire Kent family, the first witness was Sarah Cox, their housemaid, who was called forward to give evidence.

Cox's story was already well-known locally, and under oath she reiterated the tale of how she had closed up the house the previous night, but on coming down the next morning had discovered that the drawing room door, shutters and window had been opened. She had not heard anything untoward during the night and, to her knowledge, Mr Kent was the last person to go to bed. Cox was unable to name a suspect and was released as a witness.

Next to take the witness stand was Elizabeth Gough, who, in the eyes of many, was already one of the prime suspects in the case because the boy had been taken from the room in which she was sleeping. Despite the pressure she must have been under, Gough was calm and answered clearly all the questions put to her clearly. Most of what she had to say was already known to the police and, in response to questions from the coroner, she outlined her movements on the night of the murder, explaining that she went to bed at eleven but did not miss Francis until the next morning. She testified that there could have been no-one hiding in her room on the night in question and that Francis was a very heavy sleeper. When asked how someone could have crept past her during the night, Gough explained that the room was carpeted and that her door opened silently (this contradicted Mrs Dallimore's earlier observation that the door was squeaky, but nothing was made of this). Like Cox, Gough said she had not seen any suspicious characters that day and had no notion as to who could have committed such a dreadful crime. She was released by the coroner.

Over the coming couple of hours several other witnesses were called to give evidence about the discovery of the body. They included Thomas Benger and William Nutt, who discovered the child; Superintendent John Foley, who produced in court the bloodied flannel recovered from the cesspool; and Joshua Parsons, the surgeon, who summarised his post-mortem examination.

The evidence of all these men was straightforward and known to the police already, with the exception of Mr Parsons's, who, following a discussion about the manner in which the boy's throat had been cut, suddenly ventured that the child might have been partially suffocated prior to the wounds being inflicted. He based this on two observations. The first was some bruising about the boy's face which might have indicated a hand or other object being forcibly pressed over the mouth. The second was that the pool of blood discovered on the floor in the outside privy was thought to be too small to have come from a cut such as had been seen on the body; on a living person this wound would produce great spurts of blood that could travel some distance. If the boy was partially suffocated and already on the verge of death then, said Parsons, the volume produced would have been more in proportion to that observed on the privy floor.

This new evidence excited some members of the court, as it helped to explain how the boy could have been taken out of the house with little or no noise: the murderer must have suffocated him while in the cot and then removed him to the outside closet where the throat was cut. However, one member of the public gallery was outraged at Mr Parsons's testimony: he was Joseph Stapleton, the surgeon who had assisted in the post-mortem examination and who held a firm belief that the boy had not been suffocated. Stapleton was jealous of the attention being afforded to Parsons and believed the surgeon to be hogging the limelight associated with the case; for months afterwards Stapleton would crusade against the idea of Francis having been suffocated, continually reminding the public that Parsons had not mentioned this idea during the original post-mortem examination and that this theory was based on nothing more than an afterthought. In fact, both Parsons and Stapleton had noted that there was a black discolouration about the boy's mouth, but from the outset they had disagreed about its significance. 'Second thoughts may sometimes be best,' wrote Stapleton in a critique of Parsons, 'but first impressions may be more safely relied on as a rule.'

Following this new evidence from Mr Parsons, George Sylvester turned to the jury and suggested that they should now retire to consider their verdict, which, he stated, should be one of murder. 'The police will then become responsible for its detection,' he said. At this a murmur went up both from the jury bench and the public gallery. 'Do you require more evidence?' asked Mr Sylvester of the jurymen in a somewhat irritated tone. The foreman of the jury, the Reverend Edward Peacock, stood up and, with some reluctance, expressed the views of the remainder of his fellow jurymen.

'I have been requested by some of the jury to ask that some of the Kent family be examined,' said Peacock, adding that he personally disagreed with this. 'I do not see any earthly good in examining them and feel that it is our duty to spare their feelings as much as possible.'

The coroner said that he agreed with Peacock and was inclined to refuse the request. Both men were backed up by the surgeon, Mr Parsons, who pointedly told the jurors that Mrs Kent was in no fit state to face the court. On hearing this, pandemonium broke out in the courtroom with shouts of 'one law for the rich!' being heard from the public gallery. The jurymen believed that a conspiracy was operating between the coroner, Mr Peacock and Mr Parsons, all of whom were friends of Mr Kent. Despite efforts to calm them, the jurors continued to call for the family to be brought before the court. Eventually juror Henry Martin stood up and addressed himself to the coroner, saying, 'We insist on it being done.'

Mr Sylvester admitted defeat. 'I can see no good that can arise from it,' he said, 'but if you insist, and are determined to examine any part of the family then I shall adjourn the inquest to the house but before doing so, I should like you to say what part of the family you would like to be examined.'

'Miss Constance and Master William, the two younger of the family,' said one person. 'Try them all,' shouted another. 'Show no respect to one more than to the other!' said someone else. But Mr Sylvester had ceased listening; he had picked up his papers and was walking from the room, expecting the jury to follow, but they did not. They wanted the family brought before them, not vice versa, and made a loud complaint about it until they were informed that Mr Sylvester had the legal power to compel them up to Road Hill House. At this the disgruntled jurors filed out of the Temperance Hall and made their way up to the large house on the hill.

In accordance with the jury's wishes, Constance and William were summoned to the kitchen and individually examined by Mr Sylvester. According to a reporter who was present, the coroner 'did not take notes, put several of his questions in a leading form and appeared to take it for granted that that the witnesses knew nothing'. The examination lasted only a few minutes, with neither child being able to offer anything new; both merely stated that they had gone to bed as usual and slept soundly until the next morning. Against the jury's wishes, the elder daughters were not interviewed; nor were Mr and Mrs Kent, and in the late afternoon the court returned to the Temperance Hall, where Mr Sylvester started his summing up by addressing the jury with the facts of the case:

> This is one of the most mysterious murders of which I have heard, but I see no reason to attach suspicion to anyone in particular. The total absence of motive for the horrible deed renders the sad affair almost inexplicable. The circumstances have been concealed from every eye but that of Providence but I believe that the day will come when the truth will be revealed and the murderer brought to justice.

Having said this, Sylvester told the jury that 'they could do no more than return an open verdict.'

This speech did not go down well and a murmur went up from the bench. James Morgan, the parish constable, reminded the jury that, under the coroner's direction, they had no choice but to give an open verdict. This prompted Henry Martin to stand up: 'It is the opinion of the major part of the jury that the murder was done by some inmate of the house.' He was swiftly joined by another juror, Edward West, who rose and solemnly placed his hand across his breast. 'I feel that we have not done our duty,' he said, looking directly at the coroner. 'We ought to have further witnesses for the satisfaction of the neighbourhood and the country at large.'

Mr Sylvester's patience had by then worn thin. 'The grand object of the jury is to find out how the child came by its death,' he said angrily. 'It must be left to the magistrates to determine who perpetrated the crime and I have no doubt that they will immediately attend to that.'

He was quite correct. The jury in a coroner's court are primarily there to determine a cause of death, not to help solve criminal cases, but in the heightened atmosphere produced by the murder, this point had been missed by the jurors, many of whom had their own theories concerning it.

It was Edward Peacock who broke the stalemate by directing his fellow jurors to bring an open verdict. One by one the jurors were asked to sign a document acknowledging the verdict, but many did so very reluctantly. 'I have never signed anything so against my inclination,' said a juror named Marks out loud. But he had no choice in the matter and nor did the rest of the bench; in doing so they closed the inquest into the death of Francis Savill Kent.

George Sylvester was visibly relieved to be parted from the jury and directed that the little boy's body be released from the custody of the court and given back to his family. A short while later Superintendent Foley made his way up to Road Hill House and, on meeting Mr Kent, handed him the key to the laundry room. None of the family could face the sight of seeing Francis's body, which remained in its bloodied nightclothes, and so Mr Kent arranged for Mrs Silcox from the village to finish laying out his son. She unlocked the door and carefully carried Francis to one of the upstairs rooms where Sarah Cox and Elizabeth Gough were already assembled. The three women then cleaned and dressed little Francis in preparation for his funeral.

Outside the Temperance Hall several members of the jury remained in discussion; all were fuming with anger. At least nine of the twelve men believed that they had been railroaded by the coroner into giving a verdict that conflicted with the evidence they had heard. 'Some sort of undue pressure was placed upon us,' said Edward West, 'which meant that we did not do justice to ourselves or give satisfaction to the country. We are not at all satisfied with the way in which the inquest has been conducted.'

Others in the village agreed with these sentiments. Many people saw a conspiracy at work in which the local judiciary were contriving to shift the search for Francis's murderer away from Road Hill House and into the surrounding countryside. Had they been given more time to question the Kent household, argued West, then the culprit would surely have been found.

The jury were not the only ones who were dissatisfied with the way events had proceeded during the inquest; Rowland Rodway, who had been asked to attend the inquest in place of the Kent family, was greatly troubled by all that he had heard. Following the jury's verdict he trudged up to Road Hill House and requested a private interview with Mr Kent. The two men disappeared into the library where Mr Rodway advised his client that events that day had not gone altogether well and that it was evident that popular opinion believed that the killer or killers came from within the household. Mr Kent must have expressed his by then well-worn belief that a tramp, neighbour or a former servant had broken into the house, but Mr Rodway openly disagreed with him. The lawyer had listened to all the evidence given at the inquest and somewhat boldly stated to Mr Kent that it was patently obvious that the murderer would be found among the current inmates of Road Hill House. He suggested that Mr Kent should abandon all notions of the killer being an outsider and instead assist the police in finding the guilty party.

Mr Kent was outraged at this suggestion, and before long the two men could be heard arguing. A short while later Mr Rodway was shown abruptly to the front door: after encountering irreconcilable differences he had resigned from his job as Mr Kent's legal adviser. 'I found that our views of the crime, and the mode and direction of its investigation, widely differed,' he explained later, 'and as I could not adopt Mr Kent's views, nor he mine, I abstained from further interference.' When news of this reached the wider world, it only served to confirm what many had long felt: that there was something very unusual indeed about this murder and the residents of Road Hill House were conspiring to hush it up.[16]

Earlier in the day another unusual event had occurred at Road Hill House, this time concerning the washing that Sarah Cox had so carefully gathered and sorted into baskets. At around midday Hester Holley, a washerwoman from Road village, had called at the Kent residence to pick up the two laundry baskets. She arrived shortly after the inquest jurymen had departed and went round to the back of the house, where the cook let her through the kitchen door. The cook and Mrs Holley went upstairs to the lumber room where the two baskets had been left earlier by Cox.

'The cook brought down one basket and I the other,' recalled Mrs Holley later. 'The clothes were in the same state as I always received them. Mrs Kent's dress was on one basket and something else on the other.' Once outside, Mrs Holley gave one of the baskets to her daughter Martha and together they walked down the hill and directly to their house.

Like most of the villagers, Mrs Holley and her daughter were excited at the events of the previous few days and had been listening to the rumours circulating through the neighbourhood. Being the Kents' washerwomen, they were especially interested to learn that a bloodied nightdress had been discovered by the police and, even though the blood on had been deemed to be of natural origin, the women wanted to see the garment for themselves. Mrs Holley had even invited her two elder daughters to her house so that they could witness the unpacking of the Kents' dirty laundry.

Once inside the house, Mrs Holley and her daughters began to rummage through the baskets, searching for the infamous bloodied garment. However, and despite a thorough search, it could not be found among the dirty laundry (in fact, it was still in the possession of the police), but they did discover something else: one of the girls' nightdresses was missing from the basket. The laundresses checked again, but there was no doubt about it, according to the laundry book there were supposed to be three dirty nightdresses in the children's basket, but only two could be found. Mrs Holley and her daughters had been washing the Kents' clothes for years and knew who owned each item; from this it was easy to deduce that the missing nightdress belonged to Constance Kent.

Mrs Holley was not unduly alarmed, and assumed that a mistake had been made by the housemaid or perhaps by Constance herself. She decided that she should inform the family of the error and so set off on foot to Road Hill House, where Mr Kent received her straight away. However, instead of being gracious about the missing nightdress, Mr Kent went into a towering rage with the washerwoman, directly accusing her of having stolen the garment. Mrs Holley denied this vehemently, but her employer said he did not believe her.

'You have two days in which to return the item,' he told Mrs Holley, 'or I shall obtain a special warrant against you!'

The laundress was highly affronted. 'I am certain that I do not have the dress,' she said before walking out of the house. She expected that the nightdress would be found and sent to her in due course, at which time an apology could be expected from Mr Kent. In the meantime she kept the incident to herself, perhaps because she was nervous of being more widely accused of having stolen it.[17]

TUESDAY 3 JULY 1860

The coroner's inquest may have been locally controversial, but it had served its purpose. By establishing that Francis Kent had been murdered by persons unknown, the coroner had performed the principal task required of him under law; it was the job of the police to identify the murderer and to find sufficient evidence to bring them to court.

On Tuesday morning the police continued their inquiries at Road Hill House, but in a low-key fashion. Henry Heritage, the Southwick parish constable, was busy searching the house and grounds for any sign of a murder weapon. He spent some time looking through the garden sheds in the hope of finding a knife or similar straight-bladed cutting device, but all he found were mowing implements and a scythe. He concluded that the murderer had successfully disposed of the weapon and that it would never be found. On hearing this Superintendent Foley declared that the police's physical examination of Road Hill House was complete; thenceforth, all enquiries were to be centred on the Kent family and their servants, whom Foley and his boss, Captain Meredith, believed were conspiring to shield the true identity of the killer or killers from natural justice.

As Constable Heritage was finishing his search for the weapon, Mrs Holley was being received by Sarah Cox in the kitchen. The laundress had come up to the house in order to collect her money and to return the laundry book which contained a list of the clothes in the two baskets. Given the previous night's acrimony over Constance's missing nightdress, Mrs Holley fully expected the housemaid to accuse her of having taken it, but instead she handed over the money and accepted the laundry book without comment. It was evident to Mrs Holley that Mr Kent had not yet mentioned the missing nightdress to his housemaid; this struck her as odd given his earlier threat to bring in the police. Mrs Holley had no desire to inflame the situation and so took her money and left without further ado; her hope was that Mr Kent had seen fit to drop the matter, but she couldn't have been more wrong.

In the early evening Mrs Holley received a loud knock on her cottage door and was alarmed to find Constable James Morgan and other four policemen standing on her doorstep. Mrs Holley immediately feared that they had come to quiz her about the missing nightdress, but nevertheless showed them into the house and, with some trepidation, introduced them to her daughter, Martha. Morgan started to interview both women but, to their surprise, the nightdress was not mentioned at all. Instead Morgan produced the bloodied flannel that had been recovered from the cesspool. As the laundresses to the family, asked Morgan, did Mrs Holley or her daughter recognise the flannel or know who owned it? It was with some relief that Mrs Holley was able to say that she had never before seen the flannel; Martha answered likewise.

Morgan was satisfied with this and was on the verge of leaving when he turned and asked if Mrs Holley was aware of any missing items of clothing from that week's wash. 'The clothes are all right by the book,' lied Mrs Holley, as she gratefully showed the policemen to the front door.

No sooner had the police left the house than Mrs Holley entered a state of panic. She realised that by not telling Morgan about the missing nightdress she had taken a big risk, for if the police were to learn of it from Mr Kent then her denial would look highly suspicious. There was nothing for it but to come clean, and so to rectify the situation she sent her seventeen-year-old daughter up to Road Hill House to see Sarah Cox. The housemaid was somewhat surprised to see the young laundress, who was visibly distressed, at such a late hour.

'There were three nightdresses put on Mrs Kent's book,' splurged Martha to Cox, 'but only two were sent. My mother said that it is Miss Constance's that is missing and that you must send another in its place as the police have asked her if she had the same number of clothes sent this week and my mother said that she had.'

Cox was puzzled, as this was the first that she had heard of the matter. 'Your mother must have made a mistake,' she said to Martha, 'for I am certain that I put three nightdresses in the basket and that one of those was Miss Constance's.' Cox told Martha to wait in the kitchen while she went upstairs to ask Constance about the matter.

'I am quite sure that you put my nightdress in the basket,' said Constance to Cox. 'I saw you do it. I suggest that you raise the matter with my stepmother.'

More confused than ever, Cox found Mrs Kent, who knew nothing at all about the nightdress and so suggested that she, Cox, Martha and Constance all discuss the matter in the library. A few minutes later Constance was stood in front of her stepmother repeating the assertion that her nightdress had been put into the basket. She insisted that the mistake must have been made after the laundry had left the house; this automatically placed the blame with Mrs Holley and her family. The young Martha was out of her depth, but she managed to deny having ever received the nightdress before asking if she could return home to fetch her mother. A short while later Mrs Holley arrived at the house; she was seen by Mrs Kent, who had by then taken her stepdaughter's side in the dispute, insisting that the nightdress must have gone missing while in the care of the Holley family.

That Mrs Kent should have chosen to support her stepdaughter's word over that of a laundress did not surprise Mrs Holley. She was, however, slightly amazed to discover that prior to her daughter's visit that evening, neither the housemaid nor Mrs Kent had been told of the missing garment by Mr Kent. Given his threat to take legal action, it seemed odd that he had not sought to clarify the situation with Constance or Sarah Cox; it was almost as if he were trying to keep the matter quiet.

Later that evening Mrs Kent did approach her husband to ask him exactly what was going on. It was probably this that inspired him to write to Superintendent Foley the next morning, complaining that Mrs Holley had either lost or stolen a nightdress from the family's laundry. On the Wednesday evening the police were once more banging on Mrs Holley's front door, but this time the visit was not so passive. The constables entered her house and searched it from top to toe, looking specifically for the missing nightdress. When nothing was found they went across the village to the houses of Mrs Holley's two elder daughters and searched these, but without success.

The laundress was outraged that she should be accused of stealing from the laundry and immediately refused to accept any further washing from the family. Furthermore, she ensured that none of the other local laundresses would take work from Road Hill House either. It did not take long for a backlog of dirty clothing to build up, but Sarah Cox remained adamant that she had seen Constance's nightdress go into the laundry basket and that, once left in the lumber room, nobody could have had the occasion to interfere with it. Mrs Holley was equally adamant that she had not received it; Mr Kent did not follow through with his promise to prosecute the laundress and so the affair was left unresolved.

News of the missing nightdress caused much excitement locally and added another layer of mystery to a murder whose notoriety had moved away from the West Country and into the metropolis of London.[18]

MONDAY 9 JULY 1860

The funeral of Francis Savill Kent took place on Friday 6 July in the small Wiltshire parish church at East Coulston, where the first Mrs Kent had been buried. The service was a private one with only family and a few close friends attending, including three surgeons, Joshua Parsons, Joseph Stapleton and Benjamin Mallam, plus the lawyer Rowland Rodway. It was a desperate occasion and one that was made all the more so by the probability that at least one of the people stood at the graveside was guilty of murdering the little boy inside the coffin.

For over a week Superintendent Foley had been in charge of the day-to-day investigation into the murder of Francis Kent, but he had little to show for his efforts. With so many potential witnesses and only a handful of suspects, the investigation had begun optimistically enough, but the unco-operative nature of Mr Kent and his family and a lack of physical evidence meant that progress had proved to be frustratingly slow.

Many had become impatient with Foley and none more so than the members of the magistrates' bench at Trowbridge, in whose district the murder had occurred. Trowbridge had six magistrates (also known as justices of the peace), all of whom were volunteer judges at a local court that was empowered to deal with minor crimes and disputes. Although the magistrates generally heard only small cases, they did have the power to refer more serious crimes to a higher authority (the assize court) for a full criminal trial. In practice this meant that anybody arrested for the murder of Francis Kent would first have to be examined by the magistrates before they could be sent for trial elsewhere; thus, although the investigation was being conducted by the Wiltshire Constabulary, it was the magistrates who were charged with overseeing the general direction and behaviour of the police themselves. As such, Superintendent Foley was obliged to give regular progress reports to the Trowbridge magistrates, but as the days ticked by, so some of the bench started to believe that the policeman was making heavy work out of a relatively straightforward situation.

Exactly a week after the murder, Henry Gainsford Ludlow, the chair of the Trowbridge magistrates, convened a meeting of the bench during which he expressed dismay at Foley's lack of progress. His fellow magistrates (Robert Walmsley, Peter Stancomb, William Stancomb, Samuel Bythesea and the Reverend Richard Crawley) were in agreement, and so Ludlow proposed that they should ask the Metropolitan Police for their assistance. A letter was penned to the Home Secretary, Sir George Cornewall Lewis, to request that a London detective be sent to Trowbridge at the earliest possible opportunity; they also took the opportunity of cabling Scotland Yard to forewarn them that their assistance would soon be required in Somerset.

Superintendent Foley was present at this meeting and was greatly disheartened to learn that moves were being made to circumvent his authority over the investigation. He believed that his inquiry was being hampered by the Kent family's unco-operative attitude and by a lack of any physical evidence linking any one person to the murder scene. The knife used to cut the boy's throat had not been found and nor had the killer's bloodied clothing. The flannel discovered in the cesspool had no known owner and everybody within the family insisted that the culprit had come into the house from the outside. All efforts to persuade the servants to name a suspect had come to nothing, and although three members of the household had no alibi, they had no obvious motive for the crime either. He had, however, drawn some conclusions about how the crime could have been committed.

Within hours of his arrival at Road Hill House Foley had decided that the crime could only have been accomplished by two people acting in co-operation. This notion was based chiefly on Francis's cot, which the killer had apparently left in a neat and tidy state despite having extracted the boy and his blanket. To have accomplished this the murderer would have had to have tucked in the bedclothes while holding the boy in their arms. This would have been physically difficult to accomplish and ran the risk of waking Elizabeth Gough, who, according to her account, was sleeping only a few yards away. The neat cot suggested two things to Foley: firstly, that one person must have held the boy while another smoothed the bed; and secondly, that one of these people was probably Elizabeth Gough, whose story about having slept through the kidnap was implausible. There was one other possible explanation, that Gough had made up the bed after discovering the boy was missing, but she denied having done so. Either way, Foley held a belief that the nursemaid must either have been complicit in the proceedings or held some knowledge that could crack the case.

Faced with the humiliating possibility of being taken off the case, Foley decided that the time had come to take his prime suspect in for closer questioning. The superintendent informed the Trowbridge magistrates that they should assemble at the Temperance Hall in Road village where they should expect to examine Elizabeth Gough on suspicion of murdering Francis Savill Kent.[19]

The magistrates did as they were asked and assembled in the Temperance Hall to await Foley and Gough's arrival. News of the impending proceedings had travelled around Road quickly, causing a crowd of villagers to assemble at the entrance to the hall in expectation of being allowed into the public gallery. Unfortunately for them, Foley had requested that the examination take place behind closed doors so as to encourage his witnesses to speak freely and without verbal harassment from an audience. Even when told this, the crowd did not disperse, but waited in order to watch those who had been summoned to give evidence arrive and depart.

Naturally, Elizabeth Gough was to be Foley's main witness, but other people associated with the Kent household were also to be questioned under oath, including the cook, the housemaid, John Alloway, the gardener's boy and Joshua Parsons, the surgeon. With the proceedings operating behind closed doors, exactly what was said that day remains unknown, but from general accounts given afterwards, it would appear that the evidence given differed little from that offered at the coroner's inquest a week before. At the request of the magistrates Mr Kent was required to attend, but he did so reluctantly and, for the first time, gave his version of events under oath. Some of what he said that day has since become public knowledge and it reveals the scale of the problem that Foley was facing when trying to gain the co-operation of the Kent family.

'I believe that someone well aquatinted with the child and the house, or some discharged servant, must have murdered the child,' said Mr Kent, who continued to promote the idea that an intruder was responsible. Foley had heard him expound this theory many times before and as a result had wasted much time in investigating various neighbours and several ex-servants, all of whom had been cleared of suspicion. It was pointed out to Mr Kent that all his suspects had been cleared by the police and so, not to be outdone, he threw another name into the ring, someone who had hitherto not been part of the police investigation.

'I know that a discharged servant of mine has used expressions of revenge against the child,' he said. 'She called my children "horrid children", particularly referring to the little boy, and when she left, a few days before the end of the month, she vowed vengeance against the children and threatened myself.' This was startling news to the police, who had been pushing Mr Kent to name suspects for days. Why had he chosen to wait until now to do so?

Pressed further, Mr Kent named the servant concerned, explaining that she had been with the family as a housemaid for less than a month the previous autumn before arguing with Mr Kent. 'She left in a dreadful rage,' explained Mr Kent. 'She was in a great passion; and I was warm too, but not so warm as she was.'

For his own reasons, Mr Kent had given the police a new and somewhat belated lead to follow up that drew attention away from the occupants of Road Hill House. After this, Mr Kent was released as a witness. With time pressing on, it was decided that the inquiry should be adjourned until the following day, when the evidence from Elizabeth Gough herself could be heard.

Rather than return Gough to Road Hill House, Superintendent Foley ordered that the nursemaid be placed under the 'superintendence' of Constable William

Dallimore and his wife Eliza, at whose house she was to remain 'until further notice.' This was not done with the expectation that Gough might attempt to flee from justice (there had been ample opportunity to do so already) but out of a desire by Foley to have her constantly observed in case she let something slip that would be of help in the case. Mrs Dallimore was delighted to receive Gough into her small Trowbridge cottage and immediately made it her mission to tease some useful information out of the unenthusiastic houseguest.

The first opportunity to talk to Gough came that evening when, after dinner, the two women sat together in the kitchen, candles in hand, warming themselves by the fire. Gough turned to her host and, unprompted, said: 'Mrs Dallimore, did you know that there's a nightdress missing?' The constable's wife knew this perfectly well, but feigned ignorance.

'No. Whose was it?'

'Miss Constance Kent's. You may depend upon it that nightdress will lead to the discovery of the murder.' On hearing this Mrs Dallimore became very animated.

'Did you see the nightdress put into the basket?'

'Yes,' replied Gough, but as she spoke Constable Dallimore happened to walk into the room, having just returned from Road, and he was very interested to hear the women's conversation.

'Then you saw the nightdress put into the basket, as well as Cox?' asked the constable.

'Oh no, I did not,' said Gough in alarm.

'But you have just said so,' said Mrs Dallimore.

'Oh no, I did not,' repeated Gough but this time it was Constable Dallimore who answered.

'But you just said so,' he said forcibly.

'I did not,' replied Gough, who by this time was already on her feet and heading toward the bedroom which she was to share with Mrs Dallimore. It was a puzzling incident, and when the conversation was relayed to Foley, it only served to heighten his conviction that Elizabeth Gough was somehow complicit in the murder.[20]

TUESDAY 10 JULY 1860

In the nine days between the discovery of Francis Kent's body and the start of the examination of Elizabeth Gough, news of the terrible and perplexing events taking place in the remote village of Road had spread far and wide.

The first journalist to reach the scene was local reporter Albert Groser from the *Trowbridge Advertiser*: he was at Road Hill House the morning after the crime. By the middle of the week Groser had been joined by reporters from regional newspapers based in Bristol, Bath and Devizes. Articles outlining the strange circumstances of the murder appeared locally but were soon syndicated to newspapers in neighbouring towns and cities until, by the end of the week, the stories had reached London. Here, some newspaper editors were quick to sense that the murder had the makings of a sensational story. Over the weekend special correspondents were despatched to Road from London or from regional centres such as Bath, Salisbury and Swindon. At the time of the opening of the examination into Elizabeth Gough (on the Monday morning) a handful journalists were staying in Trowbridge; by the Tuesday morning this number had increased markedly so that by lunchtime the Temperance Hall in Road was surrounded by a scrum of reporters, notebooks and pencils in hand.

Elizabeth Gough was brought to the village at around ten o'clock by Constable Dallimore, but the mass of people surrounding the Temperance Hall was leading to friction and potential crowd trouble. While this was being sorted out, Gough was asked to wait inside the parlour of a nearby house. One of those who stayed with her there later told reporters that Gough had been quite relaxed and even said that, had it not been for the murder, she would then have been enjoying herself haymaking. When asked about her possible guilt, Gough replied that she would not be afraid to come before a hundred judges and be examined.

However, the nursemaid's stoicism in the face of adversity was just a front and when finally called into the Temperance Hall her bravado soon evaporated. In a sustained examination that lasted several hours, the magistrates and Superintendent Foley bombarded Gough with dozens of questions which were designed to pick holes in the evidence she had already given to the police. The transcripts of this examination do not survive, but it appears that she was grilled extensively about how she could have slept through the kidnap (and possible suffocation) of little Francis, about the chest flannel found in the cesspool and the neat state of the child's cot. It did not take long for Gough's confidence to desert her: she became flustered and weepy but, to Foley's frustration, did not alter or contradict her previous statements. Like her employer, Gough insisted that an intruder was responsible for the murder and would not accept that anybody in the household was guilty. It was the early evening when the questioning finished, by which time the nursemaid appeared very nervous indeed.

The magistrates and Superintendent Foley asked Gough to remain at hand while they undertook a private conference to discuss all that they had heard during the previous two days. The gentlemen were gone for several hours and did not return until eight o'clock that evening, bringing with them some bad news. The magistrates announced to Gough that they were not impressed with her performance and believed her evidence to contain 'certain discrepancies' which cast doubt on her claim to innocence. Superintendent Foley stepped forward and explained that, based on her evidence, he had sufficient grounds to place her in custody until the coming Friday, when a further hearing would be arranged.

On hearing that she was to be arrested, Gough screamed out 'No! No! No!' before collapsing to the ground in a faint. It was left to Foley to pick up the pieces; he escorted a weeping Gough from the building, past an assembled crowd of villagers and into a waiting carriage. She was to be taken from Road back to the Dallimores' house in Trowbridge, where she was to be held as a prisoner. Perhaps, thought Foley, a few days under house arrest would see Gough's tongue loosen a little.[21]

The arrest of Elizabeth Gough, who was young, female, educated and attractive, gave the reporters the angle they were looking for and within hours lengthy articles about the goings on in Road were being telegraphed back to London. The *Morning Post* was quickest off the mark and on 11 July they printed an essay of several hundred words, which was more frank about the nature of the crime and its investigation than the magistrates, police or the Kent family would have liked.

'A crime has just been committed,' said the article, 'which for mystery, complication of probabilities and hideous wickedness is without parallel in our criminal records.' It went on to outline the circumstances surrounding the murder and the subsequent police investigation, about which the newspaper was less than complimentary. A list of the suspects was given, with Mr Kent being regarded with the most suspicion because he had fled straight to Trowbridge on the morning of the murder instead of choosing to organise a local search. The article finished with a comment that would soon be echoed by other newspapers across the country: 'It is clear to us that the solution of the question turns upon very delicate points, which, in their nicety, lie far beyond the powers and skill of a country coroner's jury. The case must be put into higher hands and ... this matter must not be allowed to rest till the last shadow in its dark mystery shall have been chased away by the light of unquestionable truth.'

The view that Superintendent Foley and his county constabulary were out of their depth had gained much currency locally, but this notion was not shared by either the Home Office or the Metropolitan Police, who had examined the petition sent to them by the Trowbridge magistrates a few days earlier and, after due consideration, had rejected it. After conferring with Sir Richard Mayne, the Commissioner of the Metropolitan Police, the Permanent Under-secretary, Horatio Waddington, wrote back to the magistrates explaining that bringing in Scotland Yard (as the Metropolitan Police service was commonly called) was quite irregular and would undermine public confidence in the effectiveness of the nation's county constabularies, many of which had only been in existence for a few years.

Superintendent Foley's investigation had been given a reprieve, but the national publicity had served only to increase the pressure upon him and his men and, following Gough's arrest, there had been little further progress in the case. In the meantime, Road village was becoming overrun with newspaper men and curious tourists; faced with the prospect of unrest, two additional officers had to be drafted in from the Warminster division to keep order in the district. With the atmosphere becoming ever more tense, Foley must have been aware that his superintendence over the investigation was operating on borrowed time.[22]

FRIDAY 13 JULY 1860

Ominously, Superintendent Foley had chosen Friday 13th to take one last throw of the dice; it was Elizabeth Gough's continued examination, but should she fail to provide any new information, then his investigation would be at a dead end. The only other active lead, the former servant that Mr Kent had named the previous Monday, proved to be a red herring. The girl had been traced, interviewed and, having provided the police with a cast-iron alibi, discounted as a suspect. It must therefore have been with some trepidation that Foley greeted Gough as she arrived in Road following the short journey from the Dallimore's cottage at Trowbridge. She had spent three nights under house arrest but, much to Foley's annoyance, had chosen to say nothing further about the murder to her hosts. If she should remain tight-lipped then the consequences for Foley's reputation were potentially quite serious.

The magistrates assembled at the Temperance Hall, outside which an excitable crowd had gathered, including reporters from national newspapers such as *The Times*, the *News of the World* and the *Daily Telegraph*. The journalists pleaded to be allowed into the hall but the magistrates refused. 'The ends of justice will be frustrated by the publication of the evidence,' said the Reverend Richard Crawley, one of the magistrates. A reporter protested that the publication of evidence had assisted in previous cases; Crawley rejected this and made a terse remark about the poor quality of journalism associated with the murder thus far.

While the court assembled, Elizabeth Gough was taken to the house of Ann Stokes, where she was watched over by Inspector Samuel Pitney. As they waited to be called to the Hall, word reached her that there would be a delay because the magistrates wanted to visit Road Hill House. This caused Mrs Stokes to remark that they must have discovered something of significance there. Inspector Pitney went outside to chat with some of his colleagues and, on returning, said that he too thought there had been an unexpected development in the case. On hearing this Gough became very agitated and started to pace backwards and forwards around the room. With her hands pressed to her side, Gough exclaimed that she felt faint and then made an extraordinary statement.

'I cannot hold out much longer,' she said. 'I would not have held out this long had Mrs Kent not begged me to do so.' Both Pitney and Stokes were taken aback at this, but she would not be drawn on the matter and instead complained about the effect that the investigation was having on her health. 'No one knows how I've suffered,' she said. 'If anything else should occur then I think I shall die.'

Gough fell silent again and remained so for over an hour, before word came through that the magistrates were ready to receive her. It is alleged that Gough had a rough time in the witness box and was bombarded with questions from all angles, causing her to weep on several occasions; but, try as they might, the magistrates could not persuade or compel her to change any part of her testimony. It was an exhausting experience, but Gough did at least learn why the magistrates had visited Road Hill House earlier in the day. It had been related to a statement made by Constable Alfred Urch, who mentioned that while patrolling on the night of the murder he had heard the Kents' dog barking furiously and, on looking up, had seen lights in the hallway and also the nursery. He estimated the time to be just before one o'clock in the morning, which roughly coincided with the estimated time of Francis's death. Naturally this suggested that the nurse must have been awake during the night, but she denied all notion of this and said that Urch must have been mistaken.

Following Gough's examination, the magistrates and police went into conference. Foley was anxious to proceed with Gough's prosecution, but the magistrates were more cautious: they agreed that the nursemaid's behaviour and testimony was suspicious, but pointed out that there was no evidence at all that could directly link her to the murder. Without such evidence any hope of a guilty verdict from a jury was impossible. The magistrates instructed that Gough would have to be released from custody.

'There was nothing to warrant her detention,' said a policeman to the reporters assembled outside the hall. Superintendent Foley left the hall dejected and with the expectation that Gough, his only named suspect, would immediately leave the neighbourhood for her father's house in Isleworth, Surrey. He was therefore surprised to see Gough being taken back up to Road Hill House; when asked why, she replied that she was to resume her job as nursemaid to the two youngest children 'at Mrs Kent's special request'. It was all very unusual and served to reinforce an increasing suspicion that Gough was working in collusion with one or more of the Kent family.

News of Gough's release was telegraphed back to London, where it was generally met with approval by the newspaper editors, many of whom had Mr Kent pegged as the murderer. 'A very general impression of her innocence exists out of doors,' commented one paper about Gough; others were critical of Foley's management of the case and again called for the involvement of Scotland Yard. This was true also of the Trowbridge magistrates, whose patience with the Wiltshire Constabulary had worn thin. A second request by them to the Home Office for a London officer was looked upon more favourably; although still reluctant to sideline the local police, the Home Secretary agreed that, in light of the unusual circumstances surrounding the case, an experienced detective should have charge of the investigation and be despatched right away. Much to his chagrin Superintendent Foley had been taken off the case.[23]

SUNDAY 15 JULY 1860

On the morning after his son's death, Mr Kent had asked Superintendent Foley to send for a London detective to head the investigation. Those who suspected Mr Kent of involvement in his son's murder believed that he made this request to rile the inexperienced local constabulary into taking on the case single-handedly. If so, then the ploy had allowed two weeks to pass during which time the waters surrounding Francis's murder had become greatly muddied. By the time the London detective arrived in Trowbridge, late on 14 July, much valuable time and evidence had already been lost.

London's Scotland Yard was home to the country's best-organised police force, whose officers were used to investigating complex criminal cases, including murders. The Metropolitan Police had been established in 1829 with the first headquarters being adjacent to Scotland Yard in London's Whitehall. However, it was not until 1842 that they set up a 'Detective Department,' populated with plain-clothes policemen whose sole purpose was to investigate serious crimes such as murder, kidnapping and robbery. The Detective Department quickly gained a reputation for being an effective crime-busting force whose police officers had amazing powers of observation and deduction.

Most of the county constabularies (which were established between 1839 and 1856) had neither the need nor the resources for a separate Detective Department, which meant that, in the event of an unusual or brutal crime, it was not uncommon for the local populace to request the attendance of a man from Scotland Yard. Naturally, most local forces resisted such calls for outside help, as did the Metropolitan Police themselves, but there were occasions when it was unavoidable and the public failure of Superintendent Foley persuaded the Home Office that a London detective was needed in Wiltshire. A message was despatched from the Home Secretary's office to Sir Richard Mayne, the Metropolitan Police Commissioner, ordering him to send an 'intelligent' detective to the scene. Mayne was not in a mood for taking risks and therefore decided to send out his best and most famous detective, a man named Inspector Jonathan Whicher, whose reputation as a crime-buster was legendary.

In July 1860 Jonathan (Jack to his friends) Whicher was aged forty-six and a seasoned policeman of some twenty-three years standing, having joined the London

Metropolitan force as a young man in 1837. Noted for his quick wit and deductive ability, Whicher excelled at busting apart small criminal gangs who operated scams involving breaking and entering, heists, counterfeiting and theft; he proved to be particularly adept at identifying and tracking down individual criminals and was responsible for solving a number of high-profile crimes, including several murders and thefts. He joined the Detective Department in the 1850s and soon after his reputation grew, attracting the attention of his superiors and especially Sir Richard Mayne, on whose orders he was despatched to Road village.

Mayne believed that he had placed the case in a safe pair of hands, but in choosing Whicher to head such a high-profile case, he had flattered the inspector's not inconsiderable ego. Whicher delighted in his reputation as a sleuth and was keen to show off his abilities to the assembled pressmen: solving the Road Hill House murder would be a public display of his skills and so he set off to Trowbridge with the intention of not just clearing up the crime, but of doing so in as short time as possible.

Whicher arrived too late on the Saturday to begin his investigation and so he had to content himself with checking into his Trowbridge inn and settling down for the night. The next day was a Sunday, technically a day of rest, but Whicher was not prepared to waste any more time and so made contact with Superintendent Foley, insisting that the local policeman give him a full breakdown of the information and evidence thus far obtained, including any written reports and testimonies. It is alleged that Superintendent Foley felt so humiliated at Whicher's involvement in the case that he kept his co-operation to an absolute minimum. Nonetheless, by the end of the day Foley had given Whicher enough information to allow him to draw up a plan of action that would get the investigation moving forwards again.

Of immediate concern to the inspector was that the Kent family had not thus far been properly quizzed about their respective roles on the night of the murder. This view was echoed by many local people, including most of the jury at the coroner's inquest, who believed that the authorities had conspired to keep Mr Kent and his family out of the investigation. Whicher was especially surprised to learn from Foley that Mrs Kent and one of the elder daughters (probably Elizabeth) had yet to be interviewed at all. It was a situation that could not be allowed to continue: on Sunday afternoon Whicher contacted the Trowbridge magistrates to request that they resume their inquiry the next day. One senses that within twenty-four hours of his arrival at Trowbridge, the London detective already had a suspect in mind.[24]

MONDAY 16 JULY 1860

Inspector Whicher was acutely aware that his arrival in Road would be greeted with dismay by the local police. He was also aware that, despite being invited into the investigation, he did not have a free hand in it. Prior to catching the train from London Whicher had been informed by his superiors that he would be acting under orders from the Trowbridge magistrates' bench who, together with two additional magistrates from Somerset, were expecting him to provide daily updates of his progress.

Whicher was nothing if not tactful and to help quell passions in the local constabulary he sought out the Wiltshire chief constable and asked if Superintendent Foley could be his deputy officer. The chief constable agreed and for the following week Foley accompanied Whicher as he rushed about the countryside making his enquiries. However, their first appointment was at the Temperance Hall on Monday morning, a place with which Foley had become very familiar. Here he found the Trowbridge magistrates waiting to examine the entire Kent family.

At this stage the press had not been informed of either Inspector Whicher's presence or of the intention to resume the magistrates' inquiry on the Monday morning, but it did not take long for word to travel about, drawing onlookers and journalists to the Hall. To the disappointment of many, the inquiry continued to be held behind closed doors. Whicher would probably have been pleased with this but he may have been less than delighted to learn that in place of the lawyer Rowland Rodway, Mr Kent had engaged the services of another solicitor, William Dunn from Frome, to represent his family's interests. Mr Dunn turned out to be a more aggressive character than Mr Rodway and was keen to argue over every point of law. Before the inquiry had even opened, Dunn made a complaint about the presence of the two Somerset magistrates; a lengthy debate followed which resulted in the extra magistrates being asked to leave the hall. He also objected to Whicher's request that the inquiry be temporarily moved up to Road Hill House so that the Kent family could be interviewed at the scene of the crime; this appeal Dunn lost and so yet again the magistrates, together with Whicher, Foley, Dunn, Captain Meredith and the other members of the court, made their way from Road village to the house on the hill.

The examination of Mr Kent and his family was not altogether successful, thanks largely to the frequent objections raised by Mr Dunn, which time and again served to frustrate Inspector Whicher's line of questioning. The detective was unable to obtain any useful information, but the interviews did convince him of two things: firstly, that Elizabeth Gough did not commit the murder; and, secondly, that the guilty party was undoubtedly still resident at Road Hill House.

'I have made an examination of the premises,' said Whicher afterwards, 'and I believe that the murder was committed by some inmate of the house.' He then asked if it would be possible to examine Constance's bedroom: it was with some reluctance that Mr Kent (and Mr Dunn) agreed to this request.

Whicher, Foley and Captain Meredith made their way up to Constance's second-floor room and began a systematic search of her wardrobe and linen drawers. Within the chest of drawers Whicher discovered a laundry list which had apparently been drawn up by Constance on departing from her boarding school two weeks earlier: it contained a description of all the items of clothing that were to return with her to Road Hill House. On seeing it Whicher became animated and asked that Constance be brought up to her room for further questioning. She came presently and was confronted with the scrap of paper.

'Is this list of linen yours?' asked Whicher.

'Yes,' replied the girl.

'In whose writing is it?'

'It is my own writing,' came her answer. Whicher then drew her attention to the number of nightdresses that the list contained.

'Here are three nightdresses,' said Whicher. 'Where are they?'

Constance answered coolly: 'I have two, the other was lost at the wash the week after the murder.' To prove her point, Constance took the two nightdresses from the chest of draws and handed them to the inspector. He examined them: both were clean but well-worn and had evidently been in Constance's possession prior to the date of the murder. Seeing a further nightdress and gown on Constance's bed, Whicher asked where these had come from.

'They are my sister's,' she said, explaining that because the laundress had refused to wash any more clothing from the family, a backlog of dirty linen had built up, forcing her to borrow an additional nightdress to replace the one that had been lost. Whicher made note of this conversation and then left Constance to interview the servants. Their accounts tallied with their earlier testimonies and so, satisfied with what he had heard and seen, the inspector returned the inquiry to the Temperance Hall once more.

That evening Whicher made a brief presentation to the Trowbridge magistrates outlining his early thoughts about the case and the names of those whom he intended to investigate further. His list of suspects did not include Elizabeth Gough and, after explaining his reasoning, he was given permission to continue with his enquiries. A short while afterwards the press were called into the Temperance Hall and were told that Inspector Whicher was now in charge of the investigation. They were also informed that Elizabeth Gough was no longer thought to be a suspect and that she was free to go about her business as usual. This apparent *volte face* took everyone by surprise, not least Elizabeth Gough, who was said to be as bemused as the villagers and journalists to learn that she was no longer the subject of police attention.[25]

WEDNESDAY 18 JULY 1860

Inspector Whicher's arrival caused a great deal of excitement about the neighbour-hood and generated a sense of expectation among the villagers, most of whom were clamouring for action of some sort. They were not to be disappointed: within two days of his arrival Whicher told Foley that he knew the identity of the killer and the means by which they had accomplished the deed.

Unlike the local constabulary, Whicher did not think that the crime warranted two suspects; nor did he think it strange that the nursemaid had not been disturbed from her slumber. Thus, and contrary to local opinion, Elizabeth Gough was not his prime suspect; neither was Mr Kent, nor his elder son William, whom he considered to be too frail (physically and mentally) to have committed the murder. That left just one member of the household without an alibi: sixteen-year-old Constance Kent. Although she remained near the bottom of most people's list of suspects, the odd circumstances surrounding her missing nightdress had served to convince Whicher of her guilt and as a consequence he immediately devoted his efforts to finding the evidence that could link Constance to the murder of her half-brother.

It was quickly evident to Whicher that the Kent family and their servants were not going to expand on their testimonies and so, rather than focus his investigation on Road Hill House as Superintendent Foley had done, the London detective decided to broaden his horizons. In his review of Foley's paperwork Whicher found a number of letters written by members of the public that contained sto-ries and snippets of information relating to the case. With so much gossip around Superintendent Foley had placed little weight on the public correspondence, but amongst the tittle-tattle Whicher believed that he could discern some information that could be of genuine help. As soon as the examination of the Kent family had finished, Whicher began chasing up these leads, some of which he hoped would provide him with the evidence he needed to link Constance Kent to the crime.

One of the letter writers was a woman named Emma Sparks, who had been nursemaid to the younger Kent children in the year before Elizabeth Gough took up the post. Sparks had come forward with a most extraordinary story that had happened while she was at Road Hill House in the autumn of 1858. On this occa-sion Francis Kent was just two years old and slept in the same room as Miss Sparks and his older sister Mary Amelia. It was a particularly cold night and so Mrs Kent, who was then pregnant with Eveline, insisted that Sparks put Francis to bed in a pair of knitted socks so as to keep the chill from his feet. On retiring to bed, Sparks and Mrs Kent observed that Francis was still wearing his socks, but when the nursemaid awoke in the morning, she discovered that the boy's feet were bare.

At first Sparks assumed that the boy had taken the socks off himself, but on searching the cot she could not find them. A wider search led to the discovery of one sock on the nursery table which was some distance away from Francis's bed and quite beyond his reach. The other sock was not found until some time later when Mrs Kent discovered it secreted in her bedroom. Sparks had not been disturbed during the night but nonetheless concluded that somebody must have crept into the nursery and purposefully removed Francis's socks; there was simply no other explanation. Mrs Kent and the staff all had alibis and the only other person in the house that night was Constance Kent, who was on her school holidays and who slept alone. She was the only suspect, but nonetheless denied being involved and, given no harm had come to Francis, the matter was dropped.

News of this strange event was greeted with keen interest by Whicher, as it offered evidence not only that it was possible to creep in and out of the nursery unobserved, but also that Constance was already accomplished at doing so. Whicher confirmed Sparks's story with Mr and Mrs Kent, but they denied that Constance could have been responsible and instead suggested that their ex-nursemaid had exaggerated the story.

The next lead Whicher chose to follow up came via a letter from a Mrs Bailey, a woman from Sutton Veny, near Warminster, whose house was across the street from one of Constance's school friends, Emma Moody. Mrs Bailey was probably something of a busybody and she had certainly taken a great interest in Francis Kent's murder; it appears that she had quizzed either Emma Moody, or her widowed mother, closely about the friendship with Constance and, based on what she had been told, had written to the police. Early on the Wednesday morning Inspector Whicher set off by train from Trowbridge to Warminster and from there by carriage to Emma Moody's house in Sutton Veny. The seventeen-year-old girl was at home with her mother and was very surprised when the detective turned up to request an interview.

Emma was far from delighted at the prospect of talking to the police and proved to be reticent and hesitant. She confirmed to Whicher that she attended the same school as Constance and had known her for about six months, during which time they had talked only occasionally. Based on what he had heard from Mrs Bailey, Whicher pressed Emma to reveal details of certain conversations during which Emma and Constance had discussed their home lives. The girl became quiet and sullen and had to be prompted by Whicher, who asked her if Constance had ever discussed her half-brother Francis.

'I have heard her make such remarks about the child as this,' said Emma, 'that she disliked the child and pinched it but I believe more for fun than anything else, for she was laughing at the time that she said it.'

Naturally, the idea that Constance could have disliked her half-brother was of great interest to Whicher, but Emma would not be drawn on the matter and even sought to play it down, claiming that Constance had talked about teasing all of her stepmother's children and not just Francis. When asked why Constance should have wanted to pinch Francis, Emma said she believed that jealousy was the motive.

'I was walking with her one day towards Road and I said, "Won't it be nice to go home for the holidays so soon." She said, "It may be to your home, but mine's different." She led to infer, though I don't remember her precise words, that she did not dislike the child, but through the partiality shown by the parents, and that the second family were much better than the first. I remember her saying that several times.'

Jealousy and sibling-rivalry were certainly motives for murder, but Whicher would need much more than this if he was to obtain a warrant for Constance's arrest. The detective showed Emma the blood-soaked chest flannel from the cesspool which he had brought with him. Could it have belonged to Constance? Emma said that she thought not.

Whicher was not satisfied with this and it would appear that he had been told by Mrs Bailey that Emma held a piece of knowledge that was vital to solving the case. He pressed Emma further, but the girl was headstrong and would said say nothing else. The inspector was forced to return to Trowbridge with only circumstantial evidence of Constance's feelings towards her family and half-brother, but he reckoned that if Emma Moody were to be placed under oath in a court of law then she would probably reveal more. As things stood, though, he would need more evidence before a formal charge could be made against Constance.[26]

THURSDAY 19 JULY 1860

As far as can be gathered, it was the morning after his rather frustrating meeting with Emma Moody that Inspector Whicher chose to re-interview Mr Kent on the issue of his daughter Constance. The discussion focused on Constance's behaviour towards her half-brothers and sisters and on Mrs Kent's attitude toward her stepchildren. In neither case was Mr Kent able to confirm the allegations of ill treatment. He did, however, verify another unusual story which Whicher had discovered during his investigation, probably from a former servant such as Emma Sparks.

The story concerned the murderess Madeleine Smith, the twenty-one-year-old daughter of a wealthy Glasgow architect, whose trial had obsessed all of Britain three years previously. Miss Smith had been a bohemian character who found herself in a triangle with her secret lover Emile L'Angelier and an eminent suitor whom her parents had found for her. Madeleine stopped seeing L'Angelier and so he attempted to blackmail her, but on 23 March 1857 he was found dead of arsenic poisoning. Madeleine was arrested for murder but a verdict of 'not proven' was returned which, under Scottish law, suggested that while the jury felt that she was guilty, there was not enough evidence to secure a safe conviction.

The trial started in June 1857 and contained revelations of secret meetings, love letters and pre-marital sex. The world was agog and the newspapers printed the trial transcripts in full, which Mr and Mrs Kent read with fascination. However, when thirteen-year-old Constance started to ask questions about the case, they became coy and even hid any copies of *The Times* that contained mention of Madeleine Smith. It was therefore with some outrage that Mr Kent one day discovered that his secret pile of newspapers was missing; he directly accused Constance of taking them but she denied all knowledge and continued to do so even after they had been found under her mattress. Inspector Whicher asked Mr Kent about this: he confirmed that the incident had occurred and that the story was accurate.

This interested Whicher for two reasons: firstly, it suggested that Constance had taken an interest in the issue of murder before June 1860; but, far more importantly, it showed that she was quite capable of issuing a barefaced lie, even when the evidence of her guilt was manifest. Like the evidence from Emma Sparks and Emma Moody, this was not proof of Constance's guilt, but it did bolster the London detective's theory, as did the opinion of Mr Parsons and another local surgeon that Constance was a cunning sort of girl who displayed some signs of instability. Mental illness, noted Whicher, appeared to run strongly through the Windus side of the family and had afflicted Constance's mother, grandmother and an uncle.

That evening Whicher sat down with all the evidence and testimony that he had gathered during the previous five days. He made out a list of points which suggested that Constance was the guilty party, but proof of a link between her and the actual crime remained thin and rested almost solely on the strange circumstances surrounding the missing nightdress. Nonetheless, he felt that there was a great deal of circumstantial evidence which provided Constance with a motive and the means of committing the crime. This included the story concerning Francis's socks, the conversations with Emma Moody and the direct lie about taking her father's newspapers. On balance, Whicher believed that he had solved the case and that, as he had hoped, it had taken him less than a week to do so. All he had to do now was bring his suspect to trial.[27]

FRIDAY 20 JULY 1860

First thing in the morning Inspector Whicher travelled to Road Hill House to examine Constance Kent about the evidence he had acquired that week. He had a lengthy list of questions to ask which, as ever, Constance answered in a matter-of-fact way, not giving any indication of either guilt or remorse. Whicher noted down her replies carefully:

I am the third daughter of Mr Kent. I went to bed at quarter past ten on the Friday night. I remember my sister coming in before I went to sleep. I don't remember what she said. I have had no Lucifer match-box in my room these holidays. I was told by papa and mamma not to keep matches. I have seen a Church of England magazine in nurse's room. I was very fond of [the] deceased. When I first heard of our loss I ran by my mother's wish to Mr Peacock. I could carry the deceased by the length of this room easily. I was generally considered pretty strong at school. Deceased used to be not very fond of me; he appeared fonder these holidays. The little boy was not fond of me because I teased him. I never struck him or pinched him. My eldest sister was present when my box was opened when I came from school. I have heard that the nurse had turned the cot to take the child out. If I wanted a light in the night I should have gone to the nursery. I did not say to any of my schoolfellows that I should not go home for the holidays. I have said I should not like to be always at home for the holidays. I have said I should not like always to be at home. I did not see my brother William after we went upstairs. William is my favourite of my brothers and sisters. We write to each other when I am school. A window was left at the back of the house unfastened. My father told me of this morning. It would require a ladder. There are several ladders in the stable. The dog wouldn't fly at me if he recognised me. He would bite me if he didn't know me. My father takes a lantern when he goes out to let the dog loose. I have a cat but I don't care anything for it. I am not considered very timid. I don't like being out in the dark.

I once did cut off my hair and fling it down the same place where my little brother was found. I cut part of my hair and my brother cut the rest. I thought of the place to put it in. I and my brother William went to Bath by an indirect road. This was about four years ago. I didn't behave well and I went off because I was cross at being punished. I persuaded my brother William to go with me. I went to my aunt's in London last Christmas twelvemonth. I came down from London by myself. I think it was all ladies in the carriage with me. I heard of Madeleine Smith's affair, but was not allowed to read it. I may have taken a paper but I didn't intentionally take a paper with an account of this in it. I heard Madeleine Smith's friend was poisoned. I used to hear papa talk about it. I put my nightdresses out of my room on Monday morning. Cox the housemaid took it. I don't think I have thrown out dirty linen before these holidays.

I have locked my door since because I thought it was safer. I slept with the nurse two or three times since the murder. I have never done so before. I believe the nursery door opens easily. The door falls to easily when opened. I have often tried the door. I like the cook best of the servants. I like the nurse very well. I have never taken a walk alone these holidays with the little boy that is dead. I think my father was quite well on the Friday. If he had been unwell I should have heard of it.

Inspector Whicher was generally pleased with Constance's replies and, having made his notes, left Road Hill House to meet with the magistrates in the village below.[28]

At eleven o'clock the Trowbridge magistrates met at the Temperance Hall to discuss the further developments in the case. No witnesses were called, but outside there was much excitement among the assembled reporters, many of whom were speculating about a forthcoming arrest. The anticipation heightened when, just after lunch, Inspector Whicher and one of the magistrates departed the hall and were observed to travel up to Road Hill House. Shortly after this the press were invited into the hall and told to await further developments.

At the Kents' house Inspector Whicher was shown into the dining room, where he requested Constance to be brought before him. After her arrival, Whicher turned and addressed the girl in a plain and solemn tone. 'I am a police officer and I hold a warrant for your apprehension, charging you with the murder of your brother Francis Savill Kent.'

Constance stood silently while Whicher read out the warrant in full. She then began to cry and through the tears said repeatedly: 'I am innocent! I am innocent!' Whicher took his prisoner upstairs to her bedroom, where she was permitted to put on a bonnet and a cape; they then commenced to walk down the hill towards the Temperance Hall. At around half past three in the afternoon Constance, Whicher and the magistrate were spotted entering the village by reporters. 'Constance walked with a firm step from her father's house to the Hall but she was in tears,' wrote one witness. Inside the hall the press were already assembled when

Constance entered and was shown to a seat in front of the magistrates' bench. Flanked by Whicher and Superintendent Wolfe, Constance stared down at her feet and replied in a faint voice when asked to confirm her name. Following which the circumstances behind the issuing of the warrant were read out and then three witnesses were called to give evidence in support of the warrant.

The first of these was Elizabeth Gough, the person who had herself been under suspicion the week previously. Her testimony had not changed and outlined yet again the circumstances surrounding the discovery of Francis's disappearance. She was followed by William Nutt, who told how he and Thomas Benger had come to find the boy's body. The final witness was Inspector Whicher himself: he gave an account of his investigation and arrest and then asked that Constance be held in custody for a few days.

With supreme self-confidence Whicher announced to the hall that, 'I shall be able to show the animus which existed between the prisoner and the deceased and to search for the missing nightgown which, if in existence, may possibly be found. To Wednesday or Thursday next should be ample time.'

The magistrates conferred for a short while and then remanded Constance in custody for a week, after which time she was to be returned to Road for a preliminary hearing. With the court adjourned, Inspector Whicher and Superintendent Wolfe took their shocked and trembling prisoner from the hall and into a trap which was waiting to take them to Devizes gaol. By this time most of the village was in attendance. The news of Constance's arrest came as something of a shock as she was not generally viewed as being the most likely suspect. People openly wondered whether the famous Inspector Whicher might not have made a mistake: could Constance Kent, a girl of just sixteen, really be guilty of having murdered a three-year-old boy?[29]

WEDNESDAY 25 JULY 1860

The week following Constance's arrest proved to be problematic for Inspector Whicher, whose investigation, which had hitherto moved at a quick pace, suddenly encountered several obstacles. Almost as soon as he had had Constance committed to gaol, Whicher realised that his claim to be able to find the necessary evidence in only a few days had been boastful, especially as his appointed deputy, Superintendent Foley, disagreed with both his methods and conclusion. Whicher telegraphed Sir Richard Mayne, his superior officer at Scotland Yard, telling him that: 'The magistrates have left the case entirely in my hands to get up the evidence. I am awkwardly situated and want assistance. Pray send down Sergeant Williamson or Tanner.'

Sergeant Frederick Williamson of Scotland Yard was ordered to Trowbridge and arrived on Saturday 21 July. During the next week the two detectives were rarely seen in Trowbridge or Road as they undertook a series of journeys across the local countryside in search of further witnesses. Their travels took them as far afield as Bristol, Gloucester and Herefordshire, although their reasons for visiting these places are not known. Sergeant Williamson also spent a full day in Beckington, a village about a mile from Road, chasing up a lead that apparently related to Constance having taken her brother there on 10 June. What Williamson was looking for is uncertain, but circumstantial evidence suggests that Constance was seen abusing the child, possibly while they were inside a shop.

Part of Whicher and Williamson's troubles came from the arrest of Constance. A majority of local people and the county police believed that either Mr Kent or Elizabeth Gough (or both) were guilty of the crime and that the London detective had made a terrible mistake. Whicher and Williamson found themselves isolated in their task and received little co-operation, even after the government put forward a £100 reward for information leading to the murderer's conviction. They did, however, enjoy the full support of the Trowbridge magistrates, whose opinion had been swayed away from Elizabeth Gough and towards Constance Kent. The chairman of the magistrates, Henry Ludlow, wrote to Scotland Yard in praise of Whicher and his arrest of Constance Kent.

On the Tuesday morning Whicher decided to curry local favour by staging a publicity stunt at the Temperance Hall. He announced that the bloodied (but since cleaned) chest flannel that had been recovered from the cesspool would be placed on display for several hours. The pretext was to see if anybody recognised it, but as the crowds filed into the building they were forced to pass a placard offering a £5 reward for the recovery of a lady's nightdress which might have been 'thrown in the river, burnt or sold in the neighbourhood'. No-one came forward to claim the prize.

Later in the week it was with increasing desperation that Whicher dismantled the outside privy at Road Hill House in order to search the cesspool again. He even had the Kents' dog tested for its aggressiveness towards strangers, but the animal refused to bark and merely wagged its tail at all who were placed before it. By the middle of the week Whicher had telegrammed his boss, complaining that he found himself 'very unpleasantly situated' and that the local police were at best being unhelpful and at worst unco-operative. 'I have studiously endeavoured to act in concert with them as far as possible,' wrote Whicher.

As a final act of desperation, Whicher returned to Sutton Veny to interview Mrs Bailey, the woman who lived across the road from Constance's school friend Emma Moody. She was very co-operative and told Whicher something so alarming that he immediately summoned Emma from across the road and had her questioned before Mrs Bailey.

Even under this pressure, Emma claimed to remain ignorant about whatever it was that Mrs Bailey had said to the policeman. Whicher expected as much and had come prepared with a summons to appear as a witness in the court case. The girl still kept silent and continued to do so when, a few days further on, she was berated by the local superintendent over her alleged intransigence and insubordination toward the London detective.

Despite extensive and exhaustive enquiries, Whicher's time was running out and he had little new evidence to show for his, and Williamson's, additional efforts. As the morning of the preliminary hearing dawned, he was left to hope that he had gathered enough circumstantial evidence against Constance Kent to convince the magistrates that she should be further remanded for full trial on a charge of murder.[30]

FRIDAY 27 JULY 1860

Although Constance had been charged on suspicion of the murder of her step-brother, the Trowbridge magistrates did not have the legal right to bring such a serious case to trial. Instead, they had to recommend that the case to be tried before a higher court, but before doing so, the magistrates needed to satisfy themselves that there was sufficient evidence to warrant this. Thus the purpose behind the preliminary hearing into Constance Kent's arrest was to examine Inspector Whicher's evidence, to make sure that the case was watertight. Furthermore, this inquiry was to be held in full view of the public and, of course, the many journalists that temporarily inhabited the area.

Friday morning in Road village saw riotous scenes as spectators crowded about the Temperance Hall in the hope of gaining admittance to the public gallery (adequate space had already been reserved for the press). The Trowbridge magistrates met in private for half an hour before opening the doors to the assembled mass outside. Already present in the court room were the six magistrates, Inspector Whicher and several members of the Wiltshire Constabulary, including Captain Meredith and Superintendent Foley. In response to a recommendation from William Dunn, Mr Kent's legal adviser, a separate lawyer had been hired to defend Constance; he was Peter Edlin, a top criminal barrister from Bristol, whose services did not come cheaply. Mr Kent sat next to his legal representatives, occasionally swapping notes with them; it was noted that he looked tired and haggard.

At around half past ten the court was called to order by Henry Ludlow, the presiding magistrate, and the defendant called to the dock. Constance Kent entered the room and immediately crossed to where her father sat and kissed him on the cheek. She was dressed in black, taken by many to be a sign of mourning, and, on being shown to her chair, was observed to be in tears.

The clerk to the magistrates, the appropriately named Mr Clark, began proceedings by reading through the testimonies given by Elizabeth Gough and William Nutt the previous Friday. Both Gough and Nutt were called forward and asked to confirm that what they had said was correct. Further questions were asked of them, but nothing new came forward as a result. Mr Edlin attempted to imply that William Nutt may have had some prior (or possibly even supernatural) knowledge of the whereabouts of Francis's body, but he was cut short by Nutt himself who gave a graphic description of the corpse that silenced the court room. With the witnesses from the previous week dealt with, it was time to move onto Whicher's new evidence.

First up was Constance's sullen-looking school friend Emma Moody, who had appeared in the court under a great deal of protest. Whicher had subpoenaed her in the belief that answering questions under oath might loosen her tongue. The chairman of the magistrates started to question the teenager about her conversations at school with Constance.

He began by asking Emma whether the prisoner had ever expressed any feelings towards Francis such as friendship or perhaps hatred? Emma struck to the line she had taken with Whicher: Constance did not say that she disliked the boy, but appeared to be jealous of him. Several further questions did not change her mind and so the chairman moved onto Constance's feelings towards her stepmother. This proved to be more fruitful.

'She said that the second family were much better treated than her or her brother William. She said this on several occasions,' replied Emma. Believing that he was at last getting somewhere, the chairman sought to expand on the matter. 'We were talking about dresses on one occasion,' said Emma in reply to a further question, 'and Constance said, "Mamma will not let me have anything I like; and if I said I should like a brown dress, she would let me have a black one, just for contrary."'

This statement attracted the interest of the court, but before the chairman could continue, Constance's lawyer, Mr Edlin, objected to the line of questioning, complaining that his client's relationship with her stepmother was not directly relevant to Francis's death.

'The chairman has unintentionally exceeded his duty by pressing these inquires,' said Edlin. His words were greeted with a round of applause from the public bench, a majority of whom believed Constance to be innocent. The interruption caused Emma Moody to become silent once more and, after several vague answers, the chairman gave up his examination of her. Mr Edlin then questioned her and in the process established that Constance was a well-behaved and well-liked student. He also got Emma to describe the nature of Whicher's two visits to question her, which made it sound as though the inspector had placed undue pressure on the girl to corroborate a statement given to the police by her neighbour, Mrs Bailey. On hearing this Whicher realised that his investigation methods were about to be dragged through the mud and so he interrupted the proceedings. 'As my name has been mentioned,' he said to the magistrates, 'perhaps the bench would ask the witness whether I brought anything with me?'

'The inspector brought a piece of flannel with him,' said Emma, 'but I could not identify it. The second time he brought a summons and had several times impressed upon me the necessity of speaking the whole truth upon the matter.'

On Whicher's further prompting the chairman was on the verge of telling the court about the allegation made by Mrs Bailey, which perhaps concerned Emma being able to identify the owner of the chest flannel, but Mr Edlin was quick to intervene.

'I object to the introduction of any statements made in the absence of the accused,' he said. The chairman thought for a minute and then changed his question and instead asked Emma whether she had ever remonstrated with Constance in any conversation that they had together. This brought forth another objection from Edlin: 'The witness has already said more than once that she has stated all she knows.'

The question was withdrawn and Emma Moody released as a witness; Whicher's hope that she would say something to incriminate Constance had come to nothing. If anything, Moody had portrayed his prisoner as a conscientious student who endured a troubled home life; this reinforced an opinion that many in the neighbourhood already held and so elicited further sympathy for Constance.

The next witness was Joshua Parsons, the surgeon, who was able to describe the nature of the boy's wounds and ascribe a probable cause of death. As at the inquest, Parsons asserted that, 'The mouth had a blackened appearance, and the tongue protruded between the teeth. I think this was produced by forcible pressure during life.' This allegation of suffocation was still being hotly (and somewhat vocally) contested by Joseph Stapleton, who denied ever having seen the bruising about the mouth.

There was little else that Parsons could add. He admitted to having examined the clothes at Road Hill House on the morning after the murder but said that nothing incriminating had been found. 'Constance's nightdress was very clean but I cannot say how long it had been worn,' he said when asked about the prisoner's nightclothes. The next witness was only marginally more useful. It was Constance's alleged best friend from school, a fifteen-year-old girl named Louisa Hatherall whom Whicher had also visited at her Badminton home the previous week. Like Emma Moody, she was questioned about conversations concerning Constance's home life.

'I have heard of her speak of her home, and say there was a partiality shown by the parents for the younger children. She spoke of her brother William being obliged to wheel the perambulator [pram] for the younger children, and that he disliked doing it. She also spoke of her father comparing William to Francis and saying what a much finer boy the younger would be.' However, Louisa would not be drawn on the subject of Constance's feelings toward Francis. 'She told me nothing, to my recollection,' she said before being released by the magistrates.

If Whicher had hoped to prove that Constance's dislike for her stepmother and her half-brother and -sisters was a motive for murder then he had failed. That there was tension in the family was hardly news to the villagers: the incident when Constance and William ran away together suggested as much, as did their removal to boarding school. However, Inspector Whicher was not yet finished and had one other tactic to pursue, which concerned the strange events surrounding the disappearance of Constance's nightdress.

In Whicher's mind this was the strongest piece of circumstantial evidence pointing towards Constance's guilt. He theorised that when cutting the boy's throat Constance had got blood onto her nightshirt and that she had subsequently destroyed it, probably by burning (this perhaps being why he asked questions about her owning matches shortly before her arrest). This meant that she was missing one of her three nightdresses and so to cover this up she gave a dirty nightdress to Sarah Cox, the housemaid, making sure that it was entered in the laundry book. Constance then distracted the housemaid and stole back the nightdress from the laundry basket, an action that would not be noticed until the baskets reached the washerwoman. By doing so Constance could produce two nightdresses and claim that the third one (which she had destroyed) had been lost or stolen in the wash.

Whicher was proud of this theory, but few people really believed that this was what had happened, least of all Superintendent Foley and his men. It was up to Whicher to change their minds and so he summonsed Sarah Cox, the housemaid, as a witness.

'I perfectly remember putting this nightdress of Miss Constance's into the basket, I am certain of it,' said Cox, recalling the events of 2 July. She then told the court how Constance had interrupted her to ask for a glass of water from the kitchen, but the housemaid said she had been gone only a short while and that Constance would not have had time to find and steal the nightdress from the basket. 'I think I was not gone near a minute, for I went very quickly,' she said.

For once Mr Edlin found himself facing a witness whose testimony could cast some doubt on his client's claim to innocence, but he decided that his best tactic was to establish that Constance's nightdress had gone into the washing basket. He began by questioning the housemaid's ability to distinguish the girls' nightdresses, but Cox would have none of it.

'Miss Constance's nightdresses are easily distinguishable from the other Misses Kents',' she said, 'as they have plain frills and the others have lace and work.' Edlin then asked if anybody else witnessed the nightdress in the basket; Cox replied that Elizabeth Kent had. 'Miss Kent said she was quite sure that I put Miss Constance's nightdress in the basket, as she had seen me do it ... but I can't swear that the nightdress made it out of the house, because I was not in the house at the time.'

This brought the court onto the matter of whether the nightdress had been stolen and so Hester Holley, the laundress, was called to the stand. As might be expected, she denied having stolen the nightdress in the strongest possible terms, but her testimony was constantly interrupted with objections from Mr Edlin. At one point he accused the magistrates of acting in the manner of a prosecutor, even though the case had yet to come to trial. An argument between the various learned gentleman followed, but the matter was ended by a series of skilful questions from Mr Edlin, in which it emerged that Mrs Holley had previously taken some items from the Kents' laundry.

'There were two things that went missing before,' she said, 'one a very ragged duster and the other an old towel. Those are the only things I was ever accused of having before, and that I'll swear. Mrs Kent forgave me the towel.'

Mrs Holley's admission that she had previously taken items from the Kents' laundry was exactly what Edlin needed to place doubt on the washerwoman's version of events. Just to underline his case the lawyer asked his witness to confirm that one of her daughters was married to the brother of William Nutt. Edlin attached no meaning to this, but it was well known locally that the Nutt family had a dislike of Mr Kent following his prosecution of two of their number for trespass. Indeed, Mr Kent had requested that some members of the family be considered as suspects for the murder. Mr Edlin's implication was obvious: Mrs Holley had taken the nightdress either to get the Kent family into trouble or possibly to divert suspicion away from someone within her own extended family.

Mr Edlin turned and addressed the magistrates' bench:

I ask that the Bench instantly liberate the accused and restore her to her friends! There is not a tittle of evidence against her – not one word on which the finger of infamy could be pointed against her. Although a most atrocious murder has been committed, it has been followed by a judicial murder no less atrocious … The fact respecting the missing bed-gown has been cleared up to the satisfaction of every one who has heard the evidence here today and no doubt can remain that this little peg, upon which this fearful charge has been grounded, has fallen to the ground.

These were strong words, but Edlin saved his greatest criticism for Inspector Whicher and his investigation:

The hunting up of her school fellows reflects an ineffable disgrace upon those who have been in the business of bringing them here. Nothing that has been elicited from these young ladies shows anything like animus on the part of the prisoner towards the deceased child; nor has any motive been established which would induce the prisoner to imbrue her hands in the blood of the poor child. I have never heard a weaker case for prosecution. I demand that you do your duty for the country: Miss Constance should at once be discharged! Liberate this young lady and restore her to her friends and her home!

This was greeted with a round of applause from the public gallery, which the chairman forcefully and somewhat angrily suppressed. Edlin was quite correct in what he said: there was no hard evidence linking Constance Kent to the murder of her half-brother. The bravado of Inspector Whicher had led the Trowbridge magistrates to lock up a sixteen-year-old girl in an adult gaol and then to present a lamentable and humiliating inquiry in which every witness seemed to provide evidence pointing towards her innocence.

The conference between the magistrates was brief and their decision unanimous. 'We have decided to discharge the prisoner,' said the chairman to loud cheering, but he asked Mr Kent to provide an assurance of £200 for his daughter's release, 'for her appearance if called upon'. The relief on Constance's face was immediate and as she was guided from the hall by her father the crowd stood up and gave them a tremendous ovation.

It had been a very long and tiring day that had seen Inspector Whicher's investigation torn apart. The outcome had been to the satisfaction of not just the Kent family, but also of much of the village, as well as the Wiltshire Constabulary, all of whom had suspects and theories of their own.

The humiliation experienced by the Trowbridge magistrates was as nothing compared to that felt by Inspector Whicher, who was immediately dismissed from the case. On leaving the Temperance Hall he was jeered and verbally abused and, with no cause to remain in the neighbourhood, wasted no time in scurrying back to the safety and anonymity of London. The Road Hill House murder was, and remained, his most public failure, and it tarnished his reputation during the remaining few years of his service with Scotland Yard's Detective Department. Whicher must have rued the day he agreed to help investigate the mysterious murder at Road Hill House, a solution to which seemed as far away as ever.[31]

MONDAY 30 JULY 1860

The weekend following Constance's discharge from the inquiry had been an eventful one for the members of Road Hill House. Any hopes that the farcical events of the past couple of weeks would lead to a period of respite were dashed when Inspector Samuel Pitney of the Somerset police visited the family early on the Saturday morning. He had been involved with the investigation since 14 July and had helped keep an eye on Elizabeth Gough following her detention, but with Captain Meredith and Superintendent Foley suddenly back in charge of events, the inspector's role had been expanded to include the gathering of new evidence. As such, Inspector Pitney had gone to the house with a view to conducting a general search of its interior, perhaps in the hope of finding the murder weapon. He was, however, immediately confronted by a hostile and angry-looking Mr Kent who was decidedly fed up with the sight of policemen.

'I have come to make an investigation of the house,' said Pitney.

'The police have had long enough in the house,' replied Mr Kent, 'it's time you made a search outside the grounds.'

'Does anyone bear you ill will?' asked Pitney, but Mr Kent merely repeated his earlier allegations against the Nutt family. 'They are very much against me,' he said to the inspector, who agreed to look at the list of names he had just been given.

The inspector did not make his search and as he made his way into the village Mrs Kent began to experience the first pains of her labour. For a while the family's troubles were forgotten as the household went into a well-rehearsed routine that saw Elizabeth Gough, amongst others, assist with the birth. Even though this was her fourth child, the labour was long and it was not until the Monday morning that the baby was delivered: it was a boy, who was immediately named Acland Savill Kent, but he had been born into family which was much troubled.

Public interest in the Road Hill House murder was such that news of the birth was covered by local and national newspapers everywhere: even *The Times* in London saw fit to mention it. Naturally, the papers also gave coverage to the bizarre hearing that had occurred the previous Friday, with a majority coming out in favour of Constance's acquittal. Many echoed the line later taken by the *Annual Register*, which wrote that, 'the grounds on which this accusation were made were so frivolous and the evidence by which it was attempted to be supported so child-ish, that the proceedings can only be described as absurd and cruel.'

The blame for what was perceived to be an attempted miscarriage of justice was laid squarely at the door of Inspector Whicher, and it was not just the Wiltshire locals who were annoyed at him. On the Monday morning Whicher had to face the wrath of Sir Richard Mayne, the Commissioner of the Metropolitan Police, who was livid at the unnecessary speed of the investigation, something which he viewed as being the function of the inspector's arrogance.

However, the public humiliation and acerbic headlines had done nothing to dent Whicher's conviction: he still believed that Constance Kent was guilty of murdering her brother Francis, and so he sat down and wrote a lengthy letter to his boss, outlining his theory about the case and the evidence he had gathered to back it up. He ended by summarising his theory, which held a surprising twist that had not been revealed to the public: Whicher suspected that not just Constance, but her brother William was also involved.

I am able to form an opinion that the murder was committed either by Miss Constance alone while in a fit of insanity, or by her and her brother William from virtue of spite and jealousy entertained towards the young children and their parents and I am strongly impressed with the latter opinion judging from the sympathy existing between the two, the fact of their sleeping in rooms alone, and especially the defeated state of the boy both before and after his sister's arrest, and I think there would not have been much difficulty for the father or some of the relatives to have obtained a confession from him while his sister was in prison, but under the peculiar circumstances of the case I could not advise such a course and if a confession should come now it would no doubt be made to some of the family and then possibly not made known.

William and Constance had been among the first to be suspected of the crime, but the opinion of the Wiltshire police and the public had shifted somewhat so that the boy was rarely talked about in connection with the case. Whicher had viewed things differently and had been greatly impressed by the children's attempt to run away, which had been largely planned and executed by Constance and which had involved her hiding her clothes and hair in the outside privy. However, a lack of any evidence at all against William had caused Whicher to keep his suspicions quiet; in light of Constance's discharge, this turned out to be a good move. William was never again to be mentioned in connection with the crime by Whicher or anybody else.[32]

THURSDAY 9 AUGUST 1860

The dismissal of Inspector Whicher gave the Wiltshire Constabulary the chance to redress their tarnished reputation. The officer in overall charge of the case, Captain Meredith, was aware that the eyes of the entire British nation were upon his organisation and so, rather than let Superintendent Foley loose on his own again, he decided to oversee the investigation personally. Foley was to be kept on the case but in a more low-profile role; he was to be joined by Superintendent Wolfe, who had been brought down from the town of Devizes to work alongside Meredith. Spurred on by the need for results, the two policemen abandoned Foley's cautious, sensitive approach in favour of more aggressive methods.

Captain Meredith took the decision to discard all of Inspector Whicher's theories and evidence and to pick up the investigation from where Foley had left it two weeks previously. The Wiltshire officers had always believed that two people were complicit in the murder and that one of these had to be the nurse Elizabeth Gough who, if not the actual murderer, knew who the guilty party was. It was with this in mind that, after lunch on 1 August, the three senior policemen returned to Road Hill House to interview the nursemaid yet once more.

Gough expressed a weariness at seeing the police, but was nonetheless asked to accompany them upstairs to the nursery to show them Francis's cot. The officers were soon joined by Mr Kent's lawyer, William Dunn, who had been summoned to protect Gough's interests and who frequently instructed her to ignore a question that had been put her.

Gough confirmed that none of the furniture had been touched since the boy's death, including the bedclothes which, according to Gough, were just as they had been when she awoke on the morning in question. The sheet and counterpane were smooth, tucked in and had been turned down; it was very neat and convinced Meredith that they must have been rearranged following Francis's removal. He also noted that it was impossible to determine whether or not the blanket was missing without disturbing the bedclothes.

'If the blanket had been abstracted the clothes must have been adjusted afterwards,' said Meredith.

'The bedclothes are in the same state now as when I found them. The first time I missed the blanket was after the child was found,' replied Gough. When asked how she noticed that the boy was missing, she said: 'I awoke about five o'clock in the morning and, seeing that the baby was lying by my side naked, raised myself to cover it over and in doing so I looked across to the little boy's cot and missed him. I raised myself onto my knees and then went to sleep again.'

Wolfe decided to replicate this scenario. Mr Dunn was asked to place a coloured garment in the cot which Wolfe, who was very tall man, attempted to see by kneeling on the nurse's bed as Gough had described. No matter what he did, he could not get a clear enough view of the cot to see the garment; this was perplexing and gave Meredith more cause for suspicion. The policeman again asked Gough to divulge all she knew, to which she responded:

> I know nothing of who came into my room that night, or who went out I can't say. I did believe, and I do now, that somebody must have been secreted in the house that night or that they got in. I only wish I knew about the murder; I would soon tell you. Do you suppose I could have kept it for seven weeks?

Soon afterwards Mr Kent intervened by offering to show the policeman about the house, suggesting where an intruder might have secreted himself. He even suggested that they might have hidden themselves underneath a sofa in the living room, but Meredith expressed some doubt about this. He and Superintendent Wolfe left Road Hill House convinced that they were on the way to solving the case.[33]

The police investigation appeared to be gathering pace when, the day after Gough's interview, Captain Meredith was granted permission to exhume Francis Kent's body from St Thomas Becket churchyard. This action caused much upset to the Kent family and only later did Meredith explain to them that he had received information that an item of clothing 'is supposed to have been concealed in the coffin and interred with the body of the murdered boy'. One supposes that he was searching either for the missing nightdress or some piece of bloodstained clothing. On this meagre information the Home Secretary granted an exhumation order (something of a rare occurrence), but the coffin was discovered to contain nothing unusual or mysterious. Meredith wrote a second letter to the Home Secretary informing him that the case had not been materially advanced by the exhumation.

The pursuit of Elizabeth Gough did not let up and two days later she found herself being examined on her knowledge of Mr Kent's behaviour concerning the murder. 'Mr Kent has never alluded to the matter to me since it occurred from first to last,' she protested, an opinion that could perhaps reinforce the family's reputation for being dysfunctional. 'The young ladies have, and so has Miss Constance, and Master William has often cried over it.'

The issue of the blanket in which Francis had been wrapped was also puzzling Captain Meredith. Going back through the original statements made by the family he noticed that while Elizabeth Gough denied having missed the blanket until after the body had been found, that Mr Kent claimed to have known that it was missing when he set off to Trowbridge some time before the body was found. Mr Kent was re-interviewed about this by Superintendent Foley.

'Were you aware that any blanket was taken away with the child before you left for Trowbridge?' asked Foley.

'Certainly not,' replied Mr Kent, who went on to deny that he had ever said any such thing. Foley pointed out that one of his officers had heard him say so on the morning that the body was discovered, but Mr Kent said that he must have been mistaken.[34]

On Thursday 9 August the investigation was stepped up a gear. Under orders from Captain Meredith, Foley requested Elizabeth Dallimore, the wife of the Trowbridge constable, to travel up to Road Hill House where he would join her with the chest flannel from the cesspool. This item had been heavily stained with blood when recovered but had since been washed clean and it was Foley's plan that all the adult women should try it on for size. There was still no proof that the flannel was connected with the murder but it seemed strange to the police that none of the women in the house had come forward to claim the garment when it patently had to belong to one of them. This in itself was considered suspicious and suggested that the flannel's owner had a connection with the disposal of the body.

As instructed, Mrs Dallimore waited in the kitchen for the arrival of Superintendent Foley but news of her presence quickly spread through the household and drew an agitated-looking Elizabeth Gough into the kitchen. 'What are you come here for?' she demanded of Mrs Dallimore.

'A gentleman will tell me what I have to do before I leave,' replied the policemen's wife.

It was some time before Superintendent Foley arrived, bringing with him the flannel. Mrs Dallimore examined it closely: it was clearly not a purpose-made garment, but had been constructed from a piece of cloth taken from an old item of clothing, probably a petticoat. From its size and shape it was evidently, as the police had supposed, a chest flannel, designed to be worn across both breasts, next to the skin. The garment had been tailored by its owner and, when in place, would have covered the chest and reached up towards the arms, stopping just underneath the woman's stays. It was thought that matching this bespoke item to the body it had been tailored to fit was a relatively straightforward task.

Foley was keen to get the examination moving and pointed at the cook and housemaid. 'Mrs Dallimore, you must try this piece of flannel on them girls and the nurse.' She did as she was asked and took the two women upstairs to their bedrooms, where they were asked to undress partially and to try on the flannel for size. Both girls were large-chested and it was apparent that the flannel was too small for them. Mrs Dallimore returned to the kitchen to collect Elizabeth Gough, who somewhat reluctantly accompanied her upstairs to the nursery.

Mrs Dallimore asked the nurse to pull off her things so that she might try on the flannel, but Gough was reluctant to do so. 'It is of no use taking off my clothes,' she said. 'If the flannel fits me, that's no reason that I should have done the murder.' She removed her stays and permitted Mrs Dallimore to place the flannel onto her chest: it fitted perfectly.

'You see, nurse,' said Dallimore, 'the flannel exactly fits you, which it did not the other servants.'

'If it fits me,' replied Gough, 'that's no reason I done the murder.'

'Well, it might fit a great many,' countered Dallimore, 'but there's no-one in the house I have fitted it on but you.'

The policeman's wife returned to the kitchen with the flannel and reported back to Superintendent Foley. He was not surprised and had expected the flannel to fit Gough, but, to be on the safe side, he asked Mrs Dallimore to try it on the elder Kent daughters, Constance, Mary Ann and Elizabeth. This was swiftly done, but the flannel would not fit any of them. In his mind (and that of Mrs Dallimore) the chest flannel had to belong to Gough and as such it was the first piece of physical evidence linking a member of the household to the crime scene. This was a major move forward and there was talk of an imminent arrest, but before they could make their move, something extraordinary happened: another person confessed to having murdered Francis Savill Kent.[35]

MONDAY 13 AUGUST 1860

One of the most unusual turns in the Road Hill House murder case occurred at a sleepy railway station about forty-five miles to the north west of London. It was around midday on a warm Friday in the quiet village of Wolverton when Sergeant Edward Roden, an officer in the Railway Police, watched a man behaving oddly on the platform and went to speak with him.

'Do you know anything about the Road murder?' asked the man of the officer.

'Only what I have read in the newspapers,' replied Roden. 'Do you know anything about it?'

'Yes,' replied the man. 'I did it.'

The policeman did not need to hear this twice and without further ado he apprehended the man before shouting across to a colleague to help him. There was no struggle and the prisoner allowed himself to be taken by the police to the nearest large town, that of Stony Stratford, where he was placed before a magistrate. The man refused to divulge his name but he did elucidate on the matter of his confession to having murdered Francis Kent.

'My life is a burden to me,' he said. 'I did the deed. I committed the murder at Road. It is on my mind and I shall be hanged. It was Mr Kent who handed the child to me through the drawing-room window. He promised me £1 but he has not paid me and I am sure that the curse of God is upon me. I am determined to confess.' On hearing this the magistrate, the Reverend H. Barton, remanded the man in prison overnight and then to be taken to Trowbridge for further examination.

News of the arrest spread fast and by the time of the man's arrival in Trowbridge the next afternoon, a sizeable crowd had gathered. Locals and pressmen strained to get a glimpse of the alleged murderer as he was led from a railway carriage by two officers.

'He was dressed in the usual habiliments of a working mason' wrote one reporter, 'and is a rather short, but stout-made, man with a florid complexion, a considerable quantity of whisker, and of some forty years of age. His head is of peculiar shape, being remarkably flat at the crown.'

As the crowd pressed about him he was taken before the Trowbridge magistrates who, together with Superintendents Foley and Wolfe, examined him closely, but the man was unco-operative and would only give his name as Edward John.

'I will reserve my surname,' he explained before complaining bitterly of a headache. Edward John's story had changed somewhat from the one he had given the magistrate the previous day. Appearing somewhat dishevelled and bewildered he claimed not to know where he was or what had happened to him. When told he was in Trowbridge he claimed to be a mason from London and that he had never heard of Trowbridge and had never before been to either Road, Trowbridge or even the West of England. He then appeared to make another semi-confession: 'I did what I did in order to be hanged, which I should be,' he said. 'I believe God's curse to be upon me. I have had no peace and cannot get work. Why this should be, I don't know for I never injured anyone.'

The magistrates believed Edward John to be 'at least partially deranged,' but the policemen in the courtroom were not so sure and, on examining him, found three spots of blood on his trousers. The prisoner could not account for these and was remanded until a further examination could be made on Monday afternoon.

The reaction in the town was immediate and revealed the mood of the neighbourhood. Many were convinced that the police had got their man and that the original confession implicating Mr Kent was the perfect solution to the mystery. 'The feeling of the populace here is so strong against Mr Kent that any circumstance pointing against him is readily believed,' wrote the correspondent for *The Times*, adding cryptically that 'Superintendents Foley and Wolfe are sanguine in having obtained a clue to the murder in another quarter.'

The examination of the mysterious Edward John on the Monday afternoon turned out to be an unusual and very public affair which saw the eccentric prisoner produce a breathtaking display of ignorance and ineptitude that did little to endear him to court officials.

The magistrates knew that they were in for a tough time when their prisoner again refused to state his name and then, on hearing the statement he had given the railway policemen, denied having said half the things in it. Although more clear-headed than before, he continued to confound the court with vague answers. The magistrates were more convinced than ever that they were dealing with an idiot and sought to find any piece of evidence, no matter how small, that could remove him from the list of suspects. Eventually Edward John admitted that he was in Portsmouth on the night of the murder, but his line of reasoning proved to be very erratic.

'You now state that you were at Portsmouth on the night that the murder was committed,' said the chairman of the magistrates, who was somewhat exasperated. 'If so, how came you to place yourself in this position?'

'I was hard up and I thought it better if I could be hung. I am sick and tired of life,' replied Edward John.

'Then why did you change your story?'

'Because I should not like to die without convincing everyone that I was inno-cent,' he said, entirely missing the illogicality of this statement.

'Can you give us the name of any person who knows you personally, anyone who can speak as to who and what you are?'

'Nobody here, sir.'

'I don't mean here, but anywhere! Anyone in London?'

'I could refer to two or three, but I think I will let things take their course. I should not like them to know where I was.'

The examination continued like this for some hours, but, although it was evi-dent that they were dealing with a person of exceptionally low perception, they could not discharge him without first obtaining his name and an alibi for the night of the murder. As a last resort the chairman tried a different tactic; he showed the prisoner the press gallery and told him that, like it or not, he was going to appear in newspapers across the country. 'I should not like my mother to know I was here,' said the prisoner meekly.

'Everything that has taken place today in this court will be published to the world!' spluttered the chairman, before advising the prisoner that he would be remanded in custody for a further two days, but that he would not be charged with the murder. The seriousness of the situation suddenly sank in and shortly after being taken to his cell the man handed his guard a piece of paper on which he had written his name: John Edmund Gagg.

The sorry saga of John Gagg took several days to sort out and only ended on 22 August, when he was brought before the Trowbridge magistrates for a third and final time (having been further remanded on 15 August).

In the light of the unusual situation, the magistrates had ordered an investiga-tion into Mr Gagg's circumstances and in doing so discovered that he was a sorry sort of fellow whose wife had left him, taking the children with her. According to Inspector Whicher, who had helped in this case, she was now doing well for herself 'by her own industry' and was better off without her husband. Gagg received rep-rimand after reprimand from the magistrates: for being a bad husband and father; for being a drunkard; for making a false confession; and, most of all, for wasting everybody's time and energy in the process.

'The bench only regret exceedingly that it is not in their power to give you any severe punishment for your conduct. Had they the power to do so you would have had it to the full extent and would richly deserve it.' Instead they discharged Gagg and placed him on the first train to London with enough money for a few days' food and accommodation.

The matter had been a distraction from the job of identifying and prosecuting the real killer, but it had provided a little light relief for many in the neighbourhood, including the local police, who were, for a few brief days, able to pursue their enquiries without the press breathing down their necks. However, the release of Gagg saw the spotlight turn toward them again, and with it came renewed calls for the murderer or murderers to be brought to justice.[36]

MONDAY 27 AUGUST 1860

On the morning of the 27 August Superintendent Foley received word from Road Hill House that Elizabeth Gough had resigned her position and was preparing to leave the neighbourhood permanently. Foley was concerned to hear this and went directly to Road Hill House, where he found the nursemaid standing with her bags packed awaiting the arrival of her father, who was to take her home to Isleworth. On seeing Foley the nursemaid apologised at having to leave but promised that she would continue to offer assistance from her father's house. Foley made one last attempt at extracting some useful information from her.

'If I knew anything, I would tell you,' said Gough wearily, but Foley did not desist and asked if she thought that Constance was the murderer. Gough said that she was sure that the girl was not guilty.

'If you are so sure about Miss Constance, you must know who it was,' replied Foley. 'Was it yourself?'

'No.'

'Was it Mr Kent?'

'No. It must have been someone concealed within the house.'

'That story won't do nurse,' barked Foley. 'I can't believe it for a minute.'

But the superintendent's time was up and a short while later Gough's father arrived to collect his tired and emotionally exhausted daughter. Watching Road Hill House fade into the distance must surely have been a relief to the nursemaid, who remained the police's prime suspect and whose reputation had suffered greatly during the previous two months. Quite why she had remained in her post for such a long period of time was a mystery to most people, although, in truth, her association with the murder meant that her chances of finding a position in another household were next to zero. Elizabeth Gough's career in domestic service was effectively at an end.

A few days later Foley received a letter from Gough in which she said that she had settled into her father's house and that should she be required again then she would come forward willingly; all Foley had to do was to drop her a line and she would travel to Trowbridge.

This was some small comfort, but the removal of one of Foley's prime suspects was symptomatic of the way in which the Wiltshire police's investigation was once again losing momentum.[37]

The discharge of Constance Kent and the absence of any new suspects had lifted the Road murder to new heights of infamy; so much so that it was routinely being referred to simply as 'the Road mystery.' With little new information to print, the journalists, and their readers, filled the void by becoming amateur detectives, filling the newspapers with novel theories concerning the identity, motive and method of the culprit(s). Some of these were reasonably well thought out; others not so.

In the latter category was the notion that the murderer might have carried out the crime while sleepwalking and thus not even be aware that they were the guilty party. The idea that somnambulism might have played a part gained much popularity, although few people went so far as to suggest a name for the nocturnal wanderer. Others disagreed with this strongly: 'Somnambulism would hardly manifest itself with such startling results, unless symptoms had previously appeared which it would be the business of the police to discover, and which would go far to identify the author of the crime.'

Others picked up on what they believed to be vital bits of evidence that, in their view, were key to the solution of the puzzle. 'Two things that occurred the next morning are fraught with suspicion,' wrote one *Times* correspondence, 'the ostentatious reading of the Bible for an hour by the nurse, who knew that the child was missing, and who ought immediately to have made inquiry in Mrs Kent's room; and the decision which was at once arrived at by certain parties that the child had been murdered. If the police would follow out these two points they would, perhaps, be more successful than they were in their "fussy activity" about the nightdress of a schoolgirl.'

Nationally the general consensus was that Inspector Whicher's investigation had been a waste of time and that the real culprits were Mr Kent and Elizabeth Gough, who, it was suggested (though rarely in print), were romantically linked. This idea had arisen very shortly after news of the murder had leaked out, but a couple of weeks later a new rumour had sprung up in the region around Road village which linked Elizabeth Gough, not with her employer, but with the shoemaker William Nutt.

The theory was a consequence of Mr Kent's insistence that the Nutt family were out for revenge and that it had been William Nutt, a known enemy of the family, who had discovered the boy's body. It was suggested that Nutt had sneaked into the nursery to be with Gough but that the lovers had been disturbed by little Francis, who had perhaps observed the couple in a compromising situation. An attempt to silence the boy had, accidentally or otherwise, resulted in his death and lead to the couple staging a false break-in.

Inspector Whicher was made familiar with this rumour, but he had dismissed it out of hand. Writing to his superior officer at Scotland Yard he said that Gough 'was not acquainted with Nutt, and in the next place I do not suppose she would condescend to speak to him in any way, much less as an admirer, as she is rather a superior girl for her station in looks and demeanour, while on the other hand Nutt is a slovenly, dirty man, weakly, asthmatical and lame'.

This apparent incompatibility did not concern the Wiltshire police, who looked into this matter very seriously in the weeks following Whicher's departure, and went as far as to interview William Nutt several times. However, they too decided that there was little evidence to link the two and reverted back to the idea that it was Gough working in conjunction with another person.

One newspaper account even gave an elaborate account of how Gough's lover, this time a soldier from her home town of Isleworth, had crept into the nursery using a ladder, murdered the boy and then exited in the same manner, dumping his body in the privy on his way out. This version was little believed, of course, but common currency did hold that Gough and an unknown lover, be it Mr Kent, William Nutt or some other man, were guilty of the crime, and the lack of action on the part of the police was beginning to irritate people, including Mr Kent.

Considering that many, including the Wiltshire police, had Mr Kent labelled as a prime suspect in the case, it must have somewhat surprising to learn that he had been petitioning Sir George Lewis, the Home Secretary, to order a new inquest into his son's death. Via Mr Dunn, his solicitor, Mr Kent argued that problems with the first inquest had led his household to suffer from improper allegations; he especially complained that his family had not been properly interviewed as part of the original inquest. Needless to say, he omitted to mention to the Home Secretary that this had been at his own request and that even when the jury demanded such interviews, they were only allowed to speak to Constance and William for a few minutes.

It was of no consequence; the rules governing a coroner's inquest are very strict, which meant that George Lewis had to decline the application on the grounds that the first inquest had proceeded in a formal and legal manner and could thus not be annulled. On learning this Mr Dunn wrote back to request that the Home Secretary convene a special commission to investigate the murder again, but this too was refused as Sir George preferred to leave the matter in the hands of the local police and local magistrates. Following the public failure of Scotland Yard to solve the case, the Home Secretary preferred to keep a safe distance between his department and the strange goings on in Somerset.[38]

FRIDAY 7 SEPTEMBER 1860

The notion that the government need not dirty its hands over the Road murder slowly evaporated as Sir George Lewis's in-tray became weighed down with petitions, requests and even demands from the residents of Somerset and Wiltshire that the Home Secretary do something to move the investigation forward. Many correspondents expressed the opinion that Captain Meredith and his men had proved themselves unable to solve the crime and that help was needed from outside authorities.

It was Mr Kent himself who had been the first correspondent to demand government action in the form of a second inquest, but no sooner had this idea been dismissed by Sir George Lewis than he received a letter from a Mr Thomas Bush Saunders, a retired barrister living in Bradford-upon-Avon, who, by his own admission, had taken a close interest in the case. His letter informed the Home Secretary that 'circumstances had come to his knowledge which induced him to think that evidence could be brought forward without much difficulty or expense sufficient to justify the apprehension of two of the persons who slept in the house on the night of the occurrence'. Saunders did not state which two people, nor the nature of his evidence; instead he asked Sir George to set up a new inquiry which would, naturally enough, be chaired by Saunders himself, free of charge.

The Home Secretary replied in cordial terms, informing Saunders that if he had any new leads then 'it is your duty to communicate them to your brother magistrates and then to the chief constable of the county'. Saunders wrote back, complaining that he had already offered to assist the local magistrates but that they had turned him down. From this Sir George may have recognised that Saunders was, like so many others, seeking to attach his name to a very high-profile investigation: the barrister's letter did not receive a reply, but if the Home Secretary thought that this would be last he would hear from Thomas Bush Saunders then his was to be sorely mistaken.

No sooner had Sir George Lewis dealt with Mr Saunders than he received a memorial from William Tite, the Member of Parliament for Bath. In polite terms the memorial drew the Home Secretary's attention to the state of inertia concerning the investigation; there was especial concern that the inhabitants of Road Hill House had not been properly interviewed 'as to their complicity in that frightful transaction'. Tite requested that permission for a 'special commission for the investigation of the crime' be granted, 'as the ordinary means have entirely failed'. The memorial was signed not just by the MP, but also by the Mayor of Bath and many other local dignitaries. As such, the request could not be dismissed lightly, but the Home Secretary remained resolute on the matter:

> To supersede the established courts of justice,' he directed in his reply, 'which are governed by well-known and carefully defined rules, and to establish by Royal authority in their stead a commission exercising new and arbitrary power of examination, unknown to the English law, would be highly unconstitutional and a departure from the principles which the country has long been governed.

William Tite and the Mayor of Bath were furious at this, and promptly took their case to the newspapers, where they received much coverage and not a small amount of sympathy.

Before the ink had dried on this reply, the Home Secretary received a petition from the people of 'Frome, Trowbridge, Warminster, Westbury and adjacent villages' which also made the point that the Kent family had not yet been sufficiently examined and also requested that a 'special commission at once be appointed' to further examine the matter. This request was not new, but the Home Secretary was somewhat surprised to note that the first signature to the petition belonged to Samuel Kent himself and was followed by the names of the rest of his household. Despite this the petition was again refused, a decision that caused Mr Kent to write a separate letter requesting a personal interview with Mr Waddington, the Under-Secretary to the Home Secretary. This too was refused, and Mr Kent wrote back stating that 'I should at any time be prepared to submit myself and my household to a voluntary examination by the Chairman of our Quarter Sessions or any other official whom Sir G. Lewis might nominate.'

This was a rash promise and it may have been made by Mr Kent in the belief that a situation would never arise which would require him or his family to give evidence again. If so, then he was quickly to be disappointed when, the day after the Home Secretary's refusal of an interview, Mr Kent received a letter from a Mr Slack requesting that he and his family attend his office in Bath so that they could be separately examined as part of the murder investigation. Mr Slack asserted that he was opening a new inquiry into the case on behalf of the Trowbridge magistrates and that he was operating with the consent of the Home Office.

This was true enough and was a consequence of a complaint by the Trowbridge magistrates that the case against Constance Kent had collapsed partly because the prosecution did not have access to a solicitor who could adequately cross-examine the witnesses. The Home Secretary agreed with this analysis and consented to pay for just such a solicitor; the magistrates soon afterwards employed Edward F. Slack of Bath, a man of 'great experience in criminal proceedings' for the purpose of cross-examining existing and new witnesses and, should any charges result, to act as the official prospector in any future court case. Mr Slack had begun his inquiry from scratch, but, after reading the existing depositions, quickly decided that all the residents of Road Hill House needed to be re-examined and had written to Mr Kent to inform of this.

The result of this was a slightly farcical situation. Only a day or so previously Mr Kent had published a letter in the national newspapers stating his willingness to be examined but, on receiving Mr Slack's request, he ordered his solicitor to refuse Mr Slack permission to talk to the family.

In trying to find excuses not to be interviewed, the letter to Slack reveals a certain level of desperation: 'For ought we know,' wrote Mr Dunn, 'you may be acting under the instructions of the detective officer whose former proceedings in this case have been condemned by the almost unanimous voice of the country.'

This opinion disregarded Mr Slack's assertion that he was operating on behalf of the Home Secretary, the confirmation of which caused Mr Kent to write again to Sir George Lewis, stating that, in light of his earlier promise to comply with any new inquiry: 'I am sure that you will see that in declining to comply with this request I am in no way acting in opposition to the assurances I have given to you.'

Sir George did not look favourably upon Mr Kent's retraction of his offer to help. When an anonymous letter arrived on the Home Secretary's desk suggesting that Mr Kent was guilty of murder, Sir George scribbled across the bottom that the writer was 'not far from the mark'.

The Home Secretary does not appear to have directly instructed Mr Kent to comply with Mr Slack's inquiry, but his displeasure was somehow made known. Two days later Mr Slack received a letter from Mr Dunn confirming that the Kent household would after all be available to interview, but that this must occur at Road Hill House and not in the solicitor's offices. Within hours Slack was in a carriage heading towards Road village.

With the investigation apparently gaining renewed momentum, Superintendent Foley took the liberty of telegramming the police at Isleworth to check on the whereabouts of Elizabeth Gough. He learned that she was visiting friends in Oxford for a while; Foley instructed that as soon as she returned the local police were to keep a close eye on her whereabouts and, if possible, prevent her from leaving the town.[39]

TUESDAY 25 SEPTEMBER 1860

It was just after lunch on Friday 14 September when the Home Office-appointed solicitor, Mr Slack, drew up at Road Hill House to begin his inquiry. With him was Superintendent Foley, who was to act as his factotum during his time in the area.

Unlike the previous examinations made by the police, coroner and others, Mr Slack was determined to be both systematic and thorough in his approach to interviewing witnesses and suspects, but most of all he wanted to ensure that Mr Kent and his lawyer would not be able to disrupt the proceedings as they had done previously. It was partly due to Mr Kent's interference that some potentially valuable witnesses had yet to be properly examined: Mr Slack would brook no such trouble, but just to be on the safe side, he determined that Mr Kent, his daughter Constance and Elizabeth Gough should be examined last of all.

That Friday afternoon saw Mr Slack assemble an interview panel that consisted of Mr Slack, Superintendents Foley and Wolfe, two recorders and Mr Dunn, the Kents' solicitor. The makeshift panel first chose to examine Sarah Cox, the housemaid, who had been interviewed several times already, and Sarah Kerslake, the cook, who had yet to be formally questioned by anybody. Being a private inquiry, none of the questions asked or answers given was published, but according to one account, the two servants were examined 'most minutely'.

The next morning saw Mr Slack start to interview those members of the family who had hitherto been largely ignored by the police. This included the two elder Kent daughters and the two youngest, Mary Amelia and Eveline, who were aged just five years and thirty months old respectively. Despite press speculation to the contrary, little new information was obtained, and nor was it from the remainder of the staff and William Kent, all of whom were examined on the following Monday.

The exception to this was John Alloway, the sullen teenager whom Mr Kent had fired and whose last day of notice occurred the morning after the murder. Because he had the potential motive of revenge, Alloway had for a while been viewed as a suspect even though he had an alibi for the night of the crime. This had led to the boy being taciturn when interviewed and to his giving out some contradictory statements. 'Through sheer stupidity and obstinacy, not much importance attaches to what he may say,' was one verdict of Alloway's previous evidence, but Mr Slack seems to have fared somewhat better and was rewarded with a version of events that had not as yet featured in the investigation.

It was on Mr Slack's instructions that Superintendent Abbott of the Wiltshire Constabulary travelled out to Beckington village to interview John Alloway. Based on a rumour that Mr Slack had heard, Abbott had been given specific instructions to ask the boy about the events surrounding a lantern which had occurred in the days before the murder.

Alloway proved to be compliant and explained that during his last week at Road Hill House Mr Kent had been very anxious to get a lantern repaired in the village. The lantern itself was nothing special: it was a square, glass-sided candle lantern of a very common sort and in which one of the windows had been broken. On the instructions of Mr Kent, Alloway had taken the lantern to be repaired by Mr Fricker, the plumber and glazier, on the Wednesday morning before the murder. However, Alloway then related how he had been sent back to Fricker a few hours later to see if the lantern were mended; it was not, and over the next two days the boy was continually sent into the village to enquire when it would be ready. On the Thursday alone he made three trips, but it was not until the Friday night that the lantern was fixed. When asked why he had been sent so many times, Alloway was told by the cook that Mr Kent was very anxious that the lantern be mended by the end of the week, although for what purpose it was required, he did not know. When asked whether the lantern was an important one, Alloway replied that he had never seen it in use or, indeed, had never seen it all prior to taking it to the village and had not seen it afterwards either (although he had not been back to Road Hill House since the murder).

When he later heard this, it struck Mr Slack as being odd that Mr Kent should be so fussed about a lantern that, as far as could be deduced, was not in regular use within the house. Was it possible that the lantern had been used by the murderer? If so, then Mr Kent's urgency over its repair could be viewed as suspicious, suggesting that he might have been planning the crime for some while beforehand.

This was certainly an idea that crossed Mr Slack's mind: he was able to confirm with Mr Fricker that Alloway's version of events was correct and later let slip to reporters that Alloway's evidence 'tended at first sight to incriminate some members of the household'.

On the evening of Wednesday 19 September Mr Slack had a lengthy meeting with some of the Trowbridge magistrates, at which he summarised his progress and then read from some of the interview transcripts that had been made during the previous few days. Mr Slack then presented some additional background evidence he had garnered from other sources, including an interview with a former nurse-maid to the Kents, whose account 'contradicts the statements which have been made as to the harmony existing in the family'.

After much deliberation, the Trowbridge magistrates were agreed that Mr Slack's evidence as it stood pointed towards a suspect, although they refused to publicise who this was. It was agreed that the inquiry should conclude with the examination of the remaining members of the Kent household plus Elizabeth Gough; this process began the following morning when Mr Slack interviewed Mrs Kent. She was questioned continually from eleven in the morning until four o'clock in the afternoon, but nothing new was discovered. Afterwards Mr Kent was called in and was questioned for two hours that day and then for most of Friday as well, but he refused to alter his view that an intruder had killed his son out of revenge against himself.

On Friday evening it was Constance Kent's turn before the panel; she bore the inquisition with 'great self-possession and fortitude' and was not released until the Saturday evening. As with her father and stepmother, she revealed nothing of material use to the inquiry and it was with some exasperation that Mr Slack announced the termination of his interviews at Road Hill House.

Scarcely pausing to draw breath, Mr Slack compiled his evidence into a report which he forwarded to the Attorney-General for comment. Unlike Inspector Whicher, the solicitor did not want to make a prosecution based solely on his own instinct: he wanted a wider consensus before ordering an arrest. If nothing else, this would allow any blame to be spread across several heads rather than just one, as had happened to the London detective.

On the Monday and the Tuesday Mr Slack made two final visits. One was to see Mr Joshua Parsons, the surgeon who had performed the post-mortem examination on Francis's body; and the other was to Isleworth, to see Elizabeth Gough, who remained at her father's house. Both were closely questioned and by the time of Mr Slack's return to Trowbridge he had received word from the Attorney-General, who requested an urgent meeting with him and an official from the local assize court. Mr Slack left for London without delay.[40]

FRIDAY 28 SEPTEMBER 1860

The mysterious murder at Road Hill House had many unusual aspects to it, but perhaps the most extraordinary of all was its ability to sustain completely different opinions about the identity, motive and method of the murderer or murderers. It seemed as though every person in the country had their own theory as to who might have wielded the knife and why they should have wanted to do so. Some followed Inspector Whicher's reasoning and put Constance Kent in the frame; a minority of others saw her brother William as the suspect, or some outside agent; but a majority believed that Mr Kent was the killer and that he was working in conjunction with Elizabeth Gough. Given the known evidence and the evasive behaviour of Mr Kent, this theory seemed to fit the bill.

It was not just the patrons of coffee houses and idle fireside gossipers that thought this; the police and other authorities also generally thought that Mr Kent and his nursemaid were guilty, although which of them actually did the deed was still debated. To this number was added the weighty voices of Mr Slack and Sir Richard Bethell, the Attorney-General, both of whom were more familiar with the evidence than almost anybody else in the country. They likewise laid the blame on Kent and Gough, but the real question was whether there was sufficient evidence to permit one or both of them to be brought to trial. It had been with this in mind that Mr Slack, the Attorney-General and the Recorder of Bath, Mr Thomas William Saunders (who should not be confused with the Bradford-upon-Avon magistrate Mr Thomas Bush Saunders, whom we shall meet again shortly), met on the morning of Wednesday 26 September to consider the strength of the case against Kent and Gough.

What passed between them is not known, but based on hints and nudges given in the press, it appears that, while the men believed both parties to be guilty, they considered that there was insufficient evidence against Mr Kent to permit his arrest and trial. However, the case against Elizabeth Gough was somewhat stronger: she had made a number of inconsistent statements and was, by her own admission, in the room when the boy was taken. There was also some circumstantial evidence linking her to crime, including the chest flannel from the cesspool which appeared to fit her and her alone.

That she knew more about the crime was undoubted, but as to whether it was her that had inflicted the fatal wounds was less certain, as it appeared that this was a job better suited to Mr Kent's disposition and physical strength. This uncertainty raised another issue: if Gough were to be arrested then what crime should she be charged with? There were three choices: she could be charged as the principal murderer; as an accomplice to the murder; or as an accessory after the fact. The matter must have been debated long and hard, but eventually a conclusion was reached: based on the evidence he had been shown, the Attorney-General would recommend that Elizabeth Gough alone be arrested and charged with the murder of Francis Savill Kent.

A document was drawn up which stated that there were sufficient *prima facie* grounds for issuing a warrant for the apprehension of Elizabeth Gough and that it was in the interest of public justice that she should be examined in public on the matter. Both Bethell and Saunders signed the document and handed it to Mr Slack, who at once returned to Trowbridge to speak with the magistrates there.[41]

The next morning saw the Trowbridge magistrates' bench convene at an early hour in the town's court-house building. Mr Slack placed before them the document from the Attorney-General recommending the arrest and examination of Elizabeth Gough. This must have led to some debate amongst the magistrates who, just two months earlier, had universally believed Constance Kent to be guilty of the crime. However, the wishes of the Attorney-General were not be taken lightly and, following a lengthy exchange of opinions, it was agreed that a warrant for Gough's arrest should be drawn up. Its wording stated that:

> Elizabeth Gough, of Isleworth, in the county of Middlesex, single woman, charged that she, on the 29th or 30th June last at Road, in the parish of North Bradley, in the county of Wiltshire, did feloniously, wilfully, and of malice afore-thought kill and murder one Francis Savill Kent, against the peace of our Lady the Queen.

It was signed by the chief magistrate Henry Ludlow and endorsed by all those present. The charge was to be for murder, but few among them believed that Gough alone was solely responsible; it was later hinted that the accusation had been made in the hope that Gough's fragile nerves would crack under questioning and that she would implicate her likely accomplice, Mr Kent, in the crime.

The warrant for Gough's arrest was handed to Superintendent Wolfe who was told to travel to Isleworth in order to serve it. This he did and the next day placed Elizabeth Gough in his custody before taking her to Devizes gaol, where she would remain over the weekend until an examination could begin on the following Monday. Unsurprisingly, the nurse was said to be deeply upset at finding herself in the frame once more, but she held her tongue and would not be drawn to comment on either her current circumstance nor those that surrounded the murder of Francis Kent. Any hope of her offering a voluntary confession would have to wait until the examination itself.

While Superintendent Wolfe was transporting Gough across the countryside, Mr Slack and the Trowbridge magistrates started to make their preparations for the inquiry that the magistrates would need to hold into her arrest before she could go before a higher court. They were determined not to see a repeat of the farce that surrounded Constance Kent's inquiry and so, rather than relying on a police officer to act as prosecutor, the magistrates employed the services of Thomas William Saunders, who, under instruction from Mr Slack, would conduct the case on behalf of the Crown. A list of around twenty witnesses was drawn up and letters despatched to them notifying them that their presence in court would be required during the following week.

As soon as Mr Kent learned of this he notified the magistrates that he had again engaged the services of the Bristol solicitor Peter Edlin, who, together with Mr Dunn, would be watching the proceedings on behalf of his family, but not Gough. At the same time Gough's father contacted a local firm of lawyers, who arranged for William Ribton, a London-based solicitor, to defend his daughter. This collection of so many legal brains in one court room, all acting for different parties, was hardly to be welcomed, but it was hoped that Mr Slack's careful preparation would avoid any nasty surprises. As an added assurance the magistrates asked the Chairman of the Wiltshire Quarter Sessions, Sir John W. Awdry, to act as judge; he had a great experience of criminal trials in both England and India, including many for murder, and could be expected to keep good order in the court.

With all the pieces apparently in place, Mr Slack and the magistrates informed the press of the new developments and assured them that the inquiry would take place in public. He also announced that many of the testimonies were being given in public for the first time. Naturally this generated much speculation and over the weekend journalists from across the country started to make their way towards the formerly quiet country town of Trowbridge. Most travelled in expectation of witnessing the solution to one of the longest-running murder investigations ever to be seen in Victorian Britain; others suspected that, based on the case's previous history, there may yet be some surprises in store.[42]

MONDAY 1 OCTOBER 1860

By mid-morning the streets leading towards the police court in Trowbridge were lined with crowds of people, all anxious to gain a glimpse of the prisoner or the members of the Kent family as they arrived at the examination. The crowds were for the most part to be disappointed, as both Gough and the principal members of the Kent family were smuggled into the court room using disguised carriages. When this was discovered the onlookers took their anger out on the other witnesses, such as the cook and the housemaid, at whom they directed hisses, groans and shouts of indignation.

Inside the small courtroom the atmosphere was a good deal calmer. Captain Meredith and Superintendent Foley had purposefully reserved a large portion of the public gallery solely for journalists and reporters, of whom a great many had turned up. As well as getting the press on his side, this had the added benefit of greatly limiting the public seating area, which in itself lessened the possibility of heckling or other unwanted intrusions occurring.

At eleven o'clock sharp the magistrates entered the court and, following the usual formalities, such as reading out the arrest warrant and the introduction of the various legal representatives, the examination began. Superintendent Wolfe entered the court and led Elizabeth Gough to her seat in the dock, which was positioned within reach of Mr Ribton, her attorney. She was dressed entirely in black and wore a thick crape veil across her face. One reporter described her as being, 'a young woman, aged twenty-two, tolerably good-looking and appeared to have been crying. She was thinner and more pale and careworn than at the commencement of the investigation.' In her hand were a notebook and pencil which, as the examination progressed, she used to make notes or to pass letters to Mr Ribton.

Another series of formalities followed, which included a request by Mr Ribton to see any written evidence relating to the case. With this dealt with, Mr Thomas Saunders, who was acting in the role of prosecutor, opened the examination by summarising the circumstances surrounding Francis Kent's murder and the reasoning behind the arrest of the boy's former nursemaid.

As regards the murder, there was nothing new to add. Saunders stated the events leading up to the child's bedtime and then the events as they occurred the next morning, including a graphic description of the injuries inflicted and the likely manner of his death. When doing so he struck to Joshua Parsons's assertion that the boy had been wholly or substantially suffocated at the time of his throat being cut. Saunders was also mindful of the examination of Constance Kent which, he stated, was the work of an over-enthusiastic London detective. 'I believe that from first to last there was not the slightest ground for justifying suspicion against her,' said Saunders, 'and I believe that young lady to be as clear of suspicion as any one of the gentlemen whom I now have honour of addressing.'

With the facts behind the case laid out, Mr Saunders took the known evidence and used it to speculate about how the murder could have been committed and by whom. There were, he said, four main possibilities: that the murderer broke in from outside, for which there is no evidence; that it was done by somebody secreted inside the house, but again the evidence did not support this; that it was committed by a lone member of the Kent household and the scene disguised to make it look like a break-in; or that it was committed by two or more members of the Kent household and disguised as a break-in. It was these last two theories that Mr Saunders chose to focus on, stating that in either case Elizabeth Gough must have been complicit in the murder.

However, Mr Saunders further narrowed the list of possibilities by bringing into play an entirely new line of evidence which made clear his belief that Elizabeth Gough had an accomplice. His proof for this came from a confused series of events surrounding the blanket that had been recovered from the lavatory with Francis's body. He told the court:

When the nursery came to be examined, it was found that the deceased had been sleeping in a cot, and was covered over in this way: immediately over [the boy] was a sheet, over that again was a blanket, and at the top of all was a counterpane. The sheet was folded over the blanket and a portion of the counterpane, so that the blanket was entirely obscured from view. When the child was discovered in the privy, it was found to be wrapped up in the blanket. It is impossible to suppose that one person could have committed the murder; the boy was a heavy boy four years of age; the parties who were concerned in that murder must have taken the child from his bed, must then have wrapped him in the blanket, perhaps have smothered him at that time; but whether wrapped or not, must have then taken the child downstairs, and made an exit some way or other. One person could not have done that. It is idle to suppose that one person could have taken the child from the cot, could have taken the blanket from between the sheet and counterpane, wrapped the child in it, and then gone off, leaving the sheet and counterpane smoothly re-arranged, so as to present the appearance of not being interfered with. In taking the blanket from between the sheet and counterpane, a disturbance of the clothes must have taken place, and he or she who had taken the murdered child from the cot could not have so re-arranged the clothes, and any person who had murdered the child and was going away would not have had a motive for re-arranging the clothes. There must have been a second person in the room assisting in taking out the child, withdrawing the blanket, and rearranging the bedclothes afterwards.

This conclusion having been reached, Saunders went on to state that one of those persons must have been Gough:

Is it within the bounds of probability that any person could have gone in the room, and opened that door, which unless opened carefully made a creaking noise, without her [Gough] knowing it? The suggestion is almost absurd, though it is said that she knew nothing about it ... The prisoner is not the only person engaged in the murder, she is one of two who are concerned in it.

Saunders did not speculate about the name of the other supposed guilty party, but it was apparent to every person in the court that he had in mind Mr Kent. This matter being dealt with, Saunders continued to outline his case for the prosecution by moving on to the only piece of physical evidence connecting Gough to the crime scene: the chest flannel recovered from the cesspool, which, Saunders noted, had only fitted the nurse and none of the other women in Road Hill House:

That, no doubt, is not a very strong fact against her, because there might be other persons whom the flannel might also fit; but when they found that it was in the privy beneath the child, soiled with the blood that had come from it, they would find from that circumstance that it must have been put there about the same time the child was deposited in the privy, and they would find that, in point of fact, it did fit an inmate of the house, and also, in further confirmation of that circumstance, the prisoner's flannel petticoat was composed of flannel of the same character and texture as the chest flannel.

Saunders finished by stating that Elizabeth Gough had thus far produced a tissue of lies which he would expose as such and that whether or not she committed the actual deed, it was doubtless that the nurse was party to the unnatural death of Francis Kent.

Mr Ribton replied briefly for the defence, stating that his client had already been examined once and released without charge and that, given an apparent lack of new evidence, he expected the same outcome to occur again. He then suggested that the sensible course of action was to abandon the inquiry and, on being refused this, then set about determining under whose authority the court was acting. After establishing that the prosecution was operating on behalf of the Attorney-General, Mr Ribton allowed Mr Saunders to call his first witness: he chose to call Mr Kent to the stand.[43]

Mr Saunders's aim in examining Mr Kent was not so much to try and get him to implicate his nursemaid in the murder, for it was likely that he would remain tight-lipped on the subject, but to use certain new pieces of information to make the witness's behaviour appear distinctly suspicious.

The questioning began simply enough and revolved around the names and sleeping arrangements of the household members on the night of the murder. Saunders soon changed tack and began to ask Mr Kent about the presence in Road Hill House of the policemen Morgan and Urch on the night following the murder; Mr Kent suddenly became unsteady in his answers, offering as little information as possible. It quickly became clear why: Mr Saunders had discovered that the two policemen had been unwittingly locked inside the kitchen by Mr Kent for most of the night. This embarrassing incident had thus far been kept quiet by the Wiltshire police for fear that it might add to their reputation for incompetence, but the story had somehow come to Mr Slack's attention and was to be used by him to make Mr Kent look decidedly untrustworthy.

'The policemen could have left the kitchen and house if they had unbolted the doors,' protested Mr Kent in defence of his actions. Mr Saunders pointed out that the only unlocked door led into the courtyard, where the guard dog had been let loose. There followed a series of objections by both Ribton and Edlin, during which Mr Kent first denied, but was then forced to confirm, having locked the two policeman in the kitchen. Finally, the chairman intervened and asked Mr Kent if anything had occurred to cause him to lock the kitchen door that night.

'I bolted the door that the house might appear as usual, and that no-one might know that there was a policeman in the house,' he said. The matter was dropped for a while, but Mr Kent was not off the hook; he was made to appear suspicious by Saunders when it was revealed that he had been unco-operative with the police and had refused them permission to draw a plan of the premises. Further questions were then asked about the locked door, but Mr Kent complained that he only did it to conceal their presence from the rest of the family.

When asked to give an account of his movements on the morning after Francis's death Mr Kent became confused as to whether he had or had not spoken to Gough about the murder. He first claimed to have done so, which contradicted Gough's version of events, and so he then said that he had not, which contradicted his original statement. A final round of questioning left him claiming that that he might have spoken with Gough about the murder, but not at length.

The final humiliation came via Mr Ribton, who asked Mr Kent how it was that on his journey to Trowbridge he had come to mention that the boy's blanket was missing to the lady manning the tollbooth? According to other witnesses, nobody had been aware that the blanket had been taken until after it had been discovered with the boy's body, which was some time after Mr Kent had set off in his carriage. This implied that Mr Kent had some detailed knowledge of the crime a good while before his son's body had been recovered, an assertion that made him look very guilty indeed.

'On that morning,' said Mr Kent, 'before I started for Trowbridge, I knew that there was a blanket missing. When I went to wish Mrs Kent goodbye, previous to starting, she told me so and seemed pleased with the idea as it would keep the child warm. I told the turnpike woman of the circumstance: I never have, that I am aware of, denied knowing anything about the blanket.' With this, the witness was released, but Mr Kent's performance had been far from convincing and had made him look like a suspect.

Mrs Kent was next in the stand, but her examination was rather routine. She confirmed that Francis's blanket was hidden from view beneath the quilt which led on to the question as to whether she knew the blanket to be missing before the boy's body had been found and, if so, did she tell her husband, as he had earlier claimed? Mrs Kent confirmed that this was the case.

'It was before the child was brought in that I knew the blanket had been taken,' she confirmed. 'I told Mr Kent of it when he came to my door to say he was just going to Trowbridge.' This appeared to corroborate Mr Kent's version of events, but for some reason the prosecutor did not pursue the matter further and did not ask her how she herself knew the blanket was missing. If she had been told about it by Elizabeth Gough, as Mr Kent claimed, then this begged the question as to how the nursemaid could have known this before the body had been found.

Much of the rest of Mrs Kent's testimony concerned her opinion of Francis's personality and his relationship with the rest of the family and staff. When asked about Gough's relationship with young Francis, Mrs Kent was surprisingly generous. 'This girl, to the best of my belief, was particularly kind to the child and seemed very fond him. He was very fond of her.'

She did, however, think it odd that Gough, on finding Francis missing, should have believed that Mrs Kent had come into the nursery and taken him to her bedroom. 'I had never gone and taken the child from the room whilst the nurse was asleep,' protested Mrs Kent. 'I had instructed her, if the child was ill or if anything uncomfortable occurred in the nursery with regard to the children, she was to come to me immediately, which I frequently repeated. I said I would rather be called for a trivial cause than not be called when I was wanted. I had given her these general orders repeatedly.'

The chairman released Mrs Kent from the witness stand, but before stepping down she asked if she could say a few general words to the court. Mr Ribton immediately made an objection, which was countered by Mr Edlin; the two lawyers became embroiled in a bad-tempered exchange, during which Ribton described Edlin as being like 'a troubled spirit wandering about without a resting place'. The chairman stepped in and found in favour of Mr Ribton: whatever was on Mrs Kent's mind would remain a secret from the court.

The final witness of the day was Sarah Cox, the housemaid, who repeated how she had secured the house only to discover that the drawing-room shutters had been opened up during the night. She confirmed that she had checked all the spare rooms but had not seen anyone hiding in them and that she knew nothing of the whereabouts of Constance's missing nightdress.

By this time it had gone five o'clock and the chairman was restless. 'How long do you expect this inquiry to continue?' he asked Mr Saunders. The prosecutor said that it was difficult to say as he had many more witnesses yet to call.

'If my friend examines the witnesses in the same manner in which he had examined those whom we have already heard,' quipped Mr Ribton, 'then the inquiry will last a month!' This joke did not go down well with either Saunders or the chairman, and shortly after the session was adjourned.

A large crowd remained outside the court and as each blacked-out carriage passed by it was greeted with hoots and hisses, just in case a member of the Kent family should be inside.[44]

TUESDAY 2 OCTOBER 1860

The second day of Elizabeth Gough's examination began much as before: the occupants of passing carriages were heckled by the crowd; the lawyers squabbled amongst themselves; and the prisoner arrived dressed in deep mourning.

The first witness of the day was Sarah Kerslake, the cook, who had yet to be examined in public, but it was soon apparent that she had played a relatively minor part in the proceedings. After confirming some of what the housemaid had said, she was released.

The gardener, James Holcombe, was interviewed next. He lived just down the lane from Road Hill House and was able to confirm that at night he was frequently woken by the Kents' dog, which would bark at strangers, but not members of the family. When asked about the night of the murder, Holcombe replied that he had not been disturbed by its barking.

Following Holcombe's testimony came a series of witnesses who, while evidently connected to the family, were unable to provide any information of merit. This included Emily Doel, an assistant nursemaid, and the two elder Kent daughters. It became apparent to the chairman that Mr Saunders was intent on calling every person possible to the witness stand, no matter how irrelevant their evidence. It was a policy that pleased neither him nor Mr Ribton, who took to dismissing each witness with a mildly sarcastic comment. 'Your evidence comes to nothing,' he told Miss Doel, and he did not even trouble himself to ask any questions of Elizabeth Kent, merely dismissing her with a wave of his hand.

The mood of the court changed with the arrival of Constance Kent in the witness box. She was to be questioned about just one aspect of the police investigation: her missing nightdress. Mr Saunders, who had already stated that he believed Constance to be innocent, got her to recount the version of events she had already given to police, i.e. that the nightdress had been taken after it had been included in the household laundry. On being handed the witness, Mr Ribton sat in quiet contemplation for two or three minutes before standing up to address her. He also chose not to question Constance about the nightdress, but returned to the question of exactly when it became known that the blanket was missing.

'Did you hear that morning anything of the missing blanket till the child was found?' asked Ribton.

'I did from the nurse.'

'When did she tell you?'

'I don't know the time, whether it was before or after the child was found.'

'Just recollect, was it not after?'

'I don't remember at all.'

Mr Ribton asked Constance to recollect when she first heard Elizabeth Gough discussing the blanket, but the girl refused and, following some more mundane questions, she was released. Mr Ribton immediately asked that the proceedings be adjourned, but was refused and there followed brief examinations of James Morgan, the parish constable, Alfred Urch, the Somerset policeman, and William Nutt and Thomas Benger, both of whom had discovered the body.

Constable Urch was given a hard time over allowing himself to be locked in the kitchen and, the more flustered he became, the more Mr Ribton put to effect his cutting sense of humour. 'Neither you nor PC Heritage was of much use in the house that night, except as far as the bread and cheese were concerned,' observed Ribton, to much laughter from the gallery. 'I did as I was ordered,' replied the irked policeman.

Matters became more serious with the questioning of Superintendent Foley, who gave a better performance than the majority of witnesses that day. He was firstly questioned about his interview with Elizabeth Gough in the nursery on the morning after the murder. In this he insisted that the nurse had told him that she had not missed the boy's blanket until after the body had been found, the complete opposite to the testimony given by Mr and Mrs Kent.

Despite a close examination from Mr Ribton, Foley could not be persuaded that he was in error and went on to state that Mr Kent had also denied knowing anything about the blanket prior to leaving for Trowbridge, again in complete contradiction to his earlier statement to the court.

'Mr Kent told me that he did not know there was a blanket taken away until he returned from Trowbridge,' said Foley and, on being further questioned, added that he had a witness to this. 'He said so in the presence of Superintendent Wolfe. I asked him twice if he was aware that any blanket was taken away with the child before he went Trowbridge and his reply was "Certainly not".'

Foley was asked to give an account of the evidence that had been found inside the cesspool, which in effect meant the blood-soaked chest flannel. Mr Ribton was aware that this was the only piece of evidence that could even vaguely link his client with the crime scene and so sought to have it disregarded as irrelevant to the case. A war of words erupted between Ribton and the chairman, which ended with the latter snapping at the lawyer: 'The court will receive in evidence the contents of the privy!'

'What, the whole contents?' joked Ribton, whose schoolboy humour had begun to grate with the chairman. Despite Mr Ribton's insistence that there was nothing to connect the flannel, which might have been lying in the privy for some time, with the murder, Foley went on to describe its recovery. He also described how helpful he had found Elizabeth Gough to be and in doing so gave the impression that he did not feel her capable of having committed the crime. He also described how he tried to get Constables Heritage and Urch dismissed from the force after discovering that they had allowed themselves to be locked in the kitchen by Mr Kent.

There followed several more witnesses, including the chimney sweep (who confirmed that he had swept all the chimneys the day before the murder), Constable Henry Heritage and Superintendent Wolfe. The latter gave two useful pieces of evidence: firstly, he confirmed that Elizabeth Gough had told him several times that she had not missed the blanket until after the body was found; and secondly, he described how one of Gough's claims was probably false.

'She said that she awoke about five o'clock in the morning, and, seeing that the baby was lying by her side naked, she raised herself to cover it over, and in doing so she looked across to the little boy's cot, and missed him. She said she raised herself on her knees. She said that she went to sleep again. I asked her why she had taken no notice of it, and she said she imagined Mrs. Kent had taken the child away. I have tried the experiment of kneeling on the nursemaid's bed. Mr. Dunn was present, and put a dark-coloured garment on the boy's cot, which I could not see. The sides of the cot are thick canework. In looking over the cot you could only see about four inches into it. I could not look through the cane, because it was at an angle of about four feet.'

Perhaps unsurprisingly, Mr Ribton chose to ignore this potentially damaging experiment and moved onto others matters until, with much relief, the chairman adjourned the session. It was half-past five and during the previous six hours the court had examined thirteen witnesses; Mr Saunders was at pains to assure his colleagues that tomorrow's session would be the last and that he had only another eight witnesses to call.

Outside the court room a large and somewhat restless crowd had gathered, many of whom were expressing a violent intent towards the nursemaid. In light of this Gough was kept inside the court for some hours until the mob had dispersed. She was, observed one reporter, looking more wan and careworn than before.[45]

WEDNESDAY 3 OCTOBER 1860

The third day of the inquiry started much as the others had and, after the witnesses had run the gauntlet of the hostile crowd outside, the session began with the examination of William Kent. The boy was described as being nervous and 'not a strong-looking youth', but he held his nerve and answered the questions put to him directly and concisely. Nothing of any apparent use could be elucidated and nor could it from the next witness, Daniel Oliver, the odd-job boy, although he did confirm that there was no sign of any footprints leading to or from the opened drawing-room window.

Mr Saunders's policy of calling everyone and anyone who had been present at Road Hill House on the morning after the murder continued unabated, to the apparent irritation of the chairman, who was becoming bothered by a lack of any new information. Several witnesses came and went without adding anything of real merit, although John Alloway, the gardener's boy, did confirm that no knives were missing from the kitchen and that when he cleaned them none held traces of blood. Joshua Parsons, the surgeon, restated his belief that Francis Kent had been suffocated prior to his wounds being inflicted and that no narcotics had been used. Another three witnesses came and went, including five-year-old Amelia Kent, who was plainly terrified and became much more so after Mr Slack warned her that if she told a falsehood in court she would go straight to hell. Immediately after this Mr Dunn intervened, refusing to let the girl be examined any further.

Soon after lunch it was apparent that the inquiry would not be completed that day, as had been promised and that at least one more session would be necessary to allow the lawyers to deliver their closing statements. It was late afternoon by the time Mr Saunders called forward what he believed to be one of his star witnesses: Eliza Dallimore, the wife of the Trowbridge policeman William Dallimore. By her own admission, Mrs Dallimore took a great interest in her husband's work and had been especially keen to help out with this case. Luckily for her, there were certain aspects of the case that could only be handled by a woman and on these occasions it had been Mrs Dallimore to whom the Wiltshire Constabulary had turned for help.

Once sworn in, Mrs Dallimore proved herself to be an over-enthusiastic witness who was incapable of answering any question directly or concisely. She seemed particularly keen to demonstrate her amateur detective skills to the court and did not hide her belief that Elizabeth Gough was undoubtedly guilty of murdering the boy. Mrs Dallimore told the court about the several occasions on which she had been asked by the police to attend the nursemaid, either to mind her or because she needed to be physically examined. Any conversations between Mrs Dallimore and Gough were repeated in detail, with the policeman's wife taking care to highlight what she felt were incriminating statements made by the nursemaid.

After some general questioning the prosecution produced the chest flannel as an exhibit in court, stating that it was the one piece of evidence that could demonstrate that Elizabeth Gough had been present in the outside privy at the time of the murder. It was, in Mr Slack's view, his strongest piece of evidence, and he hoped that by using Mrs Dallimore to demonstrate its value he would be able to convince the court of the nursemaid's guilt.

Mrs Dallimore played her part to the full and immediately launched into a lengthy description as to how she had taken the chest flannel to Road Hill House and tried it upon all the women there. 'It fitted the nurse exactly, and was a good fit,' she said, and then told the court how Gough had protested about being made to try it on. During this time Gough was observed to look concerned and passed several written notes to Mr Ribton who, in contrast to his client's apprehension, did not look to be fussed by Mrs Dallimore's testimony. The reason for this self-assuredness was revealed when Mr Ribton came to cross-examine Mrs Dallimore.

'You seem to have a marvellously good memory. A very good one,' remarked Mr Ribton to Mrs Dallimore, who took the comment to be a compliment.

'Well, it's given to me,' she said, 'and perhaps it's better than some folks. I am not to be baffled out of the truth.'

More gentle banter followed, which confirmed to Mr Ribton that the witness's enthusiasm could be used against her. Referring to the flannel, Mr Ribton then said: 'I am told she [the nursemaid] never wore a flannel in her life. It is usually old ladies who wear flannels, is it not?'

Mrs Dallimore immediately took offence at the suggestion that the flannel might not belong to Gough. 'Many young persons wear them. I wear one myself.'

This produced much laughter from the gallery and caused one court reporter to note that by anyone's measure Mrs Dallimore could not be called young. 'I certainly am not going to ask you your age,' retorted Ribton to yet more laughter. 'Do young healthy women wear them?'

'Yes, sir! Why, I wear one myself!' An uproar of laughter ensued which caused Mrs Dallimore to turn to the gallery. 'I don't think so serious a matter should be turned to ridicule. It gives me the horrors to think about it. I'm the mother of a large family myself, sir, and know it.'

'You are very irritable, are you not?' replied Ribton calmly. 'How about the chest flannel? It fits you very nicely?'

'Yes sir.'

'Very nicely indeed?'

'Yes, sir.'

'Perhaps you have been wearing it?' More laughter ensued, but Ribton had finished playing with Mrs Dallimore and started to ask some serious questions. Referring to the two occasions that Mrs Dallimore had bodily examined female members of the Kent household, he asked if Gough had been seen wearing a flannel on either occasion.

'Yes, she wore a flannel petticoat.'

'Will you say on oath that you understood I referred to her underclothing when I asked if she wore a flannel?'

'Well, but she wore a petticoat.'

'But did she wear a chest flannel?'

'No, sir.'

'Did you search her other clothes. In her boxes?'

'No, I didn't.'

Mr Ribton was starting to make Mrs Dallimore look like an unreliable witness whose desire to see Gough convicted was interfering with her judgement. The chairman appeared to be thinking along similar lines and commented that even if the chest flannel did belong to the nurse then this was not evidence of her having been present during the murder. He pointed out that the flannel might have been taken up when the boy was removed from the room; in doing so he gave the first hint that he was not entirely convinced by the prosecution's case.

Mrs Dallimore was the prosecution's last witness, but rather than delivering a decisive blow to the defence, she had proved herself to be hot-headed and unreliable. It was late in the day and there was just time for a couple of other witnesses to be recalled, one of them being Mr Kent, who added nothing further of merit. The court clerk then read from a sworn statement produced by Elizabeth Gough on 9 July. In this Gough had said that she had not missed the child's blanket until after the body had been found: 'The body of the deceased was brought in. The blanket was on the child. I then ran upstairs and looked at his cot and saw the blanket was gone.'

Mr Saunders turned to the chairman and confirmed that the case for the prosecution was concluded; and, it being after five o'clock, the chairman reluctantly adjourned the sitting until the following morning.[46]

1. The front of Road Hill House as it looked in 1860. The two first-floor windows on the right belong to the nursery

2. The back of Road Hill House in 1860. The opened drawing-room window was on the right of the building

3. An aerial view of Road Hill House and its grounds in 1860

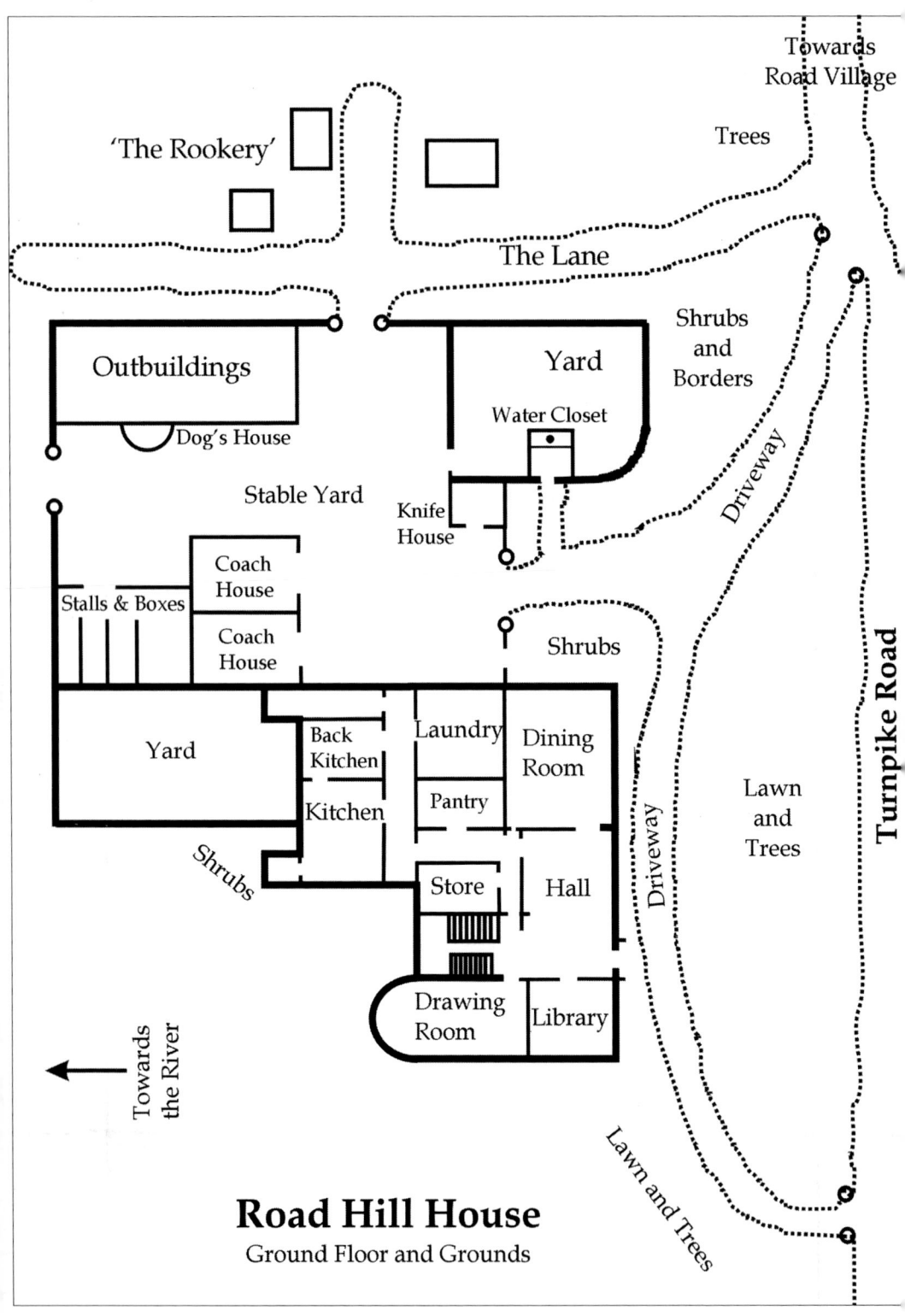

Towards
Road Village

Trees

'The Rookery'

The Lane

Outbuildings

Yard

Shrubs
and
Borders

Water Closet

Dog's House

Driveway

Stable Yard

Knife
House

Coach
House

Stalls & Boxes

Coach
House

Shrubs

Yard

Back
Kitchen

Laundry

Dining
Room

Lawn
and
Trees

Pantry

Kitchen

Shrubs

Store

Hall

Driveway

Turnpike Road

Towards
the River

Drawing
Room

Library

Road Hill House

Ground Floor and Grounds

Lawn and Trees

4. A contemporary plan of the ground floor and grounds at Road Hill House. Samuel Kent forbade the police from making such a plan, but the local newspapers produced one anyway

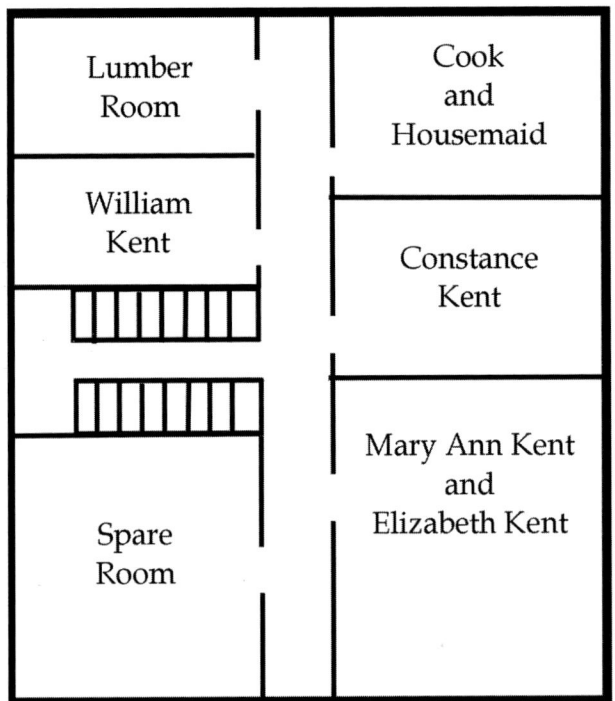

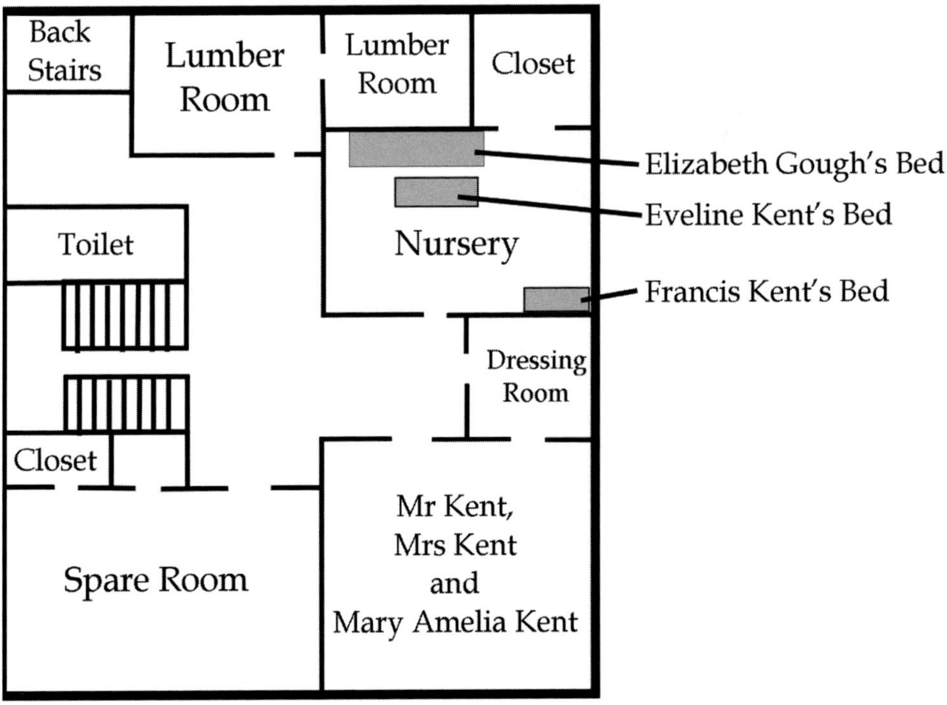

Lumber Room	Cook and Housemaid
William Kent	Constance Kent
Spare Room	Mary Ann Kent and Elizabeth Kent

Back Stairs	Lumber Room	Lumber Room	Closet
Toilet		Nursery	—— Elizabeth Gough's Bed
			—— Eveline Kent's Bed
			—— Francis Kent's Bed
Closet		Dressing Room	
Spare Room	Mr Kent, Mrs Kent and Mary Amelia Kent	

5. A contemporary plan of the first floor (lower) and second floor (upper) of Road Hill House

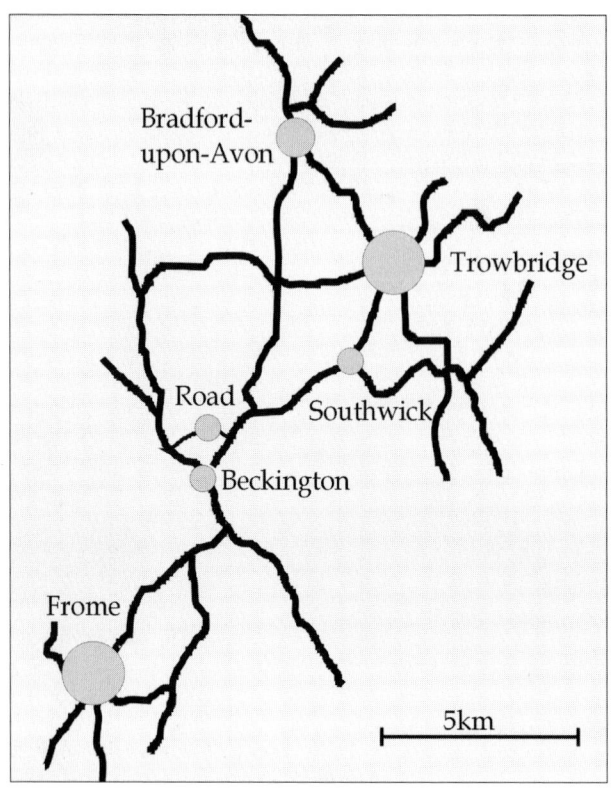

6. A map of the towns and roads surrounding Trowbridge

7. Constance Kent as she looked just prior to the murder

8. A sketch of Constance Kent made in 1865

9. A photograph of Samuel Kent taken shortly after the family moved away from Road Hill House

Above left: 10. Mary Kent (née Windus), Samuel Kent's first wife, whose early death was the subject of speculation

Above right: 11. Mary Kent (née Pratt), Samuel Kent's second wife and the mother of Francis Kent.

Left: 12. The Kents' nursemaid was at the centre of the police investigation and the subject of much gossip

sympathy existing within [...]
the fact of their sleeping in rooms
alone, and especially the dejected
state of the Boy both before and
after his sister's arrest, and I think
there would not have been much
difficulty for the Father or some of the
relatives to have obtained a confession
from him while his sister was in
Prison, but under the peculiar
circumstances of the case I could not
advise such a course, and if a
confession should come now it would
no doubt be made to some of the
Family, and then possibly not made
known.

Whicher
Inspector

13. A letter written by Inspector Jonathan Whicher in July 1860 which explained the collapse of his case against Constance Kent

14. The scene in Trowbridge court during the examination of Constance Kent in May 1860

THURSDAY 4 OCTOBER 1860

On opening what he hoped would be the final day of the proceedings, Sir John Awdry, the chairman, gave a hint that he had already made up his mind concerning the case: 'We should not determine a verdict without having heard Mr Ribton,' he said, implying that as far as he were concerned the defence's closing remarks were just a formality. However, before Mr Ribton could begin, Mr Saunders asked if he could recall Mrs Dallimore to the stand. No objection was made and so the policeman's wife returned to the witness box once more.

It turned out that Mrs Dallimore's sudden return had been prompted by the recollection of a conversation within which Elizabeth Gough appeared to confirm that she had seen Constance's missing nightdress placed inside the laundry basket. This conversation had taken place in her house in July and had been witnessed by her husband, who had just returned from work at the time. As had occurred the day before, Mrs Dallimore was very full with her descriptions and at all times implied that the nursemaid's behaviour was suspicious.

Mr Ribton was allowed to cross-examine Mrs Dallimore, but rather than tackling her on the matter of the nightdress, he asked her about another conversation that she claimed to have witnessed between Benjamin Fricker and Elizabeth Gough on the morning after the murder. In this Gough was alleged to have said to Fricker that he would not find anything incriminating inside the cesspool, a comment that, according to Mrs Dallimore, looked suspicious. Mr Ribton had, however, been contacted by Albert Groser, a local journalist, who had been in the kitchen at the time that the comment was made and who, while not denying that the conversation took place, did not remember Mrs Dallimore being present at the scene. He believed that Dallimore was lying under oath when she claimed to have been in the kitchen. If so, then this was a very serious matter indeed.

Using Groser's information, Mr Ribton set about demolishing Mrs Dallimore's reputation in a very public and humiliating manner. He started off by asking her to describe the scene in the kitchen again and then, piece by piece, took apart her account. On more than one occasion Mrs Dallimore appeared to contradict herself, giving Ribton cause to gaze across to the journalists' bench and warn that her answers 'may go forth in four and twenty hours to all parts of the kingdom.' She was so flustered that she was unable to say for certain how many people were present at the scene and whether she had, or had not, witnessed Fricker speaking to Gough. That Mrs Dallimore had lost the faith of the court could not be doubted; heckles from the gallery said as much, but worse was to come when her husband was called to the stand.

William Dallimore had not heard his wife's testimony concerning Gough's remarks about the nightdress and, when asked to corroborate it, gave an account which differed enough to discredit his wife's version of events. Observing Mr Dallimore's dejected look at having let his wife down, Mr Ribton commented that: 'You will no doubt have a curtain-lecture tonight. I fancy it won't be the first.'

If Mrs Dallimore had hoped that her appearance that morning would atone for her poor performance of the day before, then she was sadly mistaken. If anything it had only served to exasperate the situation further and gave Mr Ribton the near-perfect platform upon which to build his summary for the defence which, was by no means to be an abbreviated speech.

In an address that lasted over two hours, Mr Ribton stated his client's innocence in the strongest possible terms, claiming that almost all the evidence put forward by Mr Saunders had no relevance to elucidating the identity of the murderer.

'As respects the time when this murder was committed. Whether it was early in the night, or whether it was perpetrated at the approach of morning, has nothing to do with the prisoner at the bar. And so also as regards the wounds inflicted after death. Whether they were inflicted after death, or whether they were inflicted whilst the child was still living and breathing, has nothing to do with the prisoner at the bar.' Introducing elements such as this into the case was, said Ribton, 'laboured ingenuity of reasoning' on the part of the prosecution.

In place of the idea that Elizabeth Gough had stolen and murdered Francis Kent, Mr Ribton put forward another theory concerning the case. In doing so he chose to adopt the scenario that the police, and just about everyone else in the country, thought least likely to have occurred. He held that a stranger bent on revenge against Mr Kent had hidden in the house and stolen his son, breaking out through the drawing-room windows. Mr Ribton speculated that the criminal had not intended to kill the child, as was evidenced by the fact that he had wrapped him in the blanket to keep him warm. He also believed that the chest flannel had been stuffed into the boy's mouth, to keep him from crying out, but in the process he was accidentally suffocated. In a state of panic the assailant slit the child's throat and attempted to dispose of the body down the outside privy. This, said Ribton, explained all the known facts and offered a viable alternative to the idea that Gough, who had no known motive against the child, could have committed the crime with or without the assistance of second person.

This theory was expounded at some length, but it was Mr Ribton's quotation of a simple point of law concerning capital offences that carried the most weight:

'The guilt of a person is not to be proved by reasons, or by inferences, or by straining of wit, but by plain, and clear, and satisfactory testimony.'

By these standards in no way could Mr Saunders have been said to have proved his case; all the evidence he had presented was of little value, especially that given by Mrs Dallimore. Concluding, Ribton appealed to the magistrates for the immediate discharge of the prisoner.

The magistrates retired to consider their decision, but it was only a short while before they returned to the bench. The chairman rose to speak, but before announcing their verdict, he chose to rebuke Mr Ribton for some of the comments he had made during the trial which appeared to cast doubt on the professional reputations of Mr Slack and Mr Saunders. The defence lawyer was suitably contrite.

The Chairman then announced that Elizabeth Gough would not be placed on trial before a higher court and that she should be released on payment of a bond of £100. Gough was visibly relived at the verdict and a cheer went up from the gallery on her behalf; the bail money was immediately offered by two of her uncles, both of whom had been present in court throughout the inquiry. The chairman, however, had not finished, and went on to hint that there were parts of the hearing that had a great relevance to discovering the identity of the murderer. 'I do not say there is no material evidence before us which may hereafter, perhaps, with additions, be in some way or other acted upon,' he said cryptically.

The chairman then admonished Mrs Dallimore for 'framing every hypothesis' and commented that in locking up the two policemen, Mr Kent had been very ill advised. With that, Elizabeth Gough was discharged and taken directly to Trowbridge station, where she would catch the next train to Isleworth.

The court room emptied and, while the prosecutors went off to lick their wounds, the journalists retired to their hotel rooms so that they could write up the latest extraordinary twist in the Road Hill House mystery which, at that moment, look as far from being solved as ever.[47]

WEDNESDAY 10 OCTOBER 1860

News that the case against Elizabeth Gough had failed was greeted with incredulity by the press.

'A coroner's inquest, three magisterial inquiries and a private inquisition,' wrote the editor of the *Morning Star*, 'have been brought to a close leaving us very little wiser than we were before. The criminal still continues to elude the grasp of justice. Of the two individuals who have been accused, one [Constance Kent] comes forth from the ordeal pure and stainless, and against the other [Elizabeth Gough] there exist no proofs sufficiently conclusive to serve as a safe basis for the verdict of a jury.'

Even the editor of *The Times*, who had hitherto been quite restrained in his comments, was forced to express surprise at the turn of events:

Although the circle of suspicion is strangely narrowed, we are in the dark on every point. We cannot so much as conceive to ourselves either the motive or the manner or any other circumstance of the crime without some violence to probability or reason. It is hard to presume innocence as guilt, and guilt as innocence … It is a terrible thing for a land when crimes like these remain unpunished. Then life becomes cheap indeed, and cheapness of life means destruction of morals and debasement of national character.

The collapse of the inquiry against Elizabeth Gough heightened the public's fascination with the crime, but during the four days of court proceedings an odd thing had occurred. At the start a majority of people looked on Elizabeth Gough as a callous, calculating killer, but as the inquiry progressed so the mood of the public started to shift markedly. By the time of the verdict the nursemaid was being widely viewed as a victim of the unusual circumstances surrounding the crime rather than a fugitive from justice. Most people maintained a belief that the nursemaid knew something further about the murder, but many now thought that she was not directly involved in its perpetration. That honour went to Mr Kent, whom a majority of Britons held to be the lover of Elizabeth Gough and who had killed his own son in order to cover up their affair. To the public, Mr Kent was very much an *homme fatal*, whose lustful behaviour towards the innocent nursemaid had placed her in a position of great danger.

This swing in opinion came about chiefly because of Mr Kent's behaviour in the witness box. His two examinations before the court took place on the first and the second-to-last days of the inquiry and were considered to be far from satisfactory by all who heard them. Mr Kent's general approach and tone were considered to be defensive and his answers gave the appearance of being evasive or, in some instances, contradictory. To those who read the transcript of his testimony, Mr Kent gave every impression of being a man who was trying to wriggle his way out of trouble. This process started with the admission that he had been unco-operative with the police, but it was the revelation that he had deliberately locked two investigating policemen in his kitchen that caught the public's imagination. Why had he done so? The only logical reason was so that he would be free to undertake some deed about the house unobserved. More perplexing still was the business over the missing blanket, which placed both Mr Kent and Elizabeth Gough in a strange light.

This inconsistency arose when Mr Slack, in his thoroughness, decided to interview everyone and anyone associated with the case, including Ann Hall, the woman manning the tollbooth on the turnpike to Trowbridge. She recalled that on the morning after the murder Mr Kent had told her that his boy had been kidnapped and 'carried off in a blanket', an event that occurred some time before Mr Kent knew of the discovery of the body. Mr Slack realised that this contradicted an earlier statement given to Foley and Wolfe in which he denied knowing the blanket was missing until after his return from Trowbridge.

A similar contradiction occurred following a conversation that Elizabeth Gough had had with Constable Urch before the boy's body had been found. She told him then that a blanket had been taken with the boy which, like Mr Kent, contradicted a later statement which said that she only knew of the blanket's removal after the body was found. That both Mr Kent and Gough should have made the same contradiction seemed suspicious. Mr Kent explained that his wife had told him about the blanket and she, in turn, had said that Gough had told her. Gough refused to testify and was never officially asked about it; thus the matter of the blanket was left hanging in the air, entirely unresolved, with its significance to the case (if any) entirely unknown.

People speculated if both Mr Kent and Gough had known that the blanket was missing from the outset then this suggested that they had seen the body before it had been recovered by William Nutt and Thomas Benger. The implication was that Mr Kent and his nurse had colluded in the murder and disposal of the boy.

Mr Ribton had been quick to recognise that the matter of blanket did not look good for his client, and so sought to play the matter down:

Why, these contradictions have long been known before she left Road Hill House at all – what's the value of them? If I were to speculate upon them I should say, "It is very likely. She must have missed the blanket before the body was found.

Grasping at the crib or grasping at the bedclothes, she must have found that the blanket was gone." That is my own speculation – that she says so afterwards to the constable, who asked if anything was taken; she says nothing was taken but the blanket. The body, undoubtedly, is found afterwards with the blanket: and she says she did not know the blanket was missing until the body was found. There are various ways of reconciling it. In the first place, would the Bench like to attach any very great importance to any apparent contradiction which might be made in the statements of the inmates of that house on that morning, recollecting the state of anxiety, apprehension, tumult, in the minds of everybody? And who had more reason to be alarmed than this poor girl, under whose care the child was?

The public did not know what to make of it all, but these revelations served to turn the spotlight away from Elizabeth Gough and instead placed it squarely on Mr Kent, whose every move was suddenly viewed in a suspicious light, including the initial journey he made to Trowbridge, during which he might have disposed of evidence such as the murder weapon or nightdress. One correspondent commented:

Mr Kent is stated to have left the house in a carriage to seek a policeman who lived at a distance. What sort of a carriage did he travel in? Who ordered it? Who prepared it? Who saw Mr Kent enter it? Did he leave the premises alone or accompanied by a servant? Who did he meet with on his journey? Is the precise road he took known? Has it been searched thoroughly? What sort of horse did he drive? Was it a spirited animal that would not stand while its master absented himself for a short time, or a quiet, dull beast?

A similar range of questions was asked by others about the incident involving the two policemen ('why did Mr Kent lock them up?') and why the family continued to employ Elizabeth Gough for several weeks following the murder (and, indeed, why did she choose to stay at Road Hill House?). Of course, the answers to such questions were not forthcoming from the family and it looked to many as though the investigation had hit a dead end and that the mystery might never be solved. There was, however, one person who was not prepared to tolerate this idea, and in the days following the release of Elizabeth Gough, he sought to take matters into his own hands.[48]

TUESDAY 16 OCTOBER 1860

It was almost two weeks before the members of the Wiltshire Quarter Sessions met in the town of Marlborough to discuss the implications of Elizabeth Gough's release. In attendance were a great many respected persons, including Sir John Awdry, who had chaired the inquiry, plus three MPs, Captain Meredith of the county constabulary, a law lord and several QCs.

The Constabulary Committee (the public body that oversaw the police's operations and conduct) had prepared a report on the inquiry which was read out to the assembled court. It was generally supportive of the Wiltshire police's investigation, with the exception of Constables Urch and Heritage, whose willingness to be locked into the kitchen by Mr Kent was criticised. Captain Meredith was quizzed about this but he sought to defend the men, saying that neither knew they were locked in until it was too late. Following a quip from one the QCs, who said that it was gratifying to know that only one of the men came from the Wiltshire force (Urch was from Somerset), the matter was dropped.

Immediately afterwards one of the magistrates from the Bradford-upon-Avon district stood up and addressed the court. This was Thomas Bush Saunders, the man who had six weeks earlier written to the Home Secretary volunteering to lead a new inquiry into the murder (again, Thomas Bush Saunders should not be confused with Thomas William Saunders, who earlier led the prosecution at Elizabeth Gough's inquiry). Unlike his colleagues, Mr Saunders announced himself to be far from satisfied with the conduct of the police and felt that there was much to be discovered about the case.

'I beg, therefore,' he said, 'to move that a special committee be appointed to investigate the circumstances connected with the death of Francis Savill Kent and the proceedings taken by the police thereto and to report thereon to the next sessions.'

The idea of a yet another inquiry did not meet with general approval; Captain Meredith was particularly annoyed at the idea and spoke against this proposition, saying that he and his men had left no stone unturned. Mr Saunders disagreed and, while acknowledging that he had played no official role in the investigation, started to cite instances which he felt needed further examination.

'I have been informed that there was a light burning over the hall-door during the whole night when the child was taken away.'

'There is a light burning there every night,' replied Meredith, but Saunders disagreed and said that this was not the case. He went on to imply that the garden scythe might have been the murder weapon (Meredith said not) and that there were many witnesses who had yet to be interviewed (Meredith said there were none). Finally, Mr Saunders gave the court the benefit of his theory regarding the murder.

'My own impression of this case is that the deceased saw something improper in the nursery, and that it was that which led to the commission of the foul deed. The instrument with which it had been committed might have been disposed of in the neighbourhood.'

On hearing this, Lord Thomas Sotheron-Estcourt, the MP for Marlborough and a former Home Secretary, stood up and made an impassioned objection to the idea of a new inquiry:

> What good then, would result from having another and separate inquiry? Having read the report of the last examination, I am at a loss to conceive what fresh witness could be put into the box, or what fresh clue there was to follow up. The real difficulty in the case is that there is no clue at all. It is the lack of evidence, the want of any clue, that forms the real impediment in the case … Under these circumstances I feel bound to oppose the motion of Mr Saunders; I feel assured that it will only lead to a useless and profitless investigation.

This was greeted with shouts of 'Hear, hear!' around the room. Sir John Awdry then pointed out that as Mr Saunders did not have anybody to second his motion, there was no need even to vote on the matter. Mr Saunders admitted defeat but made one last remark.

'I reiterate my belief that unless some further proceedings are taken, the public mind will not be satisfied.' Awdry waved the comment aside and the meeting turned to other matters.

It turned out that in slapping down Mr Saunders's ambition, the Wiltshire Quarter Sessions was echoing the opinions of many around the country who, despite the oddities of the case, found themselves to be content with the investigation made by the local police.

'We are bound to say that, though the case was mismanaged at first, there has been no negligence in any quarter since then,' said *The Times*. However, Mr Saunders remained far from happy and, despite being snubbed by the Home Secretary and then the entire Wiltshire Quarters Sessions, he was determined to get his new inquiry even if it meant resorting to subversive means to do so.[49]

SATURDAY 3 NOVEMBER 1860

In the weeks following the meeting of the Wiltshire Quarter Sessions the furtive figure of Thomas Bush Saunders started to become a common sight around Road village. From time to time Saunders would be spotted entering various houses or, more commonly, stood in the lane outside Road Hill House, staring up at its windows.

It was rumoured that Mr Saunders had begun his own investigation into the murder and that he had been using his position as a magistrate on the Bradford-upon-Avon bench to gain people's co-operation. In fact, being a magistrate did not give Saunders any powers of compulsion, but most of the villagers did not know this and, assuming that he was part of the official investigation, allowed him into their houses. He could not, however, get into Road Hill House itself: Mr Kent forbade Saunders from setting foot in the grounds and so the magistrate took to making his notes from the gates and surrounding fields and roads, perhaps trying to imagine what could have occurred within on that fateful night at the end of June.

To Mr Saunders every little detail was significant and potentially incriminating. On Halloween night he and Inspector Pitney of the Somerset police were stood outside Road Hill House gazing at its burning lights when they saw a woman dressed in black dither outside the gate and then enter the property; a few minutes later the same woman could be seen in an upper window combing her hair. To Saunders this was a high drama and over the next few weeks he sought to identify the mysterious woman and even stated publicly that 'she was not one of the young Misses Kent'. Quite who he did think she was is not known, but it turned out that the woman in black was known to the family (it may actually have been Constance Kent). Such set-backs did not dent Mr Saunders's self-confidence and he continued to tour the neighbourhood listening to every scrap of gossip and to every conspiracy theory in the hope of drawing together enough evidence to support his own preconceived views about the case.

It was in all likelihood Mr Saunders who wrote the pseudonymous letter (signed 'Common Sense') that was published in *The Times* on 22 October. It outlined many of Mr Saunders's ideas about the case and suggested that Mr Kent and Gough were the murderers. However, the facts cited by the letter were often erroneous and it was left to the local journalist Albert Groser to write his own letter correcting the inaccuracies.

Most believed that Mr Saunders was acting as an amateur detective, but in truth he was doing far more than this and, on the morning of Saturday 3 November, he convened a special meeting of the six (including himself) Bradford magistrates to confront them with his findings. Exactly what occurred at this meeting is a matter of dispute. The Bradford magistrates later claimed that they listened to Mr Saunders but offered him no encouragement in his investigation. Saunders, on the other hand, went away believing that his fellow magistrates had given him their full support in his quest to open a new inquiry into the murder of Francis Kent.

It was with this belief in mind that Mr Saunders requisitioned the Temperance Hall in Road village and, with no warning, requested the attendance of Captain Meredith and several of his officers. Messages were sent to the newspapers informing them that there was to be a re-investigation of the murder which would begin at noon that day. The editor of *The Times* believed the message to be a hoax, but despatched a reporter, just in case; the editor of the *Bristol Daily Post* summed it up for many when he exclaimed: 'What next?'

What next indeed. Given the short notice, there was a scramble by journalists to reach the Temperance Hall in time for the inquiry's opening. The first reporter to arrive found himself in a building that was empty apart from Mr Saunders, Captain Meredith and Superintendents Foley and Wolfe, all of whom sat on a platform at the end of the room. Within a short time local people and reporters started to flood through the doors and into the public gallery, so that by half-past twelve the place was full. Only then did Mr Saunders rise to his feet in order to address the assembly.

'The proceedings I intend to take have been adopted with the full sanction of the Bradford bench of magistrates,' he stated, explaining that both he and the magistrates felt that there was much that could be done to track down the murderer of Francis Kent. In the speech that followed, which was noted by one reporter to be 'of considerable length', Mr Saunders was at pains to stress his authority and yet he was also very vague about just who had sanctioned him to carry out the inquiry in the first place. He asserted boldly that the Home Secretary had told him 'that it is your duty to give every information and assistance' with regard to the murder. This was true, but Mr Saunders had taken the phrase out of context; the Home Secretary had in fact been writing in reply to a letter and was directing him to given any information he had to the local police. Saunders also claimed to have the full support of the Wiltshire Constabulary, many of whom were sharing the platform with him, but this too may have been an exaggeration; Captain Meredith seemed at pains to distance himself from the Bradford magistrate and would frequently interrupt Mr Saunders to object or to correct him over certain matters.

By the time Mr Saunders had finished speaking, many in the room were highly confused, as it was far from clear whether this new inquiry had the backing of anyone other than Mr Saunders himself. It was evident that even the police were not sure where they stood: was this an official investigation or not? Given that Mr Saunders had a list of witnesses whom he wished to interview, Captain Meredith had erred on the side of caution and agreed to co-operate. After all, if somebody did say something useful then a police officer would need to be there to hear it.

And so the unorthodox inquiry got underway, albeit in a somewhat chaotic fashion. Mr Saunders declared grandly that his first witness, one Arthur Langley, had never before been examined, but Captain Meredith interrupted saying that he had been interviewed many times by the police. Saunders amended his statement to say he had never before been examined in public and went on to call Mr Langley to the witness stand. He was met with silence: Langley was not in court and so a policemen was sent to find him.

Saunders was just about to call another witnesses when the proceedings were interrupted by the arrival of a Mr George Sheppard, a magistrate from Frome, who insisted on speaking with Mr Saunders in private. However, the pair remained on stage and as their conversation became heated so the audience was able to hear every word.

Mr Sheppard berated Saunders for convening the inquiry and accused him of abusing his position as a magistrate. 'I am not here in my magisterial capacity,' said Saunders, explaining in couched terms that he had the authority of the Bradford magistrates and the Home Secretary. Mr Sheppard was far from satisfied with this, but he chose not to interfere any further and left Saunders to resume the proceedings.

The list of witnesses called into the Temperance Hall that day revealed much about the nature of Mr Saunders's inquiry. None of the key players was present, including the Kent family and their servants (current and former), nor any of the central witnesses from the previous inquiries. Each and every person examined by Saunders was on the periphery of the case; most were villagers who had heard or seen something unusual that may, or may not, have had some relevance to the murder. The only exception to this were members of the police force, some of whom agreed to be examined; however, no senior officers consented to do so and it was soon apparent that Captain Meredith was only remaining in the building so that he could correct Mr Saunders when he said something that was inaccurate (which was quite frequently).

In the space of only a few hours nine witnesses were examined, but few offered any evidence that could be described as ground-breaking. Many just repeated local gossip or gave vague stories about strangers in the neighbourhood or mysterious lights seen near Road Hill House.

Mr Hatherfield, the postmaster of Road, was typical of this. He recounted receiving 'a certain letter from a certain person in which a person confessed to a participation in the murder'. However, none of these persons could be publicly named by Mr

Saunders and all had refused to be interviewed on the subject, making Hatherfield's testimony next to useless. Many other titbits of information also added up to nothing, including that given by Arthur Langley who, when he finally arrived, recalled seeing Mr Kent in a field near Road Hill House on the evening before the murder.

Many of the reporters present recorded that Saunders appeared to be randomly scratching about in the dirt for clues, hoping that something of importance might turn up. It did not and he instead found himself confronted with hearsay evidence and reluctant witnesses who point-blank denied rumours that had been attributed to them by others.

One such was Susanna Quance, the wife of a Richard Quance, who was to say the least irritated at being dragged before the inquiry. She listened as Mr Saunders asked her to confirm that from their bedroom window her husband had seen Mr Kent wandering in the grounds of Road Hill House at dawn on the morning after the murder.

'My husband cannot see Mr Kent's grounds at all,' snapped Mrs Quance. 'Such a statement is false, whoever made it. I know nothing at all about the murder, except the talk of the village.'

Saunders was evidently disappointed at this and ended the session by quoting some theories and stories from various letters he had received about the murder. Captain Meredith gently pointed out that he had received over 200 letters from all parts of Britain that contained all manner of rubbish, including a confession from a person living in Wales. The inquiry was adjourned until the Monday morning.[50]

MONDAY 5 NOVEMBER 1860

The commencement of Mr Saunders's inquiry was so unexpected that few people really knew what to make of it. The question as to whose authority he was operating under was particularly unclear, but an analysis of the situation by *The Times* revealed the truth. It would seem, they said, that Mr Saunders had 'appeared in the Temperance Hall at Road in a private, rather than a magisterial capacity, and to have held, as it were, a public conference on the inscrutable mystery'. In other words, the new inquiry had no legal standing whatsoever and was merely a public meeting; this meant that those who appeared as witnesses did so under their own volition and could not be made to attend. Those who had seen the proceedings thus far seriously doubted that any good could come of them. 'They will, in our opinion, result in making the case more inexplicable than ever,' wrote the *Daily Post*.

Nonetheless, at eleven o'clock Mr Saunders re-opened his 'inquiry,' but this time he was alone on the stage; Captain Meredith was absent, as were those Bradford magistrates who had attended on the Saturday. Only Superintendents Foley and Wolfe remained, and they appeared to be there in order to keep an eye on matters.

Mr Saunders's first action of the day was to adjourn the inquiry until midday. He returned just after twelve, looking flustered, and said that he would be a few more minutes yet.

'Hadn't you better adjourn for half an hour, sir?' asked Foley.

'Oh no,' replied Saunders. 'Just for a few minutes.' According to one reporter Mr Saunders then 'opened a bulky portfolio, from which he produced various papers and a note-book, and from his pocket came forth a bottle containing a liquid which had very much the appearance of brandy. He poured a small quantity into a tumbler and placed it upon the table before him.'

It was one o'clock before matters were resumed, but little was achieved that day. The three witnesses that were called had little of interest to say and on those occasions when something of a sensational nature emerged, its relevance and/or accuracy would be disputed by either Superintendent Foley or Wolfe. The journalist Albert Groser, for example, told how Superintendent Summers of the Somerset police had seen smears of blood in the hallway of Road Hill House. Mr Saunders became very excited at this but, Wolfe was able to take apart the evidence with ease after Groser confessed that this had been told to him two weeks after the murder had taken place and that no-one else had found any sign of this blood.

The nature of the evidence being heard had necessitated continual interruptions and corrections by Foley and Wolfe and by the late afternoon their patience was wearing thin, leading to 'a desultory' conversation with Mr Saunders. Immediately following this he launched into a rambling and slightly nonsensical speech which again seemed to be based around gossip sent to him in a letter. According to one reporter, Saunders spoke in an 'incoherent and incomprehensible manner', the suggestion being that the brandy had taken effect. He finished by recounting the personal efforts he had gone to when investigating the case.

'I have been in the village as late as eleven o'clock,' he blustered, 'and in a young lady's bedroom.' There was an uproar of laughter at this, forcing the magistrate to add hastily, 'in the company of Inspector Pitney'. The session was adjourned and the public gallery, which consisted mostly of women and children and was not by any means full, started to empty onto the street outside.[51]

THURSDAY 8 NOVEMBER 1860

The pace of Mr Saunders's 'eccentric inquiry' did not slacken in the days that followed, but as time went on so the magistrate found himself increasingly isolated. From the Tuesday morning the Wiltshire Constabulary refused to attend, while the Trowbridge bench of magistrates released a public statement which said that they were in no way connected to the proceedings. Mr Saunders also made the mistake of complaining to the reporters that they were not giving him fair coverage and that some of them were ridiculing him. The observation that he had been drinking brandy was explained away by his having contracted a cold thanks to draughts from the windows in the hall (the clerk was told off for not having mended them), but all this only served to heighten the press's condemnation further. In describing the proceedings one newspaper wrote that: 'Mr Saunders elicited several points which he appeared to consider important, but the bearing of which on the terrible crime it is intended to elucidate is, to the ordinary mind, almost as mysterious as the murder itself.'

And so Mr Saunders's inquiry, reinvestigation or public meeting (the correct title was a matter of dispute) stumbled on, taking in an apparently endless amount of tittle-tattle and irrelevant testimony. Much time was wasted on the matter of Mr Quance having allegedly seen Mr Kent wandering about his grounds at five o'clock on the morning after the murder. However, although Mr Quance's employer swore that he had heard the story at first hand, Mrs Quance still denied the story and her husband refused to come to the hall. Mr Saunders was at this point forced to admit that he had no legal means of summoning anyone to give evidence. Much play was also made of the last-minute changes that had been made to the jury at the coroner's inquest: many viewed this as being part of a conspiracy to keep Mr Kent and his family from testifying but, as with almost everything else that came before Mr Saunders, there was no proof that this had been the case.

By the Thursday morning local interest in the inquiry was waning, but the matter remained of great interest to the newspaper-reading public and so the gallery was filled, not with bystanders, but with pressmen from every part of the United Kingdom. Given Mr Saunders's track record, few people expected his investigation to bring forth anything of any material value and viewed the proceedings more as a form of entertainment. Indeed, the Thursday session started in the same chaotic fashion as before, but after lunch the mood changed markedly when Mr Saunders, quite by accident, managed to stumble upon something of great importance.

Mr Saunders's had called forward Constable Henry Heritage, chiefly so that he could quiz him about his having been locked into the kitchen by Mr Kent. As before, Heritage defended his role in the incident, saying that he and Constable Urch had been unknowingly imprisoned so as not to alarm the family. Heritage was about to be excused as a witness when Inspector Pitney suggested to Mr Saunders that he 'ask if Sergeant Watts was there.'

Mr Saunders did so, but Heritage denied that this was the case. However, he looked most uncomfortable and so when Constable Urch came into the witness box, Saunders pursued the matter further and asked him several questions about who had been present at Road Hill House on the afternoon of 30 June. Urch too looked uncomfortable and was eventually forced to admit that Sergeant James Watts of the Frome police had indeed been present that afternoon. Saunders continued to ask Urch about Watts's instructions and movements that day; at first Urch evaded the questions, saying he couldn't recollect but eventually he said to Saunders: 'I was present when Sergeant Watts found a certain thing.'

'What was it?' asked Saunders, his interest rising.

'Some woman's night-shift.'

'Some woman's shift? I don't wish to mislead you, was it a night-shift, then, or a night or day-shift?'

'It was a shift,' replied Urch.

'Have you a sufficient knowledge of shifts?' asked Saunders. This brought forward a laugh from the gallery which he immediately cut short by shouting 'Silence!' For the first time Saunders sensed that he was on to something; he re-phrased his question. 'Have you a sufficient knowledge of such articles of dress, having seen for yourself, to say whether it was a day-shift or a night-shift?'

Urch was unwilling to commit himself and, having let the matter slip, adopted a policy of saying as little as possible about it. The reason why would soon become obvious. 'It might have been worn night and day, as it was such as is worn at all times,' he said.

'You were present with Sergeant Watts; what time was that?' continued Saunders.

'It was in the evening, I should think about five or six o'clock.'

'Where did Sergeant Watts find the article?'

'In the boiler-hole.'

'Where was the boiler?'

'In the first kitchen, going in, sir.'

'Was there anyone present?'

'Well, no.'

'Was it at the entrance of the boiler-hole, or pushed far up?'

'It was in as if to light the fire.'

'Was it dry or was it wet?'

'It was dry but very dirty,' said Urch, but Saunders sensed that there was more to it than this.

'What do you mean by dirty?' he asked the constable.

'I mean as if it had been worn a long time.'

'What was that dirt upon?' he asked again.

'It had some blood about it,' admitted Urch.

'Was it much blood or little, a large quantity or a small quantity?'

'There were several places with blood upon them.'

'Did they appear to have been there for some time?'

'Well, sir, I did not touch it myself. Sergeant Watts unfolded it, looked at it, and carried it to the coach-house,' said Urch who was becoming increasingly unwilling to discuss the subject.

'Were there any initials on that shift?'

'I do not know, sir; I did not see any.'

'Was it a coarse article, or a fine article of dress, such as servants wear, or more like what young ladies wear?'

'I should think, sir, it was one of the servants'.'

'Was it the size for a full-grown servant, or a young woman, a full-grown woman-servant, or a nurse-girl? Was it of a large size?'

'No, it was not a large one. We remarked, two or three of us who were there, that it was a small one.'

Saunders was interested to learn that there were others present. 'Who was there?'

'The sergeant, and I believe Dallimore was there.'

'Was Foley there?'

'Yes,' replied Urch reluctantly. 'Sergeant Watts gave it to Foley, and I do not know what became of it.'

Urch was unwilling to say anything further about the blood-stained woman's shift, but in mentioning it at all he had suddenly thrown doubt over the entire police investigation. In a few short minutes Urch had revealed that on the first day of the investigation the police had recovered a woman's shift (possibly a nightdress) that was covered in blood and which had apparently been deliberately hidden in the kitchen boiler.

The implications of this were obvious: the bloodied shift might have belonged to the murderer and, as such, could be the only piece of evidence linking an individual to the crime scene. It also implied that there had been a conspiracy of silence amongst the police for, despite many interviews, examinations and inquiries, this was the first occasion on which the item had been mentioned, and yet, according to Urch, at least four policemen knew of its discovery. It begged two immediate questions: what happened to the bloodied shift, and why was its existence kept hidden by the police?

Neither Superintendent Foley nor Sergeant Watts were present that day and Constable Dallimore was only able to confirm that he had seen the item and that he had told Foley about its discovery. A few more perfunctory questions were asked and then the session was adjourned. Mr Saunders stated that he needed to get to the bottom of this strange incident and asked that both Foley and Watts be present for questioning the next day.[52]

FRIDAY 9 NOVEMBER 1860

Had the story about the bloodied shift come out during any of the previous inquiries then it would have caused a sensation. However, the way Mr Saunders had conducted himself had attracted such bad press that very little comment was passed on what was arguably the most important new clue to emerge from the case for some weeks. Instead, barely a murmur was raised, and so when, some time after lunch on Friday, Mr Saunders resumed his inquiry, there were comparatively few members of the public present.

The late start had been caused by the length of time it had taken Mr Saunders to persuade Superintendent Foley and Sergeant Watts to appear. Both were aware that their actions regarding the discovery of a bloodied shift looked very improper and that they might even be disciplined over it.

The proceedings opened with another examination of Constable Urch who, in front of his superior officers, confirmed what he said the day before was the truth. In response to questions from Saunders he said that the shift had been wrapped in newspaper, though he could not remember any detail of it, and that the boiler room at Road Hill House was situated inside the kitchen.

Sergeant James Watts was next and he gave a full account of how he had found the shift inside the boiler, pushed quite far back:

I took it out into the stable to examine it, and called the attention of Police Constable Dallimore to it. I think Urch was also present. On opening the bundle in the stable I found it to contain a shift in a very dirty state; it was very bloody. It was dry then, but I should not think the stains had been on it a long time. It did not appear to have been partially washed. Some of the blood was on the front and some on the back. I wrapped up the shift again, and as I was coming out I saw Mr. Kent just outside the stable door in the yard. He asked me what I had found, and said he must have it seen, and that Dr. Parsons must see it. I did not let Mr. Kent see it, but handed it over to Mr. Foley. I believe Foley was in the front part of the house when I found the shift, and he was at the back when I handed it over to him. Dallimore was present at the time. Mr. Foley took possession of the bundle containing the shift, and I have not seen anything more of it from that day to this. I asked Dallimore at last Road fair what had become of it, and he told me he was going to put it into the place from which it was taken, and one of the servant-girls was coming into the scullery, and he put it down by the side of the boiler-hole.

This appeared to answer many of the points that Urch had been so reluctant to comment on. The shift had apparently been taken outside into the yard, where Mr Kent was made aware of it, and then shown to Foley; he apparently handed it back to Dallimore, who then returned it to the kitchen, placing it down the side of the boiler. Urch was asked to confirm all this but the timid constable refused, saying he could not remember what had occurred. On hearing this Watts rose from his seat in a threatening manner and started to speak roughly at Urch, but Mr Saunders told him to sit down.

Mr Saunders must have hoped that Foley would be able to clear up some of the finer points, such as what he thought of the item and why it had not been kept as evidence. However, as the senior officer and the one who made the decisions regarding the shift, Superintendent Foley had much to lose on this matter and he was in no mood to co-operate. He refused to be drawn at all on the matter, but in reply to a few brief questions did say the following:

When the shift was handed to me, I shuddered to think the man that found it was so foolish as to expose it. By my directions it was afterwards shown to Mr Stapleton, surgeon of Trowbridge; before doing so I was satisfied that the shift had nothing to do with the murder. I cannot say where that shift is now. I told Police Constable Dallimore to keep it for the present. When Mr Stapleton looked at it he expressed his surprise at its being exhibited to him.

Other than transferring the blame to Mr Stapleton, Foley had added almost nothing to their knowledge, but he would say no more and so Saunders moved on to other matters. He found the superintendent to be a hostile witness who at one point accused the inquiry into the bloodied shift as being something of a wild-goose chase. It was a very tense occasion and, following Foley's release from the witness stand, Mr Saunders made one of his trademark bombastic speeches, informing the assembly that he had rented a house in Road and that he would at any time happily issue an arrest warrant under his own authority, if necessary.

'I have begun and shall go on with this inquiry,' said Saunders, 'regardless of comment, and mindful of the memorable words of one of this country's greatest naval heroes: England expects every man to do his duty.'

Mr Saunders was doubtless buoyed up by his having caught out Foley and his officers, and he must have felt that in the coming days he would get to the bottom of the matter. However, the discovery of the bloody shift was perhaps also to be his undoing, for, unbeknown to him, there were a number of separate forces at work who, for their own reasons, were seeking to put a stop to this most unorthodox of inquiries.[53]

TUESDAY 13 NOVEMBER 1860

The revelation of the bloodied shift had raised the hackles of Superintendent Foley, who was very angry and somewhat embarrassed that the story had made it into the limelight. Although he sought to play down the significance of the shift, he and his men knew that in losing this piece of evidence they had made a big mistake; it was probably for this reason that they had for so long colluded to hide the incident. Nobody, not even the magistrates nor Captain Meredith, had known of its existence, and the conspiracy of silence had operated perfectly well until Constable Urch had accidentally spilled the beans under questioning by Mr Saunders.

From the moment he learned that his secret was out in the open, Foley began a damage-limitation exercise that would see him, and several others of his officers, seek to muddy the waters over both the bloodied shift's significance to the case and exactly what had happened to it. However, Foley's first move was get Mr Saunders's bizarre and impromptu inquiry stopped in its tracks; he achieved this using a variety of methods.

After being cross-examined on the Friday afternoon Superintendent Foley was in a dark mood. This deepened further when he heard Saunders announce that he had taken the lease on a property in Road village: the house concerned belonged to Mr West, one of the disgruntled jurors from the coroner's inquest, and it had originally been offered to the police for use a temporary headquarters, but Foley had turned him down.

On the Friday evening, immediately after the inquiry had finished, Superintendent Foley strode up to Mr Saunders, complaining that the house he intended to rent was, after all, needed for a police station.

'Excuse me,' said Saunders, 'this house was given me for a private purpose, and, as far as it is not inconvenient with that private purpose, it shall be at the disposal of the Wiltshire and Somerset constabulary, but not as a police station.'

Foley was furious, but Saunders did not stop to discuss the matter; he had important matters to attend to and so left the village for a short while. On his return he was surprised to see that there was not a single policeman to be found in Road or its surrounding neighbourhood. It was the start of a campaign of direct action against Mr Saunders by Superintendent Foley, who had ordered all his men out of the area. In the coming days the only policeman seen in the area was Inspector Pitney of Frome, who had worked with Saunders for some time; no police would attend the inquiry and it was made clear to the villagers that they were not to attend it either. By cutting off the supply of witnesses, it was hoped that Mr Saunders's inquiry would be forced to close, although, given the man's stubbornness, this was by no means guaranteed.

Superintendent Foley's second action was to undermine Saunders's alleged power-base. The authority under which he had convened and operated his inquiry was still a matter of mystery; initial claims that the inquiry had the backing of the Home Secretary proved to be ill-founded, but Mr Saunders did still claim to have the full support of the Bradford-upon-Avon bench of magistrates. Foley sought to speak with the magistrates and on Friday night Mr Saunders received a letter which compelled him to attend a meeting of the Bradford bench the next afternoon. Saunders apparently did not see anything suspicious in this request and may even have viewed it as being a good sign, but he was in for a shock.[54]

On Saturday afternoon the Bradford-upon-Avon bench of magistrates met in the Town Hall. When he arrived, Mr Saunders found himself confronted with quite an array of people: in addition to eight of his fellow magistrates also present were Captain Meredith and several of his officers, including Foley. A large body of reporters was also present, they having been informed by William Stone, the magistrates' clerk, that the meeting would be held in public. However, one of the first actions of the chairman was to declare that the meeting would, after all, be held in private; both the reporters and Mr Saunders disagreed with this, but it was to no avail and the magistrates and police went into a separate room, shutting the doors behind them.

The exact details of what transpired inside were not recorded, but it is known that the magistrates immediately confronted Mr Saunders with their extreme displeasure at the way in which he had been conducting himself and also the way in which he had been apt to claim support from themselves. The clerk then brought forward a letter, the wording of which had been previously agreed, and asked all those present to sign it. The letter was addressed to the editor of *The Times* and read:

Sir,

Mr T. B. Saunders is reported to have said, at the opening of his inquiry at Road, that he was there at the instance, and with the sanction, of the Bradford Bench of magistrates; that his proceedings had been sanctioned by the Bradford Bench at a meeting which they had held, so that, therefore, any responsibility which he might incur was shared by the whole Bradford Bench.

I am desired by the magistrates of the Bradford Bench, specially assembled to consider this matter, to say that Mr T. B. Saunders's statement, as reported, is not founded on fact; and that the Bench have not any connexion with Mr T. B. Saunders's inquiry.

> I am your obedient servant,
> William Stone
> (Clerk to the Justices of the Bradford Petty Sessional Division)

The letter was duly signed by all except Saunders himself, who confessed to be shocked at this turn of events. It took a short while for the message to sink in, but when he realised that the letter would be sent to *The Times*, Saunders became very defensive.

'I have a certain private understanding with *The Times*,' he boasted. 'It is useless writing to that paper for anything written to them will be sent to me.'

An argument ensued, but Mr Saunders's various threats and attempted justifications were ignored and half an hour later the reporters were informed that the results of the meeting would be seen in the next edition of *The Times*. This produced a howl of protests from the local journalists, who decried such favouritism, but they picked up on the underlying message: namely, that from that moment on Mr Saunders was operating as an outcast from the magistrates' bench. To all intents and purposes it was the end of his inquiry and, in the eyes of many, the end of his crusade to single-handedly solve the Road Hill House murder.[55]

The headlines and editorials that followed pulled no punches. 'Who is Mr Saunders? And what is he doing at Road Hill?' asked the *Morning Post*. 'Mr Saunders's proceedings are remarkable,' said the *Saturday Review*, 'as showing the latent powers of mischief and folly which are lodged in magistrates. Neither in intelligence nor authority does Mr Saunders's court of inquiry range beyond a session held in the village taproom.' The *Daily Post* agreed: 'The inquiry [shows] the track which future official investigation must not follow.'

Such condemnation must have been music to the ears of the Bradford magistrates, but they were disappointed to note that their letter to *The Times* had not been published; perhaps Mr Saunders's boast of having contacts at the newspaper were not so idle. To overcome this, a copy of the letter was quietly leaked to local journalists and in the coming days its wording was reproduced widely, much to Saunders's fury.

The papers were also alive with the talk of some local gentlemen who had applied to the Queen's Bench for a writ *ad melius inquirendum* ['for a better inquiry'], which would have the effect of quashing the findings of the original coroner's inquest so that a second inquest could take place. The writ had been submitted, but it would be some weeks before the case could be considered by the courts: it was this that gave Mr Saunders an excuse to halt his inquiry.

Despite the dressing-down he received from his fellow magistrates, Mr Saunders had convened his inquiry on the Monday morning as usual. However, in the absence of the police, any witnesses and a public audience, Saunders was reduced to talking at length on his favourite subject: himself. He managed to do this for three days, speaking about how much he had achieved and how and why the world had conspired against him, before finally throwing in the towel. Not that he admitted to being defeated: he explained that his inquiry was not stopping, but that he was merely adjourning it until the outcome of the writ *ad melius inquirendum* was known.

Needless to say, the inquiry was never resumed and a few days later Saunders was called before the Bradford magistrates and, in a very bad tempered meeting, was given a severe reprimand over his behaviour and for assuming that he had the backing of the bench, the police and several other authorities. Saunders would accept no criticism whatsoever and for over an hour he defended himself against all charges and then accused his fellow magistrates of being narrow-minded and of stabbing him in the back. The matter could not be resolved and left a permanent rift between Saunders and his fellow magistrates.

'I leave the public to judge my conduct in this matter,' said Saunders grandly. He was apparently unaware that the public had long ago judged Saunders's actions and they had found his behaviour to be at best eccentric and at worst malevolent. To the relief of many he would henceforth play no further part in the story of the Road Hill House murder.[56]

FRIDAY 30 NOVEMBER 1860

Amidst the personal criticism and incredulity levelled against Mr Saunders and his inquiry, many had chosen to ignore that the erratic proceedings had managed to uncover a major new piece of evidence, namely the existence of a bloodied shift at the crime scene. Few wanted to give Mr Saunders credit for this discovery, but the matter clearly had some importance to the Road Hill House murder and, in the light of the unusual behaviour of the local police, warranted further examination.

In light of this, William Stancomb, who was one of the Trowbridge magistrates to whom Superintendent Foley directly reported, decided that the matter should be quietly but thoroughly investigated. Stancomb began by talking to Foley privately; the policeman immediately sought to dismiss the issue, hinting that the matter was a storm in a teacup whose importance had been exaggerated by Mr Saunders. Asked to explain his dismissal of the blood-stained clothing, Foley told Stancomb that Joshua Stapleton, the surgeon, had pronounced the blood to be of natural origin (i.e. menstrual) and so thereafter the garment had been excluded from the investigation.

The idea that the shift had been dismissed on a surgeon's say-so sounded reasonable enough to Stancomb and he was afterwards shown a letter written by Mr Stapleton which appeared to support Superintendent Foley's version of events. Stapleton's letter referred to 'the woman's nightdress shown to me' as having only a small amount of natural blood upon it and that it 'furnished no clue to this crime'. However, on a closer reading Mr Stancomb noticed that the surgeon made mention of just one bloodied garment when, according to Foley, two had been shown to him that day. These were: (1) the shift recovered from the boiler hole; and (2) a nightdress belonging to Mary Ann Kent. It occurred to Stancomb that Stapleton's letter might have been referring to Mary Ann Kent's nightdress and not the disputed item from the kitchen.

To resolve the issue Stancomb went to see Stapleton at his Trowbridge home and, as he had suspected, was told by the surgeon that he had only been shown one item of clothing and that this was unquestionably a woman's nightdress. When given a description of the blood-stained shift from the boiler hole, Stapleton flatly denied having ever seen it; according to him the nightdress he saw had belonged to Mary Ann Kent. Stancomb pressed him on the issue several times but got the same reply each time.

This new information was at odds with Superintendent Foley's story, which held that it was on Stapleton's advice that he had excluded the boiler-hole shift. This left him with the prospect that one of the testimonies given by Stapleton and Foley was false; it was a situation that left him in a tricky position. Both men were high-powered and well-connected and to doubt their account was not a matter to be undertaken lightly; there could be no room for error, and so Stancomb recruited the clerk to the magistrates, Mr Clark, to act as a witness to any future interviews.

The pair began by travelling to see Sergeant Watts, the man who had first found the shift, and then afterwards to see Constable Urch, who had witnessed its recovery. The policemen re-confirmed what they had said in front of Mr Saunders. Stancomb and Clark then visited Joshua Parsons, the Kent family surgeon, who, like Stapleton, denied having ever been shown the boiler-hole shift. Finally, Stancomb travelled alone to Road Hill House and to the kitchen, where he examined the boiler in detail.

On seeing the boiler he discovered that the shift's hiding place was no so much a hole, but a large space underneath a hot plate in which a fire would be lit. It was large enough to accommodate his entire arm and was of such a design that any package placed in there would not easily have been seen from the outside. He had little doubt that whoever had placed it there intended for the package to be destroyed by the next fire. The cook was not about during his visit so he later returned to interview her and to make a further examination of the kitchen area.

On 22 November Stancomb was requested to give an update of his findings to his fellow magistrates. They approved of his investigation and at their request he re-interviewed Superintendent Foley and Mr Stapleton, questioning them further about their recollection of events.

Stancomb afterwards travelled back to Road Hill House and examined the ladies' clothes there. He discovered that the description of the boiler-hole shift did not match any existing clothes in the house but he was interested to note that all Constance Kent's nightdresses were new and that she had disposed of all her old ones a few weeks after the murder. Stancomb went to interview Hester Holley, the Kents' former washerwoman, who was able to describe Constance's old nightshirts in detail; the description she gave closely matched that of the boiler-hole shift.

In the following few days, news of Stancomb's interest in the bloodied shift reached the newspapers, much to his annoyance. Having initially ignored the issue, many started to speculate that the police had found, and then lost, the famous missing nightdress upon which Inspector Whicher had based his investigation. This moved suspicion back towards the owner of that said nightdress, Constance Kent. The Trowbridge magistrates realised that their interest in this matter was set to become the subject of speculation and agreed to hold a meeting on the issue on 30 November, during which the main witnesses would be examined in public.

Whether by coincidence or not, it was at this time that Mr Kent applied to the Home Office for a permit that would allow Constance to leave the country. He claimed that in the circumstances a normal education was simply not possible in England and so he had made arrangements for her to continue studying in the French town of Dinan in Brittany. Permission was given and either on or shortly after 24 November Constance left England for the French countryside, travelling under the name Emily (or Emilie) Kent. She entered the Convent de la Sagesse as a pupil and, even though her true identity was soon discovered, she is alleged to have settled in quickly and was noted for her 'extreme tenderness to very young children'. It would be some years before Constance would set foot on British soil again.

A few days later, on 30 November, the Trowbridge court house found itself besieged by onlookers and journalists recreating the hectic scenes of the earlier inquiries.

Many were reassured to see that Sir John Awdry was to chair the proceedings; his wisdom and fair-minded nature had already been demonstrated during the examination of Elizabeth Gough and would be a breath of fresh air compared to the ham-fisted effort made by Mr Saunders. Sergeant James Watts was the first to be examined; he confirmed much of what he had said earlier and gave a full description of the circumstances surrounding the shift's discovery and of the item itself:

> The garment was in a dirty state, and there was a good deal of blood about it; it nearly covered the fore and hind parts. There were no marks of blood above the waist; the blood extended about sixteen inches from the bottom. I should think, from the appearance, the blood had been caused from the inside. I should not think the marks had been there long, but should not think they had been made that day. I should think that, from its dirty state, it had been worn more than a week. It was of coarse material ... The garment appeared nearly worn out. There were holes under the arms. It would have been fit for wear again if it had been washed and repaired. [Dallimore, Urch, Heritage and Mr Fricker] were present when I unrolled it. I subsequently rolled it up again, and showed it to Mr Superintendent Foley. I then left it with him. I have never seen it since. I know nothing more about it.

This moved the emphasis to Superintendent Foley, who had already proved himself to be somewhat obstructive and dismissive when talking on this matter. He was, however, being examined under oath by a barrister of some repute and could not risk a confrontation. Instead, Foley chose to be vague with his details, claiming that the matter was so inconsequential as to have slipped his memory:

> I received it from a policeman. I can't say if it was Sergeant Watts. I did not keep it in my possession a minute. I did not like to touch it. I was the chief officer present. I said, 'You see it is a nasty dirty chemise, so put it away.' Some said, 'It's

so-and-so's; don't expose the girl.' I gave it to Dallimore, and I don't know that I saw it again till Monday. I can't charge my memory whether I saw it then. I would not actually swear that any medical man saw it. I showed Mr. Stapleton a stained garment. He did not see the nightgown till Monday, and, if he saw one in the yard in the cart, it must be the one in question.

These last comments appeared to contradict his earlier claim that it was Stapleton's opinion that had led to the item being dismissed. This was news to Mr Stancomb, who interjected: 'I understood from you that Mr Stapleton had seen it?' The policeman's reply remained frustratingly vague:

I understood he had seen it, but can't state positively whether he did or not. I showed him one of the Misses Kents' nightgowns. I am sorry I did not keep the shift to show it to you. Mrs Dallimore had found the nightgown of Miss Mary Ann Kent on Saturday. The missing nightgown was not missed till the Monday. It was on the Monday that I showed the nightdress to Mr. Stapleton. This that I saw was an old stained chemise, not the missing nightdress.

It was now very difficult to say which items had or had not been examined by Mr Stapleton. Foley appeared to be hinting that the surgeon had seen the bloodied shift on the Saturday and Mary Ann Kent's nightdress on the Monday, but he would not commit himself to this and would not be drawn any further, claiming only that he did not wish to expose the shift's owner to the embarrassment of having her 'dirty habits' exposed to public scrutiny. He did, however, acknowledge that in not keeping the garment or telling anyone else about it he had been at fault.

The magistrates acknowledged that a mistake had been made but affirmed their continued faith in Foley's investigation. Mr Stapleton came forward and gave a much more assured performance, stating that he had been shown a garment on three separate occasions, twice on Saturday (once by a policeman, once while it lay in the cart) and once on the Monday. He stated that it was the same garment each time, but that it 'was not like the one described by Watts'. On this he was adamant and remained so for years afterwards.

Dallimore confirmed everything that Watts had said but was able to clear up what had become of the shift and appeared to confirm that Mr Stapleton had indeed examined the garment:

By Mr Foley's direction I kept it till Monday. On the Monday morning I showed it to my wife, and afterwards took it to Road. I examined it for initials, but could not find any mark on it. There was no mark on the wrapping paper. Mr Foley called Mr Stapleton aside and showed him the chemise in my presence on

Monday, after the, inquest. Mr Foley held one part of the garment, and I another, when Mr Stapleton looked at it. The stain in front was small as compared with the stain behind. Mr Stapleton examined it thoroughly, and was satisfied there was nothing on it to lead to the detection of the murder. Ultimately I put the chemise back near the place in which it was found. There were no strangers about when I put back the shift.

Dallimore's account exactly confirmed Foley's version of events but was at odds with Mr Stapleton's testimony. The water was no less muddy following the testimonies of Constables Urch and Heritage, both of whom also backed Foley's testimony; interestingly, Urch noted that as well as being wrapped in brown paper, as others had said, the shift had also been wrapped up inside newspaper. This subtle point was missed by the magistrates but it appeared to be confirmed by Mr Fricker, the only independent (i.e. non-police) witness to the affair, who told the court that he thought the shift had been wrapped in newspaper but who in most other respects backed the testimonies of the other policemen.

The next witness was Eliza Dallimore, the policeman's wife who had so disgraced herself during the inquiry into Elizabeth Gough's arrest. This time she was much more restrained and only answered in short sentences, confirming that she had seen the shift and also believed it to be unconnected with the murder. Sarah Kerslake, the cook, said that she always lit a fire in the boiler at seven o'clock in the morning and that it was out by nine o'clock. She had done so on the morning after the murder, which meant that the shift had to have been placed there after the fire had gone out. She did not see anything suspicious occurring in the kitchen and had no idea what had happened to the parcel once it had been replaced by Dallimore on the Monday.

This brought the magistrates' inquiries to an end and, after a short consultation, it was announced that they too believed that the shift bore no relevance to the murder and that although Superintendent Foley 'had been wrong in not mentioning the matter to the magistrates, still we hold that he had refrained from doing so from feelings of delicacy and decency.'

This was the last that would be said on the matter, at least in official circles, but it left a great many questions unanswered, including why it should happen to be that a blood-stained garment, possibly a nightdress, should have been hidden the morning after the murder; why the policemen's descriptions differed so widely (according to Watt and Urch it was blood-soaked; according to Foley and others there was almost no blood at all); and did Mr Stapleton really see it and what happened to it after it had been replaced? Perhaps the most important question was why, if the matter was of so minor an importance, had the police conspired to cover it up? They purposefully refused to tell anyone about it, but this cannot have been through fear of embarrassing its owner (after all, Mary Ann Kent's blood-stained nightdress was openly talked about). There was also the matter as to why, like the chest flannel, no member of the Kent household had come forward either to claim the garment or to admit that they had taken it after being replaced on the Monday morning.

Evidence that the police's conspiracy of silence over the affair had started to operate quite quickly came from Inspector Whicher, who learned about the night-shift from reading about it in the newspapers. He was furious and penned a stiff letter to the Trowbridge magistrates, claiming that he had no knowledge of the matter, suggesting that within a week of the murder Foley and his men had already decided not to mention the matter in private or public. In a further terse letter to the chief of the Bath police, Whicher openly stated his belief that the bloodied shift had been Constance Kent's missing nightdress and that this vindicated his attempt at bringing her to trial. There were, however, few people in Britain who were prepared to back Whicher; most remained convinced that Mr Kent and his former nursemaid were the guilty parties and that they had been privy to one of the great-est cases of injustice to be seen in the country.

This presumed guilt meant that there was much hostility displayed toward Mr Kent and his family. On Sundays it became a regular sport to abuse and taunt them as they made their way from Road Hill House to church. The locals made it quite clear that the Kent family were not wanted in their neighbourhood, but they con-tinued to live at Road Hill House, tolerating the open ill-will that was displayed toward them, trying to go about their daily lives as normal.

Perhaps unsurprisingly, Mr Kent's longstanding application for promotion to Full Inspector of Factories was turned down, although he was granted a period of six months' compassionate leave in early November 1860. His superior officer explained to the management that while Mr Kent 'is probably not guilty, he is the object of suspicion and not able to go about his duties'. This, combined with the expense of legal bills and other costs associated with the various inquiries, made money tighter than ever. It was speculated locally that the family would not long be able to afford to live in Road Hill House and that the cause of so much blight on their neighbourhood would soon be gone.[57]

WEDNESDAY 1 MAY 1861

The November inquiry concerning the bloodied shift turned out to be the final public examination into the circumstances surrounding the terrible murder at Road Hill House. It had taken place exactly five months after the crime had been committed and immediately afterwards the police admitted that they were not in a position to bring charges against anyone and nor were they likely to be in the foreseeable future. Although the public wished to see justice done, the patience of the authorities had been well and truly exhausted. It seemed that what should have been a relatively straightforward police investigation had dissolved in a state of total and utter chaos. Furthermore, the affair had attracted a lot of unwelcome publicity and appeared to taint the reputation of anyone who troubled themselves with it.

After November 1860 the matter was left to settle down and, while the public did not forget the circumstances relating to the murder, they came to accept that justice would not be done. The law courts recognised this also and the writ *ad melius inquirendum* desired by the Attorney-General was refused by the Queen's Bench in January 1861. It was admitted that there had been problems with the original coroner's inquest, chief of which was the refusal of George Sylvester (the coroner) to interview Mr Kent and his family, but it was judged that these would not be rectified by holding a second inquest. Thus the matter of the Road Hill House murder was left to rest by the police, the Home Office and, eventually, by the newspapers, who could wring no more out of the story.

Inevitably there were several pamphlets and booklets written about the murder, most of which sough to blame Mr Kent, but the family did have some public defenders. One of these had been their former solicitor, Roland Rodway, who wrote a number of letters criticising the newspapers for their lurid coverage; he also defended Mr Kent's seemingly odd actions during the early part of the investigation as being due to a concern for his family's privacy.

A far fuller defence of both Mr Kent and Elizabeth Gough was published on 1 May 1861. This was a full-length book on the murder, written by the local surgeon Joseph Stapleton and entitled *The Great Crime of 1860*. Mr Stapleton knew the family well and had been present during the early part of the investigation; like many he had become obsessed with the case and the resulting book was in part a defence of Mr Kent and his family and in part an excuse to scotch what he viewed to be a couple of errors connected to himself. One of these was Joshua Parsons's belief that Francis Kent showed signs of suffocation; the other that he had been shown the bloodied shift by Superintendent Foley. Both were denied at length by Stapleton, but, although he demonstrated a minute knowledge of both the case and the Kent family history, the surgeon did not name or even hint at who the guilty party might be, although he did affirm that Mr Kent and Elizabeth Gough were innocent. He devoted the second half of his book to reproducing all the transcripts relating to the various inquiries and examinations, plus some other relevant material. The implication was that by digesting these, the reader could come to his or her own conclusion.

To those who held an interest in the murder, *The Great Crime* became (and remains) a standard reference, but by the time of its publication the Kent family had broken their ties with the Trowbridge district. In March 1861 Mr Kent applied to the Home Office for early retirement on his full salary of £350, but was refused. 'He must make an attempt to resume his duties,' was the advice to Robert Baker, the Inspector of Factories and Mr Kent's boss. Mr Kent returned to work, but he was unable to settle into his old position and was permitted to move his base of employment to another region.

In April a notice announced that the contents of Road Hill House were to be placed on sale; for days after crowds of curious people filed through the house, not in the hope of buying anything, but in order to see the various crime scenes associated with the murder. It was noted that little Francis's cot was not for sale and had been removed from the premises; the privy, however, remained in place and was to receive a continual stream of visitors in search of bloodstains.

On 28 April the Kent family moved to Barnstable, Devon, where they remained for a short while before taking a long lease on a property in Llangollen, Wales. In time, normality of a sort did return. William Kent developed a passion for marine zoology and eventually left home to pursue his studies at the University of Cambridge. Mr and Mrs Kent continued to produce children, the next of which, a daughter, was born in July 1861. They, like the rest of the country, must have assumed that the investigation into the murder had been permanently suspended. They were right: it had been shelved, and there was no expectation by any of the investigating authorities of the murderer ever being brought before a court of law.[58]

TUESDAY 25 APRIL 1865

Constance Kent's residential education at the French convent had at first been troubling and she had apparently suffered from a form of manic-depression, which would see her alternate between 'a wild feverish state of mind' and feeling 'very wretched' and suicidal. In time, however, she adjusted to her surroundings and underwent what she later described as 'a change', which saw her develop two passions that would influence her future life greatly.

The first of these was an interest in religion which, despite her Anglican upbringing, seems to have erred towards Roman Catholicism. The second was a desire to work as a nurse. In August 1863 Constance had seen both these wishes fulfilled when she was accepted into St Mary's convent in Brighton as a paying guest. The convent was affiliated with a charitable hospital for distressed women, in which Constance was permitted to work as a nurse.

The person in overall charge of the convent was the Reverend Arthur Douglas Wagner, the curate of St Paul's church, Brighton. Wagner was a larger-than-life character whose outspoken views had made him locally unpopular; he was especially notorious for his desire to see a revival of Catholic practices within the Anglican church (this was the so-called 'Puseyite' or 'Oxford' Movement). Prior to her arrival in Brighton, Constance had taken the liberty of telling Wagner her real name and of her association with the Road Hill House murder. He agreed to keep these details secret, although he did tell Miss Katherine Ann Gream, the mother superior of the convent where Constance was to stay.

From the outset Wagner suspected that Constance knew more about the murder than she had hitherto admitted and, although it was denied later, he appears to have placed a certain amount of psychological pressure on her to divulge all she knew. Wagner is alleged to have refused Constance permission to be confirmed and also from donating any money towards the church. This culminated with an extraordinary event when, on 6 February 1865, Constance reached the age of twenty-one and was thus entitled to receive her mother's legacy of £1,000. She immediately offered it to the church, but Wagner refused to touch the cash, hinting that this could not be considered proper while Constance continued to remain silent about the murder.

During Holy Week in early April 1865, Constance's nerves cracked and a few days before Easter she passed a note to Wagner concerning the murder of her stepbrother.

What she had written shocked Wagner and he immediately passed the note on to Miss Gream, the mother superior. On 12 April Gream interviewed Constance closely and, for the first time in five years, she talked openly and frankly about the horrendous event that had occurred at Road Hill House. During this meeting Constance asked if she and Wagner could travel to London with the aim of making a statement to the police. Wagner agreed, but requested that they delay making the journey until a few days after the Easter festival, perhaps to give everybody concerned time to prepare themselves for what was to come.

On 24 April Constance withdrew around £800 of her legacy and crept into Wagner's church; she stuffed the money into the poor box and went back to the convent to prepare for the journey to London, which was scheduled to take place the following morning. Wagner suspected that this might occur and had asked his staff to keep an eye on the donations; that night, while Constance was writing letters to her father and another person, Wagner carefully separated out Constance's financial contribution and put it to one side, with the intention of returning it to her at a later date.

The following morning, Constance, Wagner and Gream boarded a train for London's Victoria station, a journey of about two and half hours. Thereafter the party split, with Constance and Gream taking a cab to Bow Street Magistrates' Court while Wagner went to Whitehall to inform the Home Office of their purpose for visiting the capital. Wagner's news was received with some alarm by the Home Office officials and ensured that within minutes of his arrival messengers had been despatched from Whitehall to Scotland Yard, Bow Street and the Houses of Parliament.

At Bow Street Magistrates' Court Constance and Gream were not permitted to see anyone in authority until after the petty sessions had finished, and so were asked to remain in a waiting area. Shortly afterwards they were joined by two breathless policemen who, having received the Home Office's message, had hot-footed it over from Scotland Yard. One of these was Frederick Williamson who, as a sergeant, had assisted Inspector Whicher during the original 1860 investigation. Whicher had retired to Salisbury two years previously and in his absence Williamson had risen to become Chief Inspector of the Detective Department, but he had never forgotten the Road Hill House case and had even helped Whicher review the available evidence in 1861.

Shortly before four o'clock, Constance, who was dressed head-to-toe in black, including a veil, was led into the court room, where she was placed before the chief magistrate, Sir Thomas Henry. She silently handed him a piece of paper on which was written:

I, Constance Emilie Kent, alone and unaided on the night of 29th of June 1860, murdered at Road Hill House, Wiltshire, one Francis Savill Kent. Before the deed none knew of my intention, nor after of my guilt; no one assisted me in the crime, nor in my evasion of discovery.

Henry read the confession and, without demonstrating any apparent surprise, looked down at the young woman before him.

'Am I to understand, Miss Kent, that you have given yourself up of your own free act and will on this charge?'

'Yes, sir.'

'Is this paper, now produced before me, in your own handwriting, and written of your own free will?'

'It is, sir.'

'Then, let the charge be entered in her own words.' The clerk entered a charge of murder into the book, but as this was being done, Sir Henry caught sight of Wagner, who had just then arrived at the court house. Wagner's notoriety stretched to London and his association with the case made the magistrate suspect that the confession might have been coerced.

'I will again ask you,' he said to Constance, 'if you have made this confession by your own desire, and without any inducement from any quarter whatever to give yourself up?' She swore that she had not been coerced, but Henry was still unsatisfied and asked that Wagner be sworn in and examined.

The magistrate made the priest outline his association with Constance and got him to state that everything, including the choice of coming to Bow Street, was being done by the girl's own volition and without interference from Wagner. Sir Henry was assured that this was so but he still did not entirely trust him.

'Did you in the first instance induce her to make the confession to you?' he asked the priest.

'No, sir. She thought of it herself, without my ever suggesting it.'

This discussion went on for several minutes with Wagner denying absolutely that he had coerced the confession. What had been a sombre atmosphere started to turn quite heated and even Constance herself grew tired of the magistrate, who would periodically turn to her with the offer of withdrawing the confession. Finally, he asked her if the written confession was in her own handwriting. 'Yes, it is,' she said in an irritated tone.

The confession was then read out to the court and afterwards Sir Thomas Henry informed Constance that because the crime had been committed in Wiltshire, that this was where the trial should take place. A warrant was written out and handed, with the depositions, to Inspector Williamson, who immediately placed Constance under arrest. Williamson then took her, together with Wagner and Gream, to Paddington station, where they boarded a train for the West Country. The journey was long and involved changing trains at least once, and it was not until two o'clock in the morning that the weary travellers stepped onto the platform at Trowbridge station. The local constabulary were there to meet them and to escort the party directly to the police station. It was said that during their journey from London the sight of a senior policeman travelling with a bound prisoner, a priest and a mother superior attracted a lot of passing comments from bystanders.

The next morning Constance was brought before the Trowbridge magistrates for her arraignment. Many of the faces she saw on the magistrates bench would have been familiar to her as they had been present during the examination that had been led by Inspector Whicher. Also present in court was Captain Meredith who, like many others in the neighbourhood, must have been somewhat surprised to learn that the Road Hill House mystery had apparently been solved and without any help from the police. His deputy, Superintendent John Foley, was not in attendance: he had died suddenly the previous year with his professional reputation still very much tarnished from the events of 1860.

The arraignment was a relatively straightforward affair although its start was held up by the absence of the Reverend Arthur Wagner, who arrived late. The warrant and confession were read out to the court, as was a statement from Wagner, who was again questioned on the subject of coercion, which he denied. There then followed a brief statement from Inspector Williamson, after which Constance was formally remanded in custody pending a full trial at the next Wiltshire assizes.

It was only after the carriage carrying her to Devizes gaol had left the village that word of the momentous news began to circulate more widely. A majority of people still believed that Mr Kent and his nurse were responsible for the murder and found the news that Constance had confessed to be slightly incredible. It was noted that she had as yet offered no explanation regarding why and how she committed the crime and how she managed to cover up her tracks so effectively. The Wiltshire assizes court was not due to sit for several weeks, so until then the public would, as before, be forced to subsist on a diet of rumour and speculation.[59]

FRIDAY 5 MAY 1865

News of Constance Kent's arrest dominated the public's imagination and led to a spate of lurid newspaper headlines, editorials and letters on the subject. Given that so many people had previously hinted (or stated openly) that Mr Kent and Elizabeth Gough were the murderers, there was at first a reluctance to believe the confession. Many looked at the Reverend Arthur Wagner's association with Constance and thought that they spotted his mischievous influence at work.

'It would be curious to know when Mr Wagner was first informed [of the confession],' wrote one journalist, 'in order to judge the propriety of his conduct. But one naturally asks, if he was so "perfectly passive", why did he appear at all in the civil court, in connexion with the case?' Others were equally sceptical, with the *Express* stating that 'out of the atmosphere of religious houses, girls of the age of Constance Kent have been known to accuse themselves wrongfully of terrible crimes.'

There were, however, those who were not so surprised at Constance's confession, including Roland Rodway, Mr Kent's solicitor. He wrote a long letter to the Home Secretary and Inspector Williamson to explain why he had ceased to represent Mr Kent's family after the murder: 'I was myself so impressed with the belief that Constance Kent had done the deed, that before I [resigned] I expressed my belief to Mr Kent, and warned him that in his daughter's state of mind and feeling the deceased child might not be the only victim'.

The surgeon Joseph Stapleton was also unsurprised; those who cared to re-read his book about the crime would have discovered that while he defended Mr Kent and Elizabeth Gough, any mention of Constance's possible role in the murder was very low-key indeed. Indeed, according to Mr Rodway, he, Stapleton and Joshua Parsons had met some weeks after the murder and agreed that Constance was the only likely suspect.

Naturally, the person who was the least taken aback was Inspector Whicher, who had refused to drop his opinion on the case and who, in the autumn of 1860, had remarked to a friend that 'nothing will now be known about the murder until Miss Constance Kent confesses'. The inspector's career had suffered badly because of the Road murder, but even so he still tried to re-open the investigation in 1861 after hearing a rumour that Constance had confessed her guilt to one of her relations. However, his superiors prevented him from doing so for fear of the bad publicity this would bring. Whicher was a proud (some said arrogant) man who was embittered by his treatment at the hands of the press; Constance's confession was a comfort to him, and went some way to restoring his reputation as an ace detective, but it could not give him back the years of humiliation he had suffered prior to his retirement in 1863.

One problem faced by journalists, police and others was that while Constance had confessed to the crime, she had not explained her motives or actions on that fateful night. In order to ensure that the legal procedure was followed properly, a pre-trial hearing was organised in Trowbridge police court on 5 May. The purpose of this was to hear evidence from several key witnesses associated with the crime, to ensure that there would be no surprises when the case came to trial in late July.

The police court was packed to the rafters with spectators and journalists, not least because there was a rumour that Mr Kent himself would be attending that day. This proved to be unfounded, but he had asked his former solicitor, Mr Rodway, to represent his daughter. Rodway had agreed to do so but in light of her confession, he said that he would not be seeking to examine any of the witnesses, nor would he present any defence.

The proceedings opened at eleven o'clock when Constance Kent, dressed in black and flanked by two gaolers, entered the court and took her place in the dock. She remained silent during the entire proceedings and kept her veiled head lowered, staring resolutely into her lap.

The witnesses called were all familiar to her and most had been examined several times previously. Indeed, the first witness, Elizabeth Gough, had twice been accused of the crime herself. She had kept her figure and looks but admitted to having suffered much in the previous five years; her career as a nursemaid had been utterly ruined and she had instead been forced to take work as a seamstress, a very lowly profession indeed. Her evidence had not changed, nor had that of Thomas Benger (who found the body), Sarah Rogers (née Cox, the housemaid), Hester Holley (the washerwoman) and Sergeant James Watts (finder of the bloodied shift). All confirmed that the evidence they had earlier given was unaltered.

The same was not so true of Mr Joshua Parsons, the surgeon, whose memory of events had changed considerably. On reflection, he had come round to Mr Stapleton's viewpoint and no longer believed that Francis Kent had been partially suffocated before being wounded, but when examined on the subject he appeared to be confused and could not explain what it was that had changed his mind. Inspector Whicher was also examined, but he chose not to show much emotion. Tellingly, when asked about the bloodied shift, Whicher insisted on calling it a nightdress and hinted that it was central to his theory about the murder.

So far the public had been brought no nearer to understanding what had actually happened on the night of the murder; this would partially change with the arrival of the new witness, Katherine Gream, Constance's former mother superior at Brighton. Miss Gream proved to be highly nervous and soon found herself being tied in knots by the magistrates, who wished her to confirm that no pressure had been placed on Constance regarding the confession. This she eventually did, but in a flustered state Gream revealed some details of a private conversation between her and Constance:

> Something in the conversation made her tell me that she carried the child down-stairs sleeping, that she left the house by the drawing-room window, and that she used a razor for the purpose. She said nothing else about the actual deed. She said she obtained the razor from her father's dressing-case. She spoke afterwards of the nightdress that was lost, and I think she said she had taken it out of the basket again. I don't think she told me anything else.

As these details were revealed, so gasps of shock and surprise could be heard from the gallery. Perhaps realising that she had said too much, the mother superior became vague again, denying repeatedly that she had influenced Constance to confess.

The last witnesses, the Reverend Arthur Wagner and Inspector Williamson, gave the same evidence as before, with the priest being subject to hisses and heckles from the public gallery. With the proceedings terminated, the chairman asked Constance to stand, which, following several hours of being seated, she did with some stiff-ness. Still gazing downward, she listened as the chairman confirmed that she was charged with the wilful murder of her brother and that her trial would take place in Salisbury at the next assizes. As Constance left the court one of the reporters fancied that he had seen a glimpse of her face and that it remained entirely impas-sive and unemotional.[60]

THURSDAY 20 JULY 1865

In the ten weeks between the Trowbridge examination and the full trial, many bits of gossip were bandied about. There had been much speculation about Mr Kent's reaction to his daughter's confession. A neighbour in Llangollen claimed that Mr Kent had discovered the news only after seeing a newspaper headline in a shop: 'Temporarily paralysed,' wrote the correspondent, 'his first impulse seemed to be to hide himself from human observation and rushing up the main street he entered the Wynnstay Arms Hotel, where he ordered a carriage, in which he immediately started for home.'

The Reverend Arthur Wagner, on the other hand, denied this and claimed that Constance had written to her father from Brighton to forewarn him of what was to come. Certainly Mr Kent did not abandon Constance and on at least one occasion he travelled to Devizes gaol to visit her, leaving in floods of tears.

It was widely considered that the few snippets of information given by Miss Gream did not fully fit the known facts. The idea that Constance had exited the house via the drawing room window went against one of the few universally accepted theories: namely that these had been opened purely to give the impression that somebody had broken in. There was also the report of the murder weapon being a razor: could this really have created the deep wounds seen on the boy's body? Almost everyone assumed that a knife had been used.

With so little real information, a conspiracy theory emerged which held that Wagner had used his overbearing personality to draw a false confession from Constance. This theory was very prominent and by early July was being openly promoted in the papers. Indeed, the clergyman was being so abused by the press that he was forced to write to several editors, protesting his innocence. He especially denied the notion that Constance had told him about the murder during sacramental confession and reiterated that he had not influenced her decision, nor had he drafted the confession. But it was to no avail; Wagner had become a figure of hate while, strangely, Constance received much more sympathetic treatment.

The idea that Constance's confession might have been the result of Wager's influence was of genuine concern to Inspector Williamson. He knew that if there was any risk of coercion then the trial judge might ask for further evidence before passing sentence. Consequently, the months of May and June were busy ones for the inspector, who clocked up several hundred miles in pursuit of new evidence that could back up Constance's confession. Amazingly, and despite a gap of five years, he had some success.

Williamson travelled across the country to Bournemouth, Bristol, Barnstable, Brighton, Winchester and even across the Irish Sea to Dublin. He found two vital pieces of information, the first of which came from Francis Kent's godfather, Dr Benjamin Mallam, who confirmed that Mr Kent and his second wife had treated the children from the first marriage very poorly indeed. He gave no specific information, but suggested to Williamson that he should speak to the elder Kent daughters. He also put the inspector onto a former servant at Road Hill House named Mr Stephens, who claimed that about eighteen months prior to the murder, Constance had asked him 'how she could get a razor out of her father's dressing case'. The implication from this is obvious.

Williamson's second useful piece of evidence came from Constance's former schoolmate Helen Moody, who had gone to live in Dublin. She confirmed to the policeman that before the murder Constance had used 'strong expressions of dislike and animosity towards her brother Francis'. While not being directly incriminat- ing, this did at least suggest that Constance had a motive for killing the little boy.

In addition to these facts, Williamson uncovered a startling rumour which, try as he might, could not be confirmed. He was told that during the first week of the investigation the Trowbridge police had discovered a bloodstained poultry knife hidden in one of the sheds at Road Hill House, but, like the bloodied shift in the boiler-hole, they had subsequently managed to lose it and had afterwards covered up the mistake. This was probably just a rumour, but it was of no matter to Williamson, who believed that should the matter come to a full trial, he had enough evidence to secure a conviction.[61]

Constance's trial was scheduled to take place in Salisbury on 20 July. In the weeks beforehand Mr Rodway, who continued to act for Constance, had attempted to persuade her to change her plea either to not guilty or of 'insanity at the time of the deed'. Either of these, argued Rodway, might just spare her the hangman's noose, a fate which surely awaited her if she continued to plead guilty. Constance refused to discuss the matter, insisting that neither instance was the truth, she having com- mitted the murder in a state of sanity. As for the notion of the death sentence, this was 'the only course that will satisfy my conscience'. Prior to the trial Constance's appointed counsel, Mr John Duke Coleridge, also attempted to change her mind, but she was resolute.

The possibility that Constance might change her plea had been taken very seri- ously by the Home Office, who placed an eminent Queen's Counsel, John Burgess Karslake, in charge of the prosecution. Karslake was politically well connected and would soon afterwards be appointed to the post of Solicitor-General; his brief from the Home Office was simple: do not allow the case to collapse. To this end, he prepared a full case against Constance, just in case she should change her plea or the judge demand further evidence. Using Williamson's investigative work, Karslake subpoenaed a total of thirty-one witnesses, including all the adult members of the Kent family plus their former servants and an assortment of villagers, old school friends and policemen. All were housed in a nearby hotel, waiting in case they should be needed by the prosecution.

The morning of 20 July saw a frenzy of activity around the court house, but to the frustration of a large assembled crowd, the public gallery was closed. This was so that a jury could be sworn in and addressed by the judge, Mr Justice Willes. They were then given an overview of the known facts relating to the murder of Francis Kent by Lord Henry Thynne, the chairman of the magistrates. The case was notoriously complex and it took Thynne several hours to explain the various twists and turns that had kept the nation enthralled for several months in 1860 and had allowed Constance to go undetected for five years. This being done, Mr Justice Willes adjourned the court until the following morning. That night, Rodway and Coleridge made a final attempt at getting Constance to change her plea, only to be rebuffed. Nonetheless, Coleridge would be awake until the early hours, preparing a case for the defence which, he wrote in his diary 'after all, I shall not deliver'.

Early Friday morning saw a crush of people fighting to gain admittance to the courtroom's public gallery in the certainty that Constance Kent would be seen in court that day. They were not to be disappointed, and, following the assembly of the jury and the court officials, Mr Justice Willes called for the prisoner to be brought forward. Flanked by a female prison warder, Constance stepped into the court; she was dressed entirely in black and wore a veil across her face which, at Rodway's request, was removed shortly after she entered the dock. Her face was observed to be red and puffy, which was taken to be evidence of prolonged weeping.

The court room was deathly quiet when Mr Justice Willes stood up and read out the formal charge.

'Constance Emilie Kent, you stand charged with having wilfully murdered Francis Savill Kent, at Road Hill House, on the 30th of June 1860. How say you; are you guilty or not guilty?'

'Guilty,' whispered Constance in a low tone.

The judge then spoke up.

'Are you aware that you are charged with having wilfully, intentionally, and with malice, killed your brother?'

'Yes.' He posed the question twice more; on the second occasion Constance remained silent for some minutes and had to be prompted before she replied again.

The guilty plea was recorded, after which Constance's counsel asked that two things be taken into account before sentencing: the first was that she had not committed the crime as a result of ill-treatment by either her father or stepmother; the second that she had at no point been aided and abetted by anybody else.

Turning to Constance, the clerk asked her: 'Have you any thing to say why sentence of death should not be passed upon you?'

'No,' she replied meekly. With this Mr Justice Willes assumed the black cap and, in a voice that was cracking with emotion, affirmed the guilty plea:

> I can entertain no doubt that your plea is the plea of a really guilty person. The murder was one committed under circumstances of great deliberation and cruelty. You appear to have allowed your feelings of jealousy and anger to have worked in your breast until at last they assumed over you the influence and power of the Evil One ...

At this point Willes's nerve failed him, causing him to break into a flood of tears, and for some minutes afterwards he could not speak for sobbing. This scene affected many, including Constance, who, turning her head away from the bench, started to weep audibly and copiously. Others in the court also dissolved into tears, halting the proceedings until, at last, the judge was able to regain some composure. The scene was extraordinary and, according to some, unprecedented. Few doubted that the judge held an affection for the prisoner before him, but there was only one sentence he could pass:

> It only remains for me to discharge the duty which the law imposes upon the court without alternative, and that is to pass upon you the sentence which the law adjudges for wilful murder: That you be taken from the place where you now stand to the place whence you came, from thence to the place of execution, and that you be hanged by the neck until your body be dead; that when your body be dead it be buried within the precincts of the gaol in which you were last confined: and may God have mercy on your soul.

The proceedings were finished, and as the court rose a journalist observed that among the crowd sat ex-Inspector Whicher and wrote that 'one cannot fail to express the utmost sympathy with him for the tenacity with which he clung to a conviction that no one will ever more doubt'.

Many papers displayed a sympathy towards Constance, with some suggesting that, in light of her confession and obvious maturity, the sentence should be commuted to life in prison. Only the *Daily Telegraph* gave her a rough ride, and even mounted a personal attack on her appearance, commenting that 'she has a broad, full, uninteresting face, which wears more an expression of stupid dullness than intelligence'. The paper went on to conjecture that had Constance changed her plea to not guilty then a prosecution case involving thirty-five witnesses had been assembled against her, including some of her old school friends who were prepared to swear that she had expressed a loathing of both her stepmother and half-brother in the weeks before the crime.

There was also the question of whether the death sentence would actually be carried out. There was some speculation as to whether Constance could be declared insane, a situation that would have seen her sent to an asylum rather than the gallows. However, a psychological assessment made by Dr John Bucknill, a government physician, ruled out insanity, although he did question whether Constance was mentally strong enough to withstand a lengthy spell in prison. Sir George Grey, the Home Secretary, was uneasy over the death sentence and took the matter before Cabinet, arguing that had Constance been convicted in 1860 then her age would have prevented her from being hanged. The Cabinet were persuaded and, six days after the conviction, the Home Office released the following statement:

> After deliberating upon all the circumstances of the crime and of the confession, the Home Secretary decided upon recommending to the Queen that the convict's sentence should be commuted to one of penal servitude for life. Her Majesty has been graciously pleased to act upon the recommendation, and Constance Kent will therefore not be executed.

The news was greeted with mixed opinion but Constance, who was residing in Salisbury gaol, is said to have shown little emotion when told of the decision. There was a general agreement that, if nothing else, this decision would allow Constance to stay alive long enough to give a full account of what had happened that night in Road Hill House.[62]

THURSDAY 24 AUGUST 1865

Following five years of speculation, theorising and detective work by both amateurs and professionals, Constance Kent was behind bars for the murder of her half-brother Francis. Furthermore, a month after her conviction she broke the silence surrounding her motive for the murder and the method by which she accomplished it.

Prior to the trial Constance had given detailed statements regarding the events of 30 June 1860 to both Roland Rodway, the family solicitor, and to Dr Bucknill, who had assessed her state of mind while in prison. These statements had been passed on to the family, but on 24 August Constance requested that they be released to the public. Her motive for doing so is unclear, but there was still much talk about the involvement of a third party in the murder (usually Mr Kent and/or Elizabeth Gough), and so this may have been her attempt at absolving the rest of her family of any guilt or compliance. The statements read as follows.

Sir, I am requested by Miss Constance Kent to communicate to you the following details of her crime, which she has confessed to Mr Rodway, her solicitor, and to myself, and which she now desires to be made public. Constance Kent first gave an account of the circumstances of her crime to Mr Rodway, and she afterwards acknowledged to me the correctness of that account when I recapitulated it to her. The explanation of her motive she gave to me when, with the permission of the Lord Chancellor, I examined her for the purpose of ascertaining whether there were any grounds for supposing that she was labouring under mental disease. Both Mr Rodway and I are convinced of the truthfulness and good faith of what she said to us.

Constance Kent says that the manner in which she committed her crime was as follows: A few days before the murder she obtained possession of a razor from a green case in her father's wardrobe, and secreted it. This was the sole instrument which she used. She also secreted a candle with matches, by placing them in the corner of the closet in the garden, where the murder was committed. On the night of the murder she undressed herself and went to bed, because she expected that her sisters would visit her room. She lay awake watching until she thought that the household were all asleep, and soon after midnight she left her bedroom and went downstairs and opened the drawing-room door and window shutters. She then went up into the nursery, withdrew the blanket from between the sheet and the counterpane, and placed it on the side of the cot. She then took the child from his bed and carried him down-stairs through the drawing-room. She had on her night-dress, and in the drawing-room she put on her galoshes. Having the child in one arm, she raised the drawing-room window with the other hand, went round the house and into the closet, lighted the candle and placed it on the seat of the closet, the child being wrapped in the blanket and still sleeping, and while the child was in this position she inflicted the wound in the throat. She says that she thought the blood would never come, and that the child was not killed, so she thrust the razor into its left side, and put the body, with the blanket round it, into the vault. The light burnt out. The piece of flannel which she had with her was torn from an old flannel garment placed in the waste bag, and which she had taken some time before and sewn it to use in washing herself. She went back into her bedroom, examined her dress, and found only two spots of blood on it. These she washed out in the basin, and threw the water, which was but little discoloured, into the foot-pan in which she had washed her feet over night. She took another of her nightdresses and got into bed. In the morning her night-dress had become dry where it had been washed. She folded it up and put it into the drawer. Her three nightdresses were examined by Mr Foley, and she believes also by Mr Parsons, the medical attendant of the family. She thought the blood stains had been effectually washed out, but on holding the dress up to the light a day or two afterwards, she found the stains were still visible. She secreted the dress, moving it from place to place, and she eventually burnt it in her own bedroom, and put the ashes or tinder into the kitchen grate. It was about five or six days after the child's death that she burnt the nightdress. On the Saturday morning, having cleaned the razor, she took an opportunity of replacing it unobserved in the case in the wardrobe. She abstracted her nightdress from the clothes basket when the housemaid went to fetch a glass of water. The stained garment found in the boiler hole had no connexion whatever with the deed. As regards the motive of her crime, it seems that, although she entertained at one time a great regard for the present Mrs Kent, yet if any remark was at any time made which in her opinion was disparaging to any member of the first family, she treasured it up, and determined to revenge it. She had no ill-will against the little boy, except as one of the children of her step-mother. She declared that both her father and her stepmother had always been kind to her personally, and the following is the copy of a letter which she addressed to Mr Rodway on this point while in prison before her trial:

Devizes, May 15.

Sir, It has been stated that my feelings of revenge were excited in consequence of cruel treatment. This is entirely false. I have received the greatest kindness from both the persons accused of subjecting me to it. I have never had any ill-will towards either of them on account of their behaviour to me, which has been very kind.

I shall feel obliged if you will make use of this statement in order that the public may be undeceived on this point. I remain, sir, yours truly,

CONSTANCE E. KENT.

To Mr R. Rodway.

She told me that when the nursemaid was accused she had fully made up her mind to confess, if the nurse had been convicted; and that she had also made up her mind to commit suicide, if she was herself convicted. She said that she had felt herself under the influence of the Devil before she committed the murder, but that she did not believe, and had not believed, that the Devil had more to do with her crime than he had with any other wicked action. She had not said her prayers for a year before the murder, and not afterwards, until she came to reside at Brighton. She said that the circumstance which revived religious feelings in her mind was thinking about receiving the sacrament when confirmed.

An opinion has been expressed that the peculiarities evinced by Constance Kent between the ages of twelve and seventeen may be attributed to the then transition period of her life. Moreover, the fact of her cutting off her hair, dressing herself in her brother's clothes, and leaving her home with the intention of going abroad, which occurred when she was only thirteen years of age, indicated a peculiarity of disposition, and great determination of character, which foreboded that, for good or evil, her future life would be remarkable.

This peculiar disposition, which led her to such singular and violent resolves of action, seemed also to colour and intensify her thoughts and feelings, and magnify into wrongs that were to be revenged, any little family incident or occurrences which provoked her displeasure.

Although it became my duty to advise her counsel that she evinced no symptoms of insanity at the time of my examination, and that, so far as it was possible to ascertain the state of her mind at so remote a period, there was no evidence of it at the time of the murder, I am yet of opinion that, owing to the peculiarities of her constitution, it is probable that under prolonged solitary confinement she would become insane.

The validity of this opinion is of importance now that the sentence of death has been commuted to penal servitude for life; for no one could desire that the punishment of the criminal should be so carried out as to cause danger of a further and greater punishment not contemplated by the law.

I have the honour to remain, your very obedient servant,

JOHN CHARLES BUCKNILL, M.D.

This account was all the public were to hear from the self-confessed murderess and, although it was not intricate, there was enough detail to answer most of the outstanding issues relating to the known facts of the case. Rather than a knife, as most had supposed, a razor was the murder weapon. The bloodstained night-dress that Inspector Whicher had searched so hard for did exist, but, according to Constance, it was not coated in blood; rather, it had only a couple of spots which Mr Parsons, Superintendent Foley and Mrs Dallimore appear to have missed during their initial search. The chest flannel was her own and the mysterious bloodied shift was, as Foley had maintained, nothing to do with the murder. The motive was revenge against her family, but not due to any 'cruel treatment' on their part.

In almost all respects Constance's account was a vindication of Inspector Whicher's original theory, but many felt that it did not take into account some of the unusual events associated with the case, most of which were connected with Mr Kent and Elizabeth Gough. Even *The Times*, which was usually restrained in its comment, was unhappy with Constance's explanation and devoted a lengthy editorial to the matter:

> There is nothing in this part of the story (the commission of the murder) which can be in any way questioned, unless the medical evidence should have anything to say with respect to the manner in which she describes the wounds as having been inflicted.
>
> The difficulty, if it be one, of making the terrible journey from the nursery to the closet without disturbing anyone, even the child, is inseparable from the nature of the case, and with regard to this we can only accept Constance Kent's own description. The most extraordinary part of the story commences after-wards, and relates to the nightdress, of which so much was made at the time by Inspector Whicher. She wore, she says, in committing the deed, only a night-dress, and when she got back to her room she examined this, and found two spots of blood upon it. These she washed out, pouring the water, which was only slightly discoloured, into the footpan which she had used the night before. 'In the morning her night-dress had become dry; she folded it up and put it into the drawer.' This, of itself, seems somewhat strangely at variance with the caution she had otherwise displayed. A soiled nightdress, discarded just before the end of the week, folded up, and put away in a drawer, would seem likely at once to attract suspicion; and it is easy to suppose that every sign of recent washing had been removed, while she herself subsequently discovered that the marks of blood had not entirely disappeared: 'Her three nightdresses were examined by Mr Foley, the superintendent of police, and by Mr Parsons, the surgeon of the family.'
>
> Would it have been credible that two persons of such intelligence as Foley and Parsons should have examined these three dresses, one of which had been only just taken into wear, and another had evidently been recently discarded, without being led to some suspicion? And if suspicion had once been thus awak-ened, and the soiled dress more carefully examined, must not the still lingering

stain of blood have attracted attention? The rest of the story of the nightdress is very much as Inspector Whicher imagined it, except that, strange to say, the blood-stained nightdress found in the kitchen, which seemed to give so much plausibility to his conjecture, is said by Constance herself to have had nothing to do with the matter. It still remains a mystery, therefore, to whom this nightdress belonged, and how and why it so strangely disappeared. Constance Kent's night-dress was really removed from the clothes basket while the maid-servant was sent for a glass of water, but it is not clear whether this was not the very dress in which the murder was committed on Saturday morning, and the clothes went to the wash on Monday. It was, moreover, 'five or six days afterwards that she burnt the dress'. She had meanwhile 'secreted it, moving it about from place to place.' The razor was replaced in its case on Saturday morning.

Such are the details now afforded us of this extraordinary crime, which seems not to diminish in perplexity and strangeness as it is unravelled step by step. It is evident that we have not yet obtained a complete account of all the circumstances, whether from that obliquity of mind which seems to prevent every criminal from making a perfectly accurate confession, or from mere inadvertence or omission on the part of the narrator, it is impossible to say. The motive assigned for the murder is not the least extraordinary part of the story. She repeats her assurance that she had received nothing but kindness from her father and the second Mrs Kent, and she adds that she had no ill-will whatever against the boy. It was simply that 'if any remark was at any time made which in her opinion was disparaging to a member of the first family, she treasured it up and determined to revenge it.' These trivial vexations, and nothing else, were sufficient to incite her to take such a horrible revenge. She must, indeed, as we cannot but believe for the sake of human nature, possess what Mr Bucknill calls 'great peculiarities of disposition and great determi-nation of character.' … Let us hope that the mystery which remains may soon be unravelled, and the terrible tale consigned to a quick oblivion.'

Such views were echoed in private and in public across the entire country, but, although Constance had pointedly explained the known facts of the murder and had taken sole responsibility for it, many still believed that there was an additional side to the story that somehow involved Mr Kent and Gough. There was no way to prove this and only one other version of the story would be given by Constance Kent. This she wrote on the night before her original confession in a letter to one of her most vocal supporters, Sir John Eardley Wilmot; the letter was later seen by Inspector Williamson, who, after Constance's conviction, summarised its contents in a report to his boss, Sir Richard Mayne. Its contents differed little from those given to Rodway and Bucknill, but it did give a bit more detail concerning the motive:

The substance of the confession is that she has from her earliest childhood entertained a strong dislike towards the present Mrs Kent, who was then her governess, her own mother being alive but partially imbecile from continued illness; after her mother's death Mr Kent married the governess, then Miss Pratt, and from that time all her thoughts were turned towards avenging herself on her stepmother; twice, she stated, she intended to kill her but was prevented by circumstances, and then the thought struck her that before she killed her, she would kill the children as that would cause her additional agony, that it was with these feelings in her heart she returned home from school in June 1860, that on the night of the murder before going to bed she placed a candlestick and matches in the privy ...

Thereafter, Williamson gave Constance's account of how the murder was accomplished, which does not differ from that published in the newspapers by Dr Bucknill.

Constance's proclaimed dislike of her stepmother did concur with her attempt to run away from home and with the comments she was alleged to have made to her schoolfriends in the weeks before the murder. Given this, and the emotional turmoil associated with adolescence, this motive also seemed to fit the facts, although many still looked to an affair between Mr Kent and Gough as the explanation, still believing Constance to have confessed following pressure applied by the Reverend Arthur Wagner.

There was, however, no evidence for this, and the statements given by Constance would have to suffice for both police and public alike. If there were any loose ends then it was evident that they would have to remain as such, for Constance had no intention of mentioning the murder again in public.[63]

SATURDAY 18 JULY 1885

For the first few weeks of her imprisonment Constance had been confined to the local gaol in Salisbury while a place was sought for her in one of the national penitentiaries. She was duly moved to Millbank Prison, in London, where she spent the first nine months living in solitary confinement, before being allowed to join the rest of the prisoners. There she became a model inmate whose behaviour was exemplary and who kept herself to herself. A former governor recalled Constance as being shy and 'mouse-like' in her behaviour:

> She was a mystery in every way. It was almost impossible that this insignificant, inoffensive little person could have cut her infant brother's throat in circumstances of peculiar atrocity. No doubt there were features about her face which the criminal anthropologist would have seized upon as being suggestive of instinctive criminality: high cheek bones, a lowering, overhanging brow, and deep-set, small eyes, but her manner was prepossessing and her intelligence was of a high order, while nothing could exceed the devoted attention she gave the sick under her charge as a nurse.

The good behaviour continued down the years as Constance was moved to Parkhurst prison, on the Isle of Wight, then Millbank again, then Woking and, finally, Fulham prison in London. As she passed her twelfth year behind bars, so Constance issued the first of several petitions to the Home Secretary asking for her release. However, the law required that she serve a minimum of twenty years and so each petition was refused.

While Constance served her time much was happening to her family, who continued to reside in Wales. Just over a year after her arrival in Millbank, Constance learned that her much disliked stepmother had died of pneumonia aged just forty-six years old. Mr Kent was distraught and was said never to have recovered from the loss; he was to die several years later in 1872 of liver failure aged seventy-one. By this time the children from his first marriage had left home; the two elder sisters chose to live with one another in London, where they remained for the rest of their lives, never choosing to marry and living to a great age: Mary Ann died in 1913 aged eighty-one, while Elizabeth died in 1922 aged nearly ninety. The sisters had apparently followed their brother William to London, where he had moved in

1867 to further his career as a marine zoologist at the British Museum, an institution with which he had a love/hate relationship.

Mr Kent's death may have freed William from a number of financial and social constraints, for a matter of months after his father's funeral he married and, with his father-in-law's blessing, began to campaign for his sister's release from prison. In the coming thirteen years both William and Constance would implore the authorities for her freedom in the interests of compassion, health and as a reward for her good behaviour. In her many petitions, Constance would acknowledge the horror of her original crime and of her deep regret at having committed it. However, in some of the earlier petitions she still attempted to justify her actions, explaining that she had a stepmother 'who while living in the family some years before her mother's death always treated her mother with ridicule and disdain'.

The Home Secretary dismissed all such applications, explaining that twenty years was the minimum term for those sentenced to life imprisonment. The arguments did have some effect and a few weeks before the end of her twentieth year behind bars, Constance learned that she was to be released on licence.

On 18 July 1885 Constance Kent was released from Fulham prison into an outside world that still very much remembered the Road Hill House murder of a quarter of a century earlier. Constance's terrible deed was remembered in novels, such as Wilkie Collins's *The Moonstone*, and cheap crime pamphlets. There was even a Constance Kent waxwork model at London's Madame Tussauds, although it was removed when the owners learned of her imminent release from prison. With such an infamous reputation Constance could not be released directly into the community, but would need to be placed into a safe, monitored environment where she could be watched over. The most obvious safe haven, the home of her brother William, was not open to her: he and his family had moved to Tasmania a year earlier after he had been offered the post of Inspector of Fisheries.

Fortunately, Constance had other friends who were willing to help out and on her release she is said to have been housed in the town of Buxted, Sussex, by members of Reverend Arthur Wagner's church. There was little danger of her face being recognised: prison had transformed the gentle, educated girl into a tough, ungainly middle-aged woman, but she did have to shed her real name and, while with them, went under the name of Emilie King. One of Wagner's church spoke to the author Yesult Bridges about Constance's stay in Buxted:

> She walked like a convict – flatly. Her hands were rough and hard, and she had forgotten how to sit at table and how to use a knife and fork. She wore dark spectacles, and she had to report to the police at Brighton every month. They had cropped her hair short. Things had been put on it in the prison – for insects, you know. It was harsh and almost black.

The offer of accommodation was greatly welcomed, but Constance did not plan to stay in England for long and set about making plans to depart for foreign climes, where she could be unencumbered by the burden of her past deeds.[64]

MONDAY 10 APRIL 1944

William Kent may not have been present at Constance's release from prison, but he had not forgotten his sister. In the summer of 1886, as soon as her period of licence expired, he returned to England and, following a brief stay, returned to Tasmania, taking Constance with him. She travelled under the adopted name of Ruth Emilie Kaye, a title that would remain with her for the rest of her life. After a settled period in Tasmania, William and Constance began to pursue their own separate paths, he as a marine biologist, she as a nurse. Both were to travel across Australia in pursuit of their careers before, in 1895, William returned to England to enter a period of semi-retirement that would occasionally draw him back to the South Seas. He died in England in 1908 and was afterwards widely praised as an accomplished naturalist and author.

Meanwhile, Constance had settled in Sydney, where she had taken up the role of matron in the Maitland Nurses' Home: it seems that nobody there ever guessed or learned of her real name. In fact, there appear to have been remarkably few people who ever knew the truth of Constance Kent's fate.

Following her release from prison, the public had been given no clue as to what had become of Constance, but there was much speculation on the subject. It was commonly rumoured that she had emigrated, but nobody managed to guess where she ended up. Canada and South Africa were the favoured destinations, but some maintained that she had joined a religious order in Britain or France and was shut away in a nunnery. By the time of the First World War it was assumed by many that she must have died.

In September 1928 the detective novelist John Rhode published the first full-length book about the Road Hill House murder since Joseph Stapleton's *Great Crime of 1860*. In light of what had transpired since then, it was entitled *The Case of Constance Kent* and, aside from providing the facts of the case, Rhode also gave an attentive view of what he thought had really happened that fateful night, nearly seventy years earlier. (I have dealt with this in the Epilogue.)

Like most commentators, Rhode assumed that Constance had long since died and, when speculating on her fate said: 'The truth is probably that she entered an Anglican sisterhood and died within a year or two of her release.' He was therefore somewhat surprised to receive, via his publisher, a lengthy document that had been posted in Sydney, Australia, in February 1929. The correspondent had read his book and wished to comment on it; ordinarily there would be nothing unusual in this, but in this instance the commentator appeared to have some in-depth knowledge of Constance's state of mind at the time of the murder. Rhode suspected that Constance was the author, but others disagreed, including a handwriting expert who compared the letter to examples of young Constance's script.

The letter subsequently become known as 'the Sydney Document,' the original version of which was lodged by Rhode at his London club, where it was destroyed during the Blitz. No full copy of the Sydney Document survives, but fortunately Rhode had seen fit to print large tracts of the letter in his contribution to a volume on famous murders that was published in 1937.

The author of the Sydney Document did not seek to correct the method of the murder, as given by Constance in 1865, but they did have much to say on the motive. This may be in response to Rhode's comment that, in 1865, Constance had given 'a motive for which inadequate is the mildest possible term'. The letter focuses only on incidents in the Kent children's childhoods; none of which portray the family in a particularly favourable light.

The document, which was written in the third person, openly states that Mr Kent had been conducting an affair with his governess, Mary Drewe Pratt, long before the death of his first wife. It recounted how the eldest son Edward had one day risen early and 'met his father coming out of the governess's room which was next to his. Highly indignant, he did not mince his words to his father, who promptly sent him back to school.' The letter went on to ask:

> Why was the governess taken out for drives and her [Constance's] mother never? Why was her father in the library with the governess while the rest of the family was with her mother? She [Constance] remembered many little incidents which seemed strange. One was during a thunderstorm when the governess acted as though she were frightened and rushed over to her father who drew her down on his knee and kissed her. The governess exclaimed: 'Oh, not before the child'.

The matter of the original Mrs Kent's treatment at the hands of her husband and his governess are only lightly touched upon, although it is hinted that the poor woman was purposefully excluded from the rest of the family and forced to live in a different section of the house while her children were raised by Miss Pratt. Nor did it look favourably upon the marriage between Mr Kent and his governess; the father is portrayed as not having held any interest at all in his children while their new stepmother displayed signs of jealousy and sought only to make them miserable, using a mixture of bullying and punishment that left them isolated and traumatised.

The writer recounted how as young children Constance and William had their own little gardens which they would attend to. Then one day they were distracted by merry laugher coming from the next-door garden: 'They went to the hedge and looked over longingly at the children playing with some visitors. They were invited to join but were afraid. They were seen [by their stepmother] and their disobedience punished; the little gardens were uprooted and trampled down. Constance made some futile efforts to revive hers.'

The regime of punishment and bullying was also incorporated into their schooling, the early years of which took place at home, under the direction of the new Mrs Kent:

The governess had a theory that once a child said a letter or spelt a word right it could not forget it, and she conscientiously believed it was her duty to treat any lapse as obstinacy. The letter H gave Constance many hours of confinement in a room while she listened longingly to the music of the scythe on the lawn outside. When words were to be mastered punishments became more severe. Two days were spent shut up in a room with dry bread and milk and water for tea. At other times she would be stood up in a corner in the hall, sobbing, 'I want to be good. I do, I do,' till she came to the conclusion that goodness was impossible for a child and she could only hope to grow up quickly as grown-ups were never naughty.

The onset of adolescence appears to have brought out a rebellious streak within Constance who, to judge by the letter, stopped trying to appease her stepmother and who instead sought to defy her:

Constance did not take her punishments very seriously; she generally managed to get some amusement out of them. Once after being particularly provocative and passionate, the governess put her down in a dark wine cellar. She fell on a heap of straw and fancied herself in the dungeon of a great castle, a prisoner taken in battle fighting for Bonnie Prince Charlie and to be taken to the block next morning. When the governess unlocked the door and told her to come up she was looking rather pleased over her fancies. The governess asked what she was smiling about. 'Oh,' she said, 'only the funny rats.'

'What rats?' said the governess. She did not know there were any there.

'They do not hurt,' said Constance, 'only dance and play about.'

After that, to her disappointment, she was shut in the beer cellar, a light room but with a window too high to look out of. She managed to pull the spigot out of a cask of beer. After that she was locked up in one of two spare rooms at the end of a vestibule and shut off by double doors. She liked the big room for it had a large four-poster bed she could climb about, but the little room was dreary.'

This rebelliousness and an urge to escape her family led to the disastrous attempt to run away and as a consequence the sending of Constance and William to separate boarding schools. According to the letter-writer, Constance enjoyed her schooling, but even so continued to be naughty and defiant of authority (this view contrasts with the award she is known to have been given for good behaviour); apparently Constance started to think of herself in negative terms. After reading a book by 'Baxter' (probably the puritan preacher Richard Baxter) she became convinced that 'she had committed the unforgivable sin' (doubting the Bible) and, believing that 'it was useless to try any more', she turned away from religion; she even expressed a support for the Darwinian viewpoint on evolution, much to her family's disgust. This ties in with Constance's earlier statement, in which she claimed to have stopped saying her prayers shortly before the murder was committed.

Constance did not enjoy her school life and dreaded coming home for holidays. The taunts and abuse from her stepmother did not abate:

> She was sitting at a window, rather disconsolate, when her stepmother wanted her to do some mending. She refused, and her stepmother said, "Do you know, but only for me you would have remained at school. When I said you were coming one of your sisters exclaimed, 'What, that tiresome girl!' So you see, they do not want you."

Thus the Sydney Document gave a hitherto unseen prologue to the Road Hill House murder, laying out in detail the events which were to motivate an intelligent fifteen-year-old girl from a well-off background to kill her half-brother and afterwards to have the nerve to deny it, even in a court of law.

The Sydney Document, when combined with Constance's 1865 statements, paints a picture of an abused and rebellious schoolgirl who as a teenager began to believe that she was in some way evil or, as she later put it (admittedly after she had found religion), 'felt herself under the influence of the Devil'. It was in this state that she appears to have hatched a plan to kill her stepmother, but, after twice failing, decided to murder her children instead. Constance allegedly told friends that she held a dislike of little Francis and the boy seems to have been a favourite of both Mr and Mrs Kent, so perhaps she decided to start with him, planning the event some weeks in advance before finally carrying out the terrible deed.

In light of what is now known about Constance's life after prison, there can be little doubt that she was the author of the Sydney Document. The main arguments against it were that by 1929 Constance Kent was assumed to have been dead for some years and to have been living in Canada, not Australia. Both suppositions were wrong, which, when combined with the accuracy of the letter's contents, leave most modern commentators in little doubt that it had been penned by Constance herself. She could afford to write the letter in the secure knowledge that it would not harm any of her immediate family: at the time of its writing, she was eighty-three years old and a spinster who had outlived all fourteen of her brothers and sisters.

The Sydney Document is a final unexpected twist in the story of the Road Hill House murder and if one accepts that Constance was the author then it offers a detailed glimpse into her state of mind almost seventy years after the crime. That she took the trouble to read Rhode's book suggests that she was not hiding away from her past and could live with the knowledge of her deed (it was also said that she talked about the murder frequently while in prison). That she took the time to write a letter of over 3,000 words suggests that she was keen that people should know more about the dysfunctional family situation that eventually drove her to commit murder. Perhaps more controversially, when reading the surviving extracts of the Sydney Document, one is left with the impression that even in 1929 Constance did not entirely regret what she had done and that she in some way still believed that the murder could be justified. Despite John Rhode's continued interest in the case, nothing more was heard from Constance Kent, who continued to live her anonymous Australian life.

Constance remained healthy and is said to have made the weekly walk from her rest home to church every Sunday. She made her 100th birthday in February 1944, an occasion that was celebrated with a glass of champagne: 'She is still energetic, bright and a constant reader,' wrote the *Sunday Sun & Guardian*. 'She does not wear glasses and is possessed of a particularly keen insight into politics.'

Several newspapers covered the event of Ruth Emilie Kaye's centenary, but (not unsurprisingly) none made any connection with her notorious English *alter ego*; to them she was a sweet-faced pioneering nurse who had travelled widely in Europe before settling in Australia.

The birthday was to be her last and two months later, on 10 April, almost seventy-nine years after she had been sentenced to death, Constance Kent passed away peacefully in her sleep. With no surviving family to come forward and claim the body, her minister arranged for her cremation and, following a brief church service, the last living connection to the terrible crime committed on 30 June 1860 was severed.[65]

EPILOGUE: ALTERNATIVE ENDINGS?

Nearly a century and half has passed since Constance Kent confessed to having murdered her half-brother in Road Hill House during the early hours of 30 June 1860. In that time there have been four journalistic investigations into the case, all of which have resulted in full-length books.

The first of these was by John Rhode, a writer of crime fiction, whose steadfast inquiries into the murder were published in 1929 as *The Case of Constance Kent*: it was this book that drew Constance herself to elucidate her motive for committing the murder in the first place. The second book, *Saint – with Red Hands?*, was written by the Trinidadian author Yseult Bridges and was published in 1954, a decade after Constance's death. The next book was *Cruelly Murdered*, which was based on an extensive investigation into the murder (and the life of Constance Kent) by author Bernard Taylor. This was published in 1979 and contains some interesting and important new information, especially concerning the ultimate fate of Constance following her release from prison. Finally, shortly after I had completed the first draft of this book, Kate Summerscale published *The Suspicions of Mr Whicher*, which tells the story of the murder but with an emphasis on the case's wider effect within Victorian society.

These four books were written across a period of eighty years by four people who had immersed themselves in the wealth of archive material relating to the Road Hill House murder in order both to tell its story and also to see if they could make sense of the many conflicting and confusing incidents and events that are associated with it. Each author made their own inquiries and pieced the evidence together in their own way and to varying degrees all come to the same general conclusion: that Constance Kent's confession of 1865 does not fit all the known facts of the case and that she was covering up a portion of the story. However, although this is acknowledged, these authors have different opinions as to the scale of the cover-up and as to what exactly did happen in Road Hill House on the night of the 30 June 1860. And so have I.

In this last section I should like to conclude by offering a summary of the various ideas and theories that have been expressed regarding what may or may not have occurred in Road Hill House, and to then offer my own view on the subject.

From the moment that Constance Kent's confession was released to the public in August 1865, people have questioned the version of events that it contains. It may be remembered that Constance claimed to have single-handedly devised and executed the plan to kill her half-brother and that in order to do so she stole a razor from her father; took the child and his blanket from the room; carried him downstairs and out of the drawing-room window; lit a candle in the privy; held him with one hand and killed him with the other; stabbed the body and disposed of it; cleaned her nightdress; and returned to bed. She said that after this the night-dress was examined by the police and a surgeon; that she cleaned and hid the razor; and that the nightdress was burned. She also confessed to being the owner of the chest flannel, which she claimed to be an ordinary flannel, and that the bloodied shift found in the boiler-hole was unconnected to the murder.

Even in 1865 many found this version of events hard to reconcile with the many oddities associated with the Road Hill House murder. It had already been shown that *The Times* newspaper found the confession seriously at odds with facts as they were understood, leading them to say: 'Let us hope that the mystery which remains may soon be unravelled and the terrible tale consigned to a quick oblivion.' The greater majority of people that have looked at the case since have thought likewise and it is frequently pointed out that Constance's version of events gives the impression of being a well-thought out story that is purposefully designed to take into account the main features of the case (the missing nightdress; the open window; the blanket; the lack of murder weapon, etc.), while at the same time exonerating all other members of the family of any blame.

Some have even suggested that Constance was (wittingly or otherwise) aided by Mr Rodway when drawing up the confession, although given that she apparently gave a similar account to Miss Gream and Sir Eardley Wilmot before she even contacted the authorities, this seems unlikely (see earlier). Many complained that, had Constance been placed before a jury and questioned, then a different story might have emerged. 'Had it been presented as a case for the Prosecution,' wrote Yesult Bridges, 'it would have been demolished in five minutes by Counsel for the Defence.' This may be so, but it is an academic argument as under English law Constance could be found guilty upon her confession alone without the need for any corroborating evidence.

Let us now have a look at the perceived problems with the confession and the conclusions that these have engendered.

It was John Rhode's 1929 book that was the first to suggest outright that Constance's confession might be wholly or substantially false ('She fails to prove the case against herself,' says Rhode). He takes issue with several points in her confession which he felt stretched believability beyond breaking point.

Rhode's first bone of contention concerned the journey from the nursery to the privy, which he described as being 'frankly incredible'. He questioned how, holding a large child in one hand, Constance could have extracted the blanket, put on her boots, opened the shutters and window, bent down to climb out of the window and then found and lit the candle using matches. During this time the child allegedly slept soundly which was 'a most remarkable thing'.

His second issue was with the use of a razor which, according to Constance, was used once on the throat and yet produced a wound that nearly severed the head from the body. Given the wounds to the throat and chest, a razor was seen as being a most unlikely weapon and was not even considered by the police at the time. Rhodes also questioned her comment about the blood seeming to take an age to come when, in reality, a cut throat will instantaneously produce great jets of bloods that can travel some distance. In light of this the fact that only one or two spots of blood were on her nightdress also seems odd. His other stated problem was the chest flannel was alleged to have been in everyday use by Constance and yet was not recognised by anybody in the household.

Rhode made it clear that he did not think that the confession was very satisfactory, but he stopped short of offering an alternative version of events other than to suggest that the flannel might have been used to gag the child, partially suffocating him in the process. He imagined a scenario whereby Constance had come under the influence of the Reverend Arthur Wagner and as a consequence 'conceived the idea of offering herself as a sacrifice, in order to clear away the cloud that rested on her family'. The confession was then concocted (with the help of Mr Rodway) to take into account the most obvious features of the case.

Although it is not openly stated, Rhode implied that Constance was either wholly or substantially innocent (hence his statement that her given motive was unbelievable) and that, therefore, the murder was committed either solely by or with the help of others in the house. Rhode leaves us dangling in the air and offers no theory of his own to fill the void he has created. It is, however, interesting that his views incensed Constance enough to cause her to break cover and write the Sydney Document, which implicitly took Rhode to task over her alleged lack of motive, but which had nothing to say on his questioning of her method.

Yesult Bridges produced her book twenty-five years after Rhode and came to a similar conclusion, but she stated her reasons more fully and found a total of fourteen inconsistencies with Constance's alleged confession. These are listed below:

1. *The razor was the only weapon used.* This was said to be inconsistent with the wounds produced, especially the stab to the body. 'It is,' said Bridges, 'impossible to stab with a razor'.

2. *The given timings.* Constance claimed to have left her bedroom just after midnight, but, according to Bridges, Constable Urch saw a light in the hall and nursery at quarter to one in the morning and Mrs Kent was woken by the shutters being opened when 'it was just light'.

3. *The removal of the child.* This echoed Rhode's point about the weight of the child and the need to move in the dark.

4. *Manoeuvring with the child.* Again, this referred to trying to open the drawing room window and exiting through it with a child in hand.

5. *The sleeping child.* Could a child have really slept while it was transported and manoeuvred through the house and garden?

6. *The wound to the throat.* Could someone unaccustomed to using a razor have inflicted a wound so expertly?

7. *The stab wound.* This reprised the point made in (1) above about the razor being an unsuitable murder weapon.

8. *The candle used in the privy.* No sign was ever found of it.

9. *The flannel being Constance's personal property.* Constance described having made the flannel herself some time previously for washing and yet no-one in the house recognised it. Also, Foley and others were adamant that it was a chest flannel, not a washing item.

10. *Two spots of blood on her nightdress.* Was this feasible after having cut the throat of a living child while it was balanced on her arm? There should have been blood everywhere.

11/12. *The washing and examination of the nightdress.* Could the three people who examined the nightdresses (Foley, Parsons and Mrs Dallimore) really have missed the fact that one had just been washed and had faint bloodstains on it?

13. *The hiding and destruction of the nightdress.* In a household that was full of police, where did she hide it?

14. *The bloodied shift was not hers.* Then whose was it and where did it go?

Mrs Bridges followed Rhode in thinking that Constance's given motive was poor and that she was innocent of the crime. She also followed Rhode in thinking that the confession was a consequence of undue pressure placed by Wagner, with the details of the story itself being devised with the aid of Mr Rodway. Mrs Bridges then used her knowledge of the case to put forward the following scenario.

The underlying premise was that Mr Kent was having an affair with Elizabeth Gough, an idea that was commonly put forward in 1860. Thus, said Bridges, on the night of the crime Mr Kent waited downstairs until he was certain that his wife was asleep before creeping into the nursery to be with Gough. Usually the children slept soundly but Francis's pill had made him restless and caused him to awake; peeping over the edge to his cot, the boy viewed his father *in flagrante delicto* with the nursemaid and cried out in alarm. To silence the child Mr Kent clapped Gough's chest flannel over his mouth, but, in attempting to subdue him, the child was accidentally suffocated. To cover up the crime both of them manoeuvred the body to the privy and there inflicted some post-mortem wounds using a kitchen knife; in the process Gough's nightdress became covered in blood and the body became stuck in the privy. Afterwards the pair cleaned the knife in the kitchen and hid the nightdress in the boiler-hole; the drawing-room window was opened to make it look as though the crime had been committed by an intruder. In the nursery Francis's cot was smoothed to remove signs of a struggle; Mr Kent's clothes were hidden and burnt the next night in the greenhouse furnace while the two policemen were locked in the kitchen. At the same time the lantern they used, which had also been bloodstained, was destroyed.

Variants of this theory, some of which do not feature Constance at all, were widely circulated both at the time of the murder and for many years afterwards. Most people connected with the case believed that Mr Kent and Gough were somehow involved in the crime and the idea that they were caught out by Francis was the most popular motive for his death. This scenario is plausible and goes some way to explaining Mr Kent and Gough's odd behaviour and their knowledge of the missing blanket the next morning. There are some minor inconsistencies, not least the fact that the cook lit a fire in the boiler at seven o'clock the next morning, which means that the bloodied nightshift was placed there after it had cooled, at around nine o'clock, but the biggest problem is that it entirely excludes Constance from the proceedings and yet she was the only person with an acknowledged and credible motive. The motive ascribed to Mr Kent and his nursemaid is entirely invented, as no evidence has ever been produced of an illicit liaison between them. This is its greatest trouble.

Bridges overcame this by insisting that Constance's motive is not credible and her confession an act of self-sacrifice concocted with her solicitor. However, long before she met with Mr Rodway, Constance gave details of her confession to Miss Gream (who recounted pieces of it at the arraignment) and also set it out in a letter to Sir Eardley Wilmot, written before she left Brighton. If it was devised then it was devised by her alone. Then there is the Sydney Document, which gave much more credence to the motive outlined by Constance in 1865.

Bridges only became aware of the Sydney Document (excerpts of which were published in 1937) after her manuscript had gone to the publishers. This elicited a hasty postscript in which she sought to play down its information and which stated that its author could not have been not Constance Kent or a member of her family, but probably someone who had skilfully knitted together some local gossip into a coherent narrative. In my view this total exclusion of Constance from the crime does not fit the facts and ignores the opinion of people such as Mr Rodway, Mr Stapleton and Inspector Whicher, all of whom suspected her from the outset.

This brings us onto what is probably the most in-depth modern investigation into the Road Hill House murder, undertaken in the late 1970s by Bernard Taylor. He made an exhaustive analysis of the available information and, like those that had gone before him, found the official version of events to be somewhat lacking. He found many of the same inconsistencies in Constance's confession as Rhode and Bridges, with the additional observation that in order to return the razor to her father's case in the wardrobe, she would have had to have passed through Mr and Mrs Kent's bedroom unobserved the day after the murder. Considering that Mrs Kent was confined to this room all day, this would have been difficult. Taylor also believed that the bloodied shift found in the boiler was not connected with the murder and went to some lengths to stress this point.

In his solution to the mystery, Taylor did not seek to sideline Constance, but instead combined her actions with those of Mr Kent and Elizabeth Gough to create a scenario in which the guilt is split three ways.

According to Taylor, the drama started when, on the night of the murder, Mr Kent and Gough stole away to one of the spare rooms in Road Hill House in order to indulge their passion. Meanwhile, Constance crept downstairs with the intention of killing her half-brother; she was surprised to discover that Gough was absent from the nursery but enacted her plan anyway, stifling and partially suffocating Francis using the flannel, which was left stuffed inside his mouth. The child was taken downstairs and, as Constance related in her confession, taken to the privy, where she attempted to push his limp (but perhaps not yet lifeless) body into the cesspool. It got stuck and she had to leave it momentarily, returning with a knife from the kitchen. Using this she attempted to push the body past the privy splashboard, causing the stab wound and injury to the fingers. This failed and she abandoned the body, returning to her room where she cleaned her nightdress of any blood.

Meanwhile Mr Kent and Gough returned from the spare room to find Francis gone. Both assumed that the child had started to cry and that eventually Mrs Kent was forced to come in and get him. The lovers believed that Mrs Kent, having seen that the nurse and her husband were not in their beds, would know what they had been up to. Mr Kent returned to his bedroom expecting to be taken to task by his wife, but he found Mrs Kent asleep and no sign of Francis. He exited the room again and began to search the house and garden for his son: he finally found the body in the privy and suspected Constance to be responsible. To cover up his affair and his daughter's guilt, he staged a murder scene by slitting the boy's throat with a knife and then opening the drawing-room window. He washed himself and buried his bloodstained lantern in a neighbouring field before returning to bed.

In the morning Elizabeth Gough, who still believed the child to have been taken by Mrs Kent, knocked on her employers' bedroom door, fully expecting to be lambasted and sacked for her affair. Instead she discovered that the boy was missing and thereafter that he had been murdered. Thus the two guilty parties were Constance, for committing the murder, and her father, for covering it up. Gough was merely an accomplice whose association with Mr Kent prevented her from telling all she knew about the events of that night.

Taylor's theory is well thought out and can be made to fit the facts well enough. That said, in my opinion it suffers from being unnecessarily complicated and it relies heavily on the assumption that there was an affair between Mr Kent and Gough, that they were together that night and that the injuries to Francis's body were carried out at separate times and by different people. There is no evidence to suggest that this was the case and whenever I read Taylor's version of the crime my feeling is that it is cluttered, necessitating the sustained movement of three individuals backwards and forwards through various parts of the house for several hours, all without detection. It is certainly a possibility, but I personally doubt that this is what occurred that night.

The meticulous and readable account given by Kate Summerscale accepts that Constance was the murderer, although she raises the intriguing possibility that she might have been aided by her brother William, or had at least confided in him afterwards. Summerscale suggests that many of Constance's actions were made in order to protect her brother from suspicion, including her confession which was made a year before William was due to inherit his mother's legacy. Constance's action could thus have removed all hint of gossip and allowed him to progress with his scientific career.

This is certainly possible, but I must confess that I rather fancy that Constance would not have wanted to involve her brother in the deed from the outset, he evidently being of a sensitive nature (he was also very quick to confess to the police during their attempt to run away a few years previously). The Kent family's behaviour suggests that they knew (or strongly suspected) Constance was guilty from the outset and thus, in most respects, it was actually William who, by not co-operating with the police, was protecting his sister.

I accept Constance's explanation to Sir John Wilmot that she was driven to come forward by her renewed religious belief which, perhaps in conjunction with some pressure from the Reverend Arthur Wagner, made her feel the need to make a confession. When one looks at the few statements and letters made by Constance around the time of the confession, they include such phrases as 'I felt as though Hell were in me', '[I] devoted myself body and soul to the Evil Spirit, invoking his aid' and 'I became a demon'; these suggest that the evangelised Constance was viewing her previous actions in a religious context. The next step after admitting one's sins is to confess them and seek forgiveness. As with many aspects of Constance's life, the desire to confess was probably driven by a selfish need connected to her new-found faith and not out of concern for her brother.[66]

So, given such a range of opinion, what actually did happen in the early hours of 29 June 1860? I should perhaps say that I do not know for certain the solution to this mystery and nor does any other living person. Like the Jack the Ripper case and dozens of other controversial historical events, we are too far removed from the scene of the action and possess too little knowledge to be able to say definitively what actually occurred. Of course, this does not stop us from advancing theories on these subjects and what follows is my hypothesis on the Road Hill House murder.

My feeling is that too much emphasis has been placed on some of the minutiae associated with the case and there has been too much reliance on some of the testimonies given at the 'inquiry' organised by Thomas Bush Saunders, many of which repeated village gossip or were unreliable.

When I started to investigate this case properly I took all the published witness testimonies from the various inquiries and used them to create a day-by-day, sometimes minute-by-minute, calendar of events concerning the murder. In doing so it became apparent that many of those testifying held differing memories of the same event. The timings given to individual incidents could be out by an hour or more (in one case it was out by a month); the number and names of witnesses present at a scene varied between testimonies and details of individual conversations changed with time. Such inconsistencies between different eyewitness testimonies are an everyday reality in police investigations (see the work of psychologist Elizabeth Loftus for more details): events happen so fast and emotions run so high that recalling exactly what happened, when and to whom can be difficult. The further away from the event the testimony is taken, the more inaccurate it will generally be. As an example, look at the debacle concerning the bloodied nightshift, where several witnesses recalled the same event in completely different ways. See also the testimony of Mrs Dallimore, whose eagerness to see Gough convicted led her to exaggerate the context of conversations between them. I need hardly mention again the events of Mr Saunders's 'private inquiry,' which served to convert much village gossip into what was assumed afterwards to be fact.

Unreliable or irrelevant evidence is the bugbear of every police investigation and deciding what is pertinent and what is not is problematic. Sometimes by focusing on individual details it is possible to miss the bigger picture, and so my solution has been to try and take a wide look at the proceedings and thereafter find the simplest explanation that best fits the facts. In doing so I believe the events associated with the Road Hill House murder can be separated into two distinct phases. The first of these is the murder itself, which I believe was committed by Constance Kent and by her alone, unaided by anybody else.

The idea that two people were needed to lift the child or that the nursery had to be empty in order to accomplish this feat are, in my opinion, merely assumptions that were made during the early days of the investigation. Despite protests about the weight of Francis Kent and the danger of him or the nursemaid waking, it was evidently possible for a person to creep in and out of the nursery undetected. This is evidenced by the person (assumedly Constance) who crept in and removed the boy's socks while he and the nurse slept soundly. It is certainly possible for an adult to lift a three-year-child, even a large one; Elizabeth Gough accomplished it every day of her life, as did Mrs Kent until her pregnancy intervened. It is not by any means extraordinary to think that Constance could have lifted the boy, wrapped him in his blanket and carried him out of the nursery. Once out of earshot she could do what she wanted to him with little fear of detection.

The idea that the boy was suffocated, intentionally or otherwise, before leaving his cot is based solely upon Mr Parsons's observation of bruising about the mouth, a fact that was not noted at the post-mortem examination and was strongly denied by the other surgeon present. It was also later denied by Parsons himself, who believed he had made an error. This is one of those small pieces of contested evidence on which so much store has been placed. Another is Mrs Kent's testimony that she was awoken by the noise of the shutters being opened and that it was, according to her, 'bright daylight'. This has been taken to mean that she was awoken around quarter to four in the morning, when sunrise occurred, and is used as evidence that Mr Kent was abroad in the house staging the mock break-in at this time. However, immediately after relating this, Mrs Kent testified that her husband was asleep next to her when she heard the noise. No specific time was attached to this event and it is quite conceivable that, as Mrs Kent herself suspected, it was after six o'clock and the noise she heard was the servants opening up the house.

By Constance's own admission, she had been planning this murder for some time and did not wish to be caught by the police. It seems unlikely that having plotted the murder itself, Constance would not have thought of a diversion to throw the police off her trail. The opened window was that diversion and was evidently designed to imply that a stranger had broken into the house. Before taking Francis it was probably Constance that stole downstairs and opened the window; whether she actually exited via the open window or the front door is, frankly, not relevant to the question as to whether or not she was the murderess; it is another minor detail.

Too much has also been made of Constance's insistence that a razor was used to cut the child's throat and inflict the side injury: the idea that it could not rests mostly on Mr Parsons having said that the wounds 'could not have been done by a razor', but this does not mean that (a) he was correct or (b) Constance was not the murderer. A quick look through various anthologies of criminal trials revealed to me several instances where a single razor wound in the throat had either entirely or nearly severed a person's head; and most of these cases concerned adult victims, not children. Take the example of the Welsh farmer Thomas Davies who, in May 1849, nearly severed his child's head with a single razor stroke: it took me only an hour in a London library to find nearly a dozen other examples.[67]

Furthermore, buried deep within the Metropolitan Police archive is a statement from Inspector Williamson recalling an interview with Dr Benjamin Mallam, who independently told the detective that around eighteen months before the murder Constance had asked the gardener how she could take a razor from her father's bedroom without being observed. Based on this, I am inclined to believe that Constance did use her father's razor and that she planned the murder in detail at least several months, if not years, in advance of the actual crime.

Doubtless my belief that there is little value in those little bits of testimony and evidence that others have deemed as being so important (e.g. the lantern; the various lights observed at the house; the dog barking; etc.) will have some people spluttering with indignation. However, if examined closely, the majority of these little incidents were never directly connected to the murder by the police, although many were connected to it by Mr Saunders, who saw conspiracies lurking around every corner. Saunders built his inquiry upon a teetering column of possibilities that had been extracted from contentious details and facts; when one strips out those incidents and events that were never proved to have any connection to the murder (e.g. the lantern), there are actually very few solid facts associated with the case. I remain resolute in my belief that the simplest explanation is the most probable and in this instance that means Constance Kent planned and committed the murder on her own. It is also the theory which best fits the known facts.

Now we must leave what I feel is a fairly certain course of events in order to speculate about what happened after the murder had been committed. This is the second phase of the story and one which is more contentious than the first.

Like other authors, I have looked at Constance Kent's confession and have found it wanting in some respects. I believe that the general outline she gives of the murder fits the established facts quite well, but that she left out much detail concerning what occurred afterwards: this was done in order to protect her family from accusations of collusion.

When examining the evidence associated with the investigation into the Road Hill House murder it is obvious that from the outset there was a great deal of odd behaviour displayed by many members of that household. The oddest person of all was unquestionably Mr Kent, who proved himself to be highly obstructive to the police investigation and to the efforts of the authorities to make inquiries into his son's murder. Aside from not allowing his family to testify at the coroner's inquest, stopping the police from making a plan of the house or interviewing him personally and being generally unavailable, he also maintained that all in his household were innocent and that an intruder must be responsible. He must have been the only person in the country to believe this version of events and it is said that he went to the grave maintaining it. Not once did he ever name a suspect from under his own roof, although some ex-servants and neighbours were implicated by him.

Nor was he the only one. Next on the odd behaviour list is Elizabeth Gough, who seemed permanently on the edge of a nervous breakdown and who, if the hearsay evidence is to be believed, occasionally hinted that she knew more than she had officially let on. The assumption by the police that the murder had to have been carried out by two people and that Gough could not have slept through the kidnap automatically implicated the nurse. In truth, it was Mr Kent they were after and by continually harassing Gough, his assumed accomplice, they hoped that she would implicate him. It is largely on these assumptions that the pair were presumed to be lovers who had been caught in the act by Francis.

The behaviour of Mr Kent and Gough was certainly odd, if not to say suspicious, but in my view this was partly because they had been placed at the centre of the investigation by the police and were, as a consequence, questioned more frequently and subject to a closer scrutiny than the other housemates. In fact, if you broaden the horizon a little then the behaviour of many more of those in Road Hill House starts to appear unusual.

There was Mrs Kent, who was a long time in coming to the witness stand but whose testimony supported her husband and Gough's version of events exactly. The same was true of William Kent and the elder sisters, whose brief, non-descriptive testimonies also offered support to their father, mother and the nursemaid. The only members of the household whose behaviour could be described as approaching normal were the servants: the cook, the housemaid (both of whom lived in the house) and the various gardening and odd-job staff (who lived off-site).

Many have looked at the aftermath of the murder and seen an apparent conspiracy between Mr Kent and Elizabeth Gough who, it is assumed, were anxious to cover up their affair and/or their part in Francis's death. To my mind the conspiracy is wider than this and encompasses the entire Kent family plus Gough, but it was not a sexual encounter on the night of the murder that they were covering up: they were trying to shield a member of their household from natural justice. The family was desperately trying to prevent the police from arresting Constance Kent.

There are many signs that right from the start Mr Kent and the rest of his family were perfectly aware who had committed the crime and that they sought to cover the matter up. Every attempt was made to direct police suspicion away from the residents of Road Hill House and towards others in the neighbourhood. When this tactic was seen to be failing, the family became unco-operative by making themselves unavailable for interview, by refusing access to the property and by employing attorneys to be present whenever the police were in residence.

The Kents' wall of silence was extremely difficult for the police to overcome and its effect was compounded by a number of errors made by Foley and others in the early part of the investigation. These included a willingness to enact suggestions made to them by the family, the casual treatment of physical evidence, the inability to control access to the site and a lack of organisation and discipline amongst the police. Many of these errors came about because the police wished to be sympathetic towards the family, but this provided enough time for the Kents plus Gough to form a united front that time and again confounded the police's best attempts to discover the truth.

But is there any real evidence that the Kent family were aware that Constance was the guilty party from the outset? There is quiet a lot of anecdotal information that supports this idea, including Mr Rodway's assertion that he told Mr Kent outright that his daughter was the guilty person (he apparently had the backing of Mr Stapleton, Mr Parsons and Dr Mallam). Probably the strongest suggestion that Mr Kent knew of his daughter's guilt comes from the period just after Constance's arrest, when Mr Kent hinted to journalists that Constance might be mentally ill. This was perhaps his way of laying the foundations for a plea of criminal insanity which, should she have been tried and found guilty, would have allowed her to avoid the death penalty. Elizabeth Gough also hinted that Constance might be the guilty party when she said to Mrs Dallimore that the missing nightdress would be the key to the mystery. Even Mrs Kent, who held little love for Constance, played along with the plan and, by sticking together, the family achieved their goal. Without the family's co-operation the police were unable to find any one bit of evidence that could link any one individual to the murder scene: it would only have taken one person to crack in order to effect a prosecution, but they never did. Furthermore, as soon as the last examination had been completed, Constance was sent to live in France and was effectively exiled from the family. Even after finishing school in Brittany she did not return home but instead moved to Brighton. Her banishment from the family is again suggestive that her guilt was known to them.

There is also some less certain evidence that the family's desire to shield Constance may have involved more than just keeping quiet about certain events: they may have taken more direct action. There is, for example, the distinct possibility that Mr Kent knew that his son had been murdered before he set off for Trowbridge to fetch a policeman on the morning of 30 June. This assertion rests solely on his contradictory statements concerning the blanket that was found with Francis's body in the privy. When interviewed by the police Mr Kent initially denied knowing that the blanket was missing until after his return from Trowbridge; Superintendent Foley sensed that there was something unusual about the blanket and casually pursued both Mr Kent and Gough on the subject but to no avail. It was not until Mr Slack's inquiry that it was discovered that, while on his way to Trowbridge, Mr Kent had told a woman at a tollbooth that his son and a blanket were missing from the house.

Following the arrest and examination of Elizabeth Gough, Mr Kent was faced with this fact in court; he immediately changed his testimony, explaining that his wife had told him about the blanket being missing before he set off to Trowbridge. Mrs Kent then said that it was Elizabeth Gough who had told her that the blanket had been taken with the boy. Gough, however, had earlier given a sworn statement saying that she did not know the blanket was missing until after the body was found.

It is often stated that both Gough and Mr Kent gave contradictory statements concerning their knowledge of the blanket. In fact, if one looks at the testimonies it was only ever Mr Kent that did so and in order to explain this away he blamed his wife, who then blamed Gough. However, as Gough was never interviewed on the subject (all this emerged during her own inquiry, at which she was not examined), we did not get to hear whether she contradicted herself; the statement that she gave saying she had no knowledge of the blanket until the body was discovered was never altered by her. The closest the police came was a statement by Foley, who said that he thought he had heard Gough say something about a missing blanket to some of his men but, as Mr Ribton makes clear, this was actually never established to have occurred. Once again we are left with Mr Kent at the centre of the confusion with his family and Gough acting to reinforce his version of events.

The incident over the blanket suggests (but does not prove) that Mr Kent knew of the whereabouts of his son's body prior to its formal discovery. There is, however, no proof that Gough or the rest of the household (except Constance) were privy to this information; they may only have learned of Francis's murder after the body's discovery. To my mind it is equally possible that the whole blanket affair is another red herring that became blown out of proportion by Mr Slack, who was desperately searching for something (or indeed anything) that made Gough and Mr Kent appear suspicious. I am, however, certain that the moment Mr Kent became aware of his son's murder (whether it was before or after his trip to Trowbridge), he suspected Constance. It was at this point that Mr and Mrs Kent took the decision to shield Constance, possibly to protect their own reputation, which would have suffered greatly had the tales of abuse, neglect and extra-marital activities ever been repeated in court in defence of their daughter's actions.

In fact, one of the few indiscretions made by Elizabeth Gough was her admission that it was Mrs Kent (not her husband) that had placed pressure on her to keep quiet. This admission came just before she entered court on 14 July and was witnessed by more than one person. 'I would not have held out this long had Mrs Kent not begged me to do so,' said Gough, suggesting that the pressure was not coming from Mr Kent (her supposed lover) but from his wife. It also suggests that she, like her employees, was perfectly aware that Constance was the guilty party.

Despite the probable conspiracy between these three people, I do not think that Mr Kent ever discussed the matter with Constance herself and nor do I think that he acted in collusion with her. The actions he took after the murder appear to have been made on his own and without any particularly detailed knowledge of the crime. I suspect that he locked the two policemen in the kitchen, not to dispose of any particular piece of evidence, but to make his own investigation about the house.

That night would have been the first opportunity that Mr Kent would have had to move about Road Hill House unobserved since the discovery that Francis was missing. Without a detailed knowledge of his daughter's methods he would perhaps have wanted to check that there was nothing incriminating in the house or its grounds. Trapping the policemen was certainly a risk but one that, in the circumstances, was worth taking. Mr Kent was lucky that Superintendent Foley sought first to cover up the matter and, when news of it did emerge, tried to play it down.

The stationing of the police in the house brings us on to probably the most contested piece of evidence of all: Constance's missing nightdress. This item lay at the centre of Inspector Whicher's inquiry and was his main piece of evidence against Constance Kent. With no knowledge of the nightdress's whereabouts, Whicher was left with only an unsupported theory until, several months afterwards, it was revealed that a bloodied shift had been discovered in the boiler-hole and then discarded. Some feel that the bloodied shift is a red herring and that Constance's version of events (that she washed her nightdress then destroyed it a few days later) was correct; others believe that she was lying and that the bloodied shift belonged to her after all.

I must confess that I am in the latter camp. I am not a great believer in coincidence and therefore the fact that the day after an horrific murder the police discovered an item that fits the description of a nightdress (and which, according to the washerwoman, resembled one of Constance's old nightdresses), that was covered in blood, which had been purposefully hidden that morning and which nobody came forward to claim, seems a little incredible to me. It also seems incredible that Mr Parsons, a surgeon, Superintendent Foley and Mrs Dallimore (who held some of the clothes up to the light) could have not noticed that one of Constance's had been recently washed and folded and that it, by her own testimony, still contained visible stains of blood upon it. This does not tally with their statements, which give details of a close search for the smallest spots of blood.

That the murderer had blood on them cannot be in doubt: there was a pool of it on the privy floor and a large smear of blood on the door where the murderer had touched it on exiting. There was also the piece of newspaper which had been used to clean the murder weapon, which was itself bloody. To have had that much blood about and not have got any on the clothing would be a remarkable feat indeed. I believe that Constance planned to use one of her older nightdresses for the crime (the one in the boiler-hole was described as being worn out) in the belief that it would not be missed. It was only after it became evident that the police were making an inventory of clothing that she enacted the plan to steal one back from the laundry basket.

This theory is, however, now impossible to prove thanks to Superintendent Foley's attempts to downplay the significance of the bloodied shift. Because of this we cannot be sure whether the item was a shirt, nightdress or smock; nor can we be sure how much blood was on it or, indeed, of the nature of that blood. We also cannot even say with certainty that it was examined by a surgeon and we certainly do not know what happened to it. The police returned the item to the kitchen on the Monday, but it was not seen by either the cook or housemaid, which suggests that a member of the family took (and probably destroyed) it promptly.

It is my suggestion that rather than risk apportioning blame to the police or another family member, Constance chose to gloss over the bloodied shift when drawing up her confession. After all, in comparison to her admission of having been the murderer, the matter of the nightdress was of far less relevance.

All this is, of course, conjecture, but I shall add one more observation that may have some relevance to this issue. When interviewed independently about the bloodied shift, both Sergeant Watts and Mr Fricker describe (the latter with less certainty) seeing the bloodied shift wrapped up inside newspaper. These two men were present when the item was found and their conduct meant that they had the least to lose from the debacle that followed. If the shift was wrapped in newspaper (and this was never established) then I wonder whether this could in any way be related to the scrap of newspaper that had been used to wipe the murder weapon clean.

It was established that the paper used to clean the weapon had been taken from an edition of *The Times* from 9 June but, other than acknowledging that Mr Kent subscribed to this paper, this did not otherwise feature in the investigation. One recent suggestion is that it was part of a pile of newspapers from within the privy that was used as lavatory paper: I cannot find any reference to this in the investigation notes and it is at odds with the 'laborious search' that the police said they made trying to establish the origin of this scrap of paper. I have often wondered if this small scrap could have been torn from the same newspaper in which the bloodied shift was said to be wrapped. If so then this would, of course, imply that it was the murderer who placed the clothing in the boiler-hole. This is pure conjecture and cannot in any way be proved, but it is an interesting possibility.

This then is my general thesis. To summarise, I believe that Constance planned the crime well in advance, committed the deed unaided and was afterwards shielded by Mr and Mrs Kent who conspired, with Elizabeth Gough, to shield her from justice. In comparison to most theories this is relatively simplistic, but this is far from being an original idea: I believe these are the lines that Inspector Whicher was working along just two weeks after the murder had been committed.

There is one last mystery associated with my version of events: if Constance was guilty and the family knew this, then why did Elizabeth Gough agree to co-operate in the cover up? By obstructing the police investigation she had everything to lose and, indeed, ended up being vilified in public, arrested twice and was forced to abandon her career as a nursemaid and governess to become a dressmaker. The logical thing to do would have been to help the police, all of whom ended up being convinced that she knew more than she was letting on. She did not and for five years was suspected as being Mr Kent's mistress and a murderess: why would she do this?

Again, we can only guess as to her motives, but I think that the intensity of the police investigation may have made her role seem more prominent than was actually the case. The police focused on Gough because they felt she was a weak link and would eventually cave in under pressure; they were, of course, wrong. However, the process of enacting two lengthy enquiries into Gough served to make her seem more important to the murder than was probably the case and to make her actions look more suspicious than they actually were. It must be remembered that the two main bits of 'evidence' used against her were the alleged knowledge of the missing blanket (this actually came about as a consequence of something Mr Kent said, not her) and the chest flannel (which was never proved to be hers or to have been connected with the crime). The other main accusation was that she knew more about the crime than she was letting on: this is probably true and there are some conversations which, if recalled correctly, suggest that this was the case (see Mrs Dallimore's erratic testimony).

Whether she was having an affair with Mr Kent, as many suppose, must remain in doubt. From my reading of the testimony the conspiracy to shield Constance was not driven by Mr Kent and Gough operating together but instead by Mr Kent and his wife. In the aftermath of the murder Mrs Kent appears to be the one working with her husband, refusing to be interviewed for weeks and, when she did consent, backing up her husband's viewpoint entirely. She even gave him an alibi that got him out of trouble over the missing blanket, placing the blame on Gough instead. Mr Kent mentions a number of occasions in which he took his wife into his confidence (e.g. the presence of the police in the house); in contrast Gough appears to have had relatively little contact with Mr Kent. She did, however, have a great deal of contact with Mrs Kent, whom she admitted meeting and talking to regularly.

One can suppose that rather than covering up evidence of an affair, Mr and Mrs Kent were trying to keep any mention of their past family life coming to light, especially the allegedly abusive relationship between Mrs Kent and her stepchildren. To give up Constance to the courts would be to risk her detailing the cause of her hatred towards the child. Like the other members of the family, Gough may have been asked to tell the police that an intruder was responsible and to keep quiet about any mention of tension between Mrs Kent and the children. Again, why she should have chosen to co-operate is a mystery, but once involved in the conspiracy, it would have been very difficult to get out without attracting a charge of complicity or perjury against herself. This may just have been the reason that she did not crack under questioning; after all, if her case had gone to trial then she still had the option of telling the truth. It cannot be doubted that in agreeing to help out the Kent family, Elizabeth Gough destroyed her future employment prospects, although the notion that the boy was taken while she slept may well have put an end to her career anyway. These are my thoughts on what is surely one of the most perplexing cases of murder ever to occur in Victorian England and one which, to my mind at least, can be described as a closed case.

The final word should perhaps go to Road Hill House itself, which was afterwards renamed Langham House in an attempt to disguise its terrible history. The property has changed hands many times since the Kents' departure, but the family may have left subsequent residents a spooky legacy. Local tradition says that, on moving into the house, each new occupant will hear the distinct and piteous sound of a baby crying, the source of which could never be found. The implication, of course, is that this is the ghostly wail of young Francis Kent, acting out the last moments of his short life, even though he probably did not die inside the house but in the outside privy, which has long since been removed.

There is a recent substantiation of this tale when, during the early 1990s, the author Stewart Evans interviewed Cynthia Yates, the then owner of Langham House. Mrs Yates confirmed that she and her husband had on one occasion been woken by the noise of a baby crying and that her son and cleaning lady had heard it also. She further commented that each person would hear the crying just once, after which the house would return to silence, its living occupants having been made all too aware of the terrible events of June 1860.

When I began researching and writing this book I believed the Road Hill House murder to be unique and that the strange circumstances and events that it constituted could never be repeated. It turns out that I was wrong.

In front of me as I write I have an article from *The Economist*, which informs me that: 'There is not much that fascinates the great British public more than a juicy "whodunit", especially where the victim is a beautiful child.'

These words could have been written in 1860 about the murder of Francis Kent, but they were in fact penned in September 2007 and concern three-year-old Madeleine McCann, who vanished from a holiday apartment in Portugal earlier in the year, on 3 May. The McCann case concerns the disappearance of a sleeping three-year-old child from an occupied bedroom in a crowded holiday complex. Like the Road Hill House mystery, there was near hysterical press coverage and a controversial police investigation which saw the introduction of a number of contradictory suspects that, for a time, included the girl's parents. At the time of writing the McCann case remains unresolved and it is commonly described as being unique in the annals of criminal history. This is wrong, for although the Road Hill House mystery has little to say on a possible solution to the McCann case, the frenzied events that took place in Portugal in 2007 mimic those which were seen in a quiet English village a century and a half previously.

BIBLIOGRAPHY

This is a limited bibliography of the main books consulted as part of the background reading and research undertaken for this book. Most of the specific information, such as descriptions and dialogue, came from reports given in contemporary newspapers and journals: the sources of these are listed in the next section.

Bridges, Y. *Saint – With Red hands?* London: Arrow, 1958.

Critall, E. 'North Bradley' in *A History of the County of Wiltshire*. Oxford: Oxford University Press, 1965. Vol. 8, pp 218–34.

Davies, J. *The Case of Constance E. Kent, Viewed in the Light of the Holy Catholic Church.* London: J. Masters, 1865.

Griffiths, A. *Secrets of the Prison-house: or, Gaol Studies and Sketches.* London: Chapman & Hall, 1894.

Harrison, A. J. *The Savant of Australian Seas.* Hobart: Uniprint, for the Tasmanian Historical Research Association, 1997.

Hurley, J. *Wiltshire Policemen: 1839–1870.* Devizes: Wiltshire Family History Society, 1997.

Parkinson, J. C. *Under Government.* London: Bell & Daldy, 1859.

Rhode, J. *The Case of Constance Kent.* London: Geoffrey Bles, 1928.

Simpson, H. *The Anatomy of Murder.* London: Macmillan, 1937.

Stapleton, J. W. *The Great Crime of 1860.* London: Marlborough & Co., 1861.

Summerscale, K. *The Suspicions of Mr Whicher.* London: Bloomsbury, 2008.

Taylor, B. *Cruelly Murdered: Constance Kent and the Killing at Road Hill House.* London: Souvenir Press, 1979.

Walford, E. *The Handybook of the Civil Service.* London: Longman, Green, Longman & Roberts, 1860.

NOTES AND SOURCES

The majority of the events in this book (including the quoted dialogue) were portrayed using descriptions from the many hours of eyewitness testimony that were given at the various inquiries, examinations and court cases connected to the murder. By cross-referencing the information within these testimonies it has been possible for me to build up a detailed chronology of the entire Road Hill House murder and its subsequent investigation by the police and others.

To avoid repeating any errors that may have been made by individual court reporters or typesetters, I used transcripts of the testimonies as provided in two different newspapers: one of these was *The Times* (London) and the other was the *Daily Post* (Bristol). The transcripts in both papers match well, but there are occasions when, for whatever reason, one or the other would omit certain speeches or minor details (assumedly for reasons of space, but it appears that individual reporters also missed bits of information). Those wishing to follow my research will find that the majority of *Daily Post* testimonies are reproduced in Stapleton's *The Great Crime of 1860*; this book was difficult to obtain (my copy was sourced in Canada and cost a fortune to buy) until very recently, when a version of it became available to download through Google's Book Search website. Because of this, wherever possible I have given a page number in *The Great Crime* for any cited references from the *Daily Post*.

Background information on the people and places mentioned in the book was generally obtained from newspaper reports, from the 1861 National Census data held at The National Archives: Public Record Office or from various professional or local directories. Information concerning the Metropolitan Police's investigation and the Home Office may be found in the The National Archives: Public Record Office (specifically MEPO 3/61 and HO 144/20.49113), as can references to the impact the case had on Mr Kent's career prospects (HO 45/6970). All other information was obtained from a range of additional sources, including various books, journals, genealogical materials, etc; these sources are listed in the notes below.

Other versions of this story may be found in the books of John Rhode, Yseult Bridges, Bernard Taylor and, most recently, Kate Summerscale. I purposefully did not read their accounts of the Road Hill House murder until after I had completed the first draft of my manuscript, as I wished to come to my own conclusions. Their views regarding the case are summarised in the Epilogue.

Abbreviations used:

Great Crime = Stapleton, J.W. *The Great Crime of 1860*. London: Marlborough & Co., 1861.

TNA: PRO = The National Archives: Public Record Office, Kew, Surrey.

1. Quote comes from the *Morning Post*, 11 July 1860.
2. Dialogue, events and descriptions: *The Times*, 28 July 1860; 2, 3 October 1860; 7 November 1860. *Great Crime*, pp 127–129, 170–75. Additional information: census data, *A History of the County of Wiltshire*. Oxford: Oxford University Press, 1965. Vol. 8, pp 218–34. Road village has since changed its spelling to Rode. For the sake of authenticity I have stuck with the original Victorian name.
3. Ann Hall: TNA: PRO RG9/1300, fo. 52; p. 13. *The Times*, 9 November 1860; *Great Crime*, pp 272–73. Ann Heritage: TNA: PRO RG9/1300 fo. 39; p. 16. *The Times*, 9 November 1860; *Great Crime*, pp 273–74; Going to Trowbridge: *The Times*, 2 October 1860; *Great Crime*, pp 148–49, 272–74.
4. Sarah Cox: *Great Crime*, p. 121; *The Times*, 28 July 1860. Urch and Morgan: *Great Crime*, pp 170–72. Both Urch and Morgan have taken credit for some of the questions put to Gough.
5. Edward West: PRO: TNA RG9/1300 fo. 60, p. 6. Newspaper: *The Times*, 7 November 1860; *Great Crime*, pp 105, 254–55. Joshua Parsons: *The Times*, 4 October 1860; *Great Crime*, p. 186; George Sylvester: TNA: PRO RG9/1296; fo. 56, p. 14. Gough and Mrs Kent: *The Times*, 2 October 1860; *Great Crime*, pp 144–45, 154–58.
6. John Foley: *Great Crime*, pp 176–77. Henry Heritage: *The Times*, 9 November 1860. Details of privy: *The Times*, 26 July 1860.
7. Rodway: *Morning Post*, 10 November 1860; *Great Crime*, pp 71–72; *The Times*, 2 October 1860. Foley's actions and opinions: *The Times*, 3 October 1860; *Great Crime*, pp 67–75.
8. Fricker: *The Times*, 5 November 1860; *Great Crime*, pp 225–26; TNA: PRO RG9/1300, fo. 63, p. 11. Details of privy: *The Times*, 26 July 1860. Conversation with Gough: *The Times* 4, 5 October 1860, 5 November 1860; *Great Crime*, pp 72–74, 194. N.B.: In the light of a later discovery (detailed further on in the book), the police cast doubt on Stapleton, claiming that he had not examined this particular nightdress but another one. Stapleton, however, remained adamant that he looked at only one nightdress that day and that it belonged to the elder Kent sister.
9. Mr Kent's interview: *Great Crime*, pp. 72–74; Other quotes: *The Times*, 2 October 1860.
10. Parsons and Stapleton: TNA: PRO RG9/1656, fo. 42, p. 11; RG9/1296 fo. 35, p. 19. *Provincial Medical Directory*, pp 213, 261. Both surgeons were the same age and appear to have gone through medical training together. To judge by his letters to various journals, Stapleton probably believed himself to be a superior surgeon to Parsons. Autopsy details: *Great Crime*, pp 58–65; *The Times*, 4 October 1860.
11. Nightdress: *Great Crime*, p. 106. This nightdress was the subject of great confusion later in the case; there are several different versions as to which nightdress this was and who examined it; I have chosen to follow Stapleton's version of events, which is the most consistent and best fits the sequence of events. Secret orders: *The Times*, 10 November 1860; *Great Crime*, p. 279.
12. Locked in: *The Times*, 2, 3, 18 October, 10 November 1860.
13. Rowland Rodway: TNA: PRO RG9/1300 fo. 5, p. 3. Jury selection: *The Times*, 5, 7 November 1860; *Great Crime*, pp 226, 262–63. Holding the coroner's inquest just three days after Francis's death might have appeared rather hasty, but it was not that unusual. Whenever a suspicious death occurs a coroner's inquest must be held at the earliest possible opportunity to determine the cause of death. Furthermore, the body cannot be released for burial until after an inquest has been opened.

14. Kent family history: *Great Crime*, pp 1–34; TNA: PRO HO 45/6970; MEPO 3/61.
Factory Inspector: Walford, E. *The Handybook of the Civil Service*. London: Longman,
Green, Longman & Roberts, 1860. p. 164; Parkinson, J. C. *Under Government*. London:
Bell & Daldy, 1859. pp. 86–87; TNA: PRO HO 45/6970. Birth: Whites Row Independent
church, Spitalfields; born 7 July 1800; baptised 28 July 1800. Details on the Kent carpet
business, see *The Proceedings of the Old Bailey*: t18050220–40 and t18150510–23. Additional
information from the national census returns for 1841, 1851 and 1861, GRO registers, local
trade directories and the International Genealogical Index. Thomas Windus's will: TNA:
PRO PROB 11/2205. It is said that Constance and William's attempt at running away
inspired Charles Dickens to start writing *Edwin Drood* in 1870, a work that he did not
finish (Dickens is known to have taken a close interest in the Road Hill House murder
and to have corresponded with others about the matter).

15. Meredith's tour: *The Times*, 3 October 1860; *Great Crime*, p. 96. Laundry: *The Times*, 28 July
1860; 6 November 1860; *Great Crime*, p. 241.

16. Coroner's Inquest transcript: *Daily Post*, 4 July 1860; *Great Crime*, pp 65, 121–24.
Disgruntled jury: *The Times*, 5, 7 November 1860, 1 February 1861; *Great Crime*,
pp 122–24, 342–55; *Trowbridge Advertiser*, 1 December 1860. Rodway and Mr Kent:
TNA: PRO MEPO 3/61; *Morning Post*, 10 November 1860; *Great Crime*, pp 329–41.

17. *The Times*, 28 July 1860; 2 October 1860.

18. Heritage searches: *The Times*, 5 November 1860. The nightdress: *The Times*, 28 July 1860;
2 October 1860; *Great Crime*, pp 109–11, 132–35, 158–60.

19. Funeral: TNA: PRO MEPO 3/61. Magistrates and Foley: *The Times*, 12, 14 July,
4, 5 October 1860; 10 November 1860; *Great Crime*, pp 146, 195, 280; TNA: PRO
MEPO 3/61. Foley's reasoning, see Mrs Dallimore's testimony in *The Times*, 4 October.

20. Gough's examination: *The Times*, 4, 5 October 1860; *Great Crime*, pp 201, 203–05. Gough's
outburst: *The Times*, 5 October 1860. As we shall see later on, although there is little doubt
that this conversation between Mrs Dallimore and Gough took place, there was later
some debate over the exact wording and circumstances.

21. The examination: *The Times*, 12, 14 July 1860; *News of the World*, 15 July 1860.

22. *Morning Post*, 11 July 1860. Home Office correspondence: TNA: PRO HO 144/20/49113.

23. Gough's questioning and outburst: *The Times*, 5 November 1860; *Great Crime*, p. 227. Foley
and the magistrates: TNA: PRO MEPO 3/63.

24. Inspector Whicher: background information came from numerous articles in *The Times*
archive, TNA: PRO MEPO 4/333; 3/63; HO 144/20/49113; *Great Crime*, pp 280–85.
A fuller biography may be found in Summerscale, K. *The Suspicions of Mr Whicher*.
London: Bloomsbury, 2008. pp 43–57.

25. Whicher: *The Times*, 21 July 1860. TNA: PRO MEPO 3/61.

26. Emma Sparks: *Great Crime*, p. 114; TNA: PRO MEPO 3/61. Emma Moody: *The Times*,
28 July 1860; *Great Crime*, pp 129–30; TNA: PRO MEPO 3/61.

27. Constance and the Smith case: TNA: PRO MEPO 3/61.

28. Constance's interview: TNA: PRO MEPO 3/61. The mention of the dog probably relates to
Urch's having reportedly heard the dog barking on the night of the murder. The questions
about the matches may relate to Whicher's theory that Constance burnt her nightdress and/or
Urch's report of seeing a light at Road Hill House at around the time of Francis's murder.

29. Constance's arrest: *The Times*, 21 July 1860.

30. *The Times*, 28 July 1860; TNA: PRO MEPO 3/61. Unfortunately, whatever information
Mrs Bailey gave Inspector Whicher has not been recorded, but the available evidence
implies that Emma was able to identify the bloodied chest flannel as having belonged to
Constance (see Emma's testimony mentioned later).

31. The hearing: *The Times*, 28 July 1860; *Great Crime*, pp 125–36. Additional material from TNA: PRO MEPO 3/61.

32. Newspapers: see, for example, *The Times*, 30 July 1860; *Morning Post*, 30 July 1860; *Annual Register*, 1860, p. 101. Letter and Mayne: TNA: PRO 3/61.

33. *The Times*, 3, 4 October 1860; *Great Crime*, pp 179–81, 190, 197.

34. Gough and Mr Kent: *The Times*, 3 October 1860; *Great Crime*, p. 181.

35. Flannel: *The Times*, 4 October 1860; *Great Crime*, pp 194–96. Mrs Dallimore initially claimed that the chest flannel had been tried on Gough and the servants on 9 July, but later corrected this to 9 August.

36. John Gagg: *The Times*, 13, 14 August 1860.

37. *The Times*, 3 October 1860; TNA: PRO MEPO 3/61.

38. Letters: *The Times*, 9 August 1860; at least one person took the idea of sleep-walking seriously: the author Wilkie Collins incorporated drug-induced somnambulism into *The Moonstone*, a book based on the events of the Road Hill House murder. William Nutt: TNA: PRO MEPO 3/61.

39. Home Office correspondence: TNA: PRO HO 144/20/49113; *The Times*, 4, 8, 11, 19 September 1860; 18 October 1860; 5 November 1860. Foley and Gough: TNA: PRO MEPO 3/61.

40. *The Times*, 19, 24 September 160; *Great Crime*, pp 249–53; TNA: PRO MEPO 3/61; TNA: PRO HO 144/20/49113.

41. TNA: PRO MEPO 3/61; TNA: PRO HO 144/20/49113; *The Times*, 1, 2 October 1860; *Great Crime*, p. 138.

42. *The Times*, 1, 2 October 1860; *Great Crime*, p. 138.

43. *The Times*, 2 October 1860; *Great Crime*, pp 137–60.

44. All details from: *Great Crime*, pp 137–60; *The Times*, 2 October 1860; *Daily Post*, 2 October 1860.

45. All proceedings from: *Great Crime*, pp 161–81; *The Times*, 3 October 1860; *Daily Post*, 3 October 1860.

46. All proceedings from: *The Times*, 4 October 1860; *Great Crime*, pp. 181–99; *Daily Post*, 4 October 1860.

47. All proceedings from: *Great Crime*, pp 200–22; *The Times*, 5 October 1860; *Daily Post*, 5 October 1860.

48 *Morning Post*, 6 October 1860; *The Times*, 10 October 1860; Blanket testimonies: *Great Crime*: pp 154 (Mr Kent), 156 (Mrs Kent), 169 (Constance Kent), 172 (Urch), 176, 177 (Foley), 181 (Wolfe), 198 (Gough's oath), 217–18 (Ribton); *The Times*, 22 October 1860.

49. *The Times*, 18, 20 October 1860.

50. *The Times*, 5 October 1860. N.B. Unusually, *The Times* report for this day is superior to that of the Bristol *Daily Post*, which suggests that the latter may not have got a reporter there in time.

51. *Daily Post*, 6 November 1860; *The Times*, 6 November 1860.

52. *The Times*, 7, 8, 9 November 1860; *Daily Post*, 7, 8, 9 November 1860; *Great Crime*, pp 245–78.

53. *Daily Post*, 10 November 1860; *Great Crime*, pp 278–82.

54. *Great Crime*, pp 282–84, 289–90, 292–93, *The Times*, 13 November 1860; *Morning Post*, 12 November 1860. N.B.: Separate to Foley's actions was another, more mysterious figure known as Ignatius Pollaky, whose presence at Mr Saunders's inquiry was noted by many reporters. Pollaky, who spoke with a strong Hungarian accent, was a silent figure who each day would take his place in the public gallery and solemnly make notes about Mr Saunders's conduct. He had also been seen speaking to people who were associated with the inquiry, but especially those whom Saunders claimed were supporting his efforts,

including members of the Bath and Bristol police and various magistrates. Pollaky was working for the London Detective Force, a private investigation company set up a former member of the Metropolitan Police, Inspector Charles Field. The implication was that somebody was making a private investigation into Mr Saunders, a notion that he found greatly disturbing. On a number of occasions he and Inspector Pitney attempted to speak with the mysterious Mr Pollaky, but they was never able find him in his lodgings and so his true purpose for visiting Road was (and remains) an enigma.

55. *Great Crime*, pp 286–88, 291–98, 304–17; *The Times*, 13 November 1860.

56. *Great Crime*, pp 289–02, 304–17; *Daily Post*, 15, 29 November 1860.

57. *Great Crime*, pp 317–28; *The Times*, 13, 26 November 1860; 1 December 1860; TNA: PRO HO 45/6970.

58. *Great Crime*, pp 329–79; *The Times*, 1 February 1861; Harrison, A. J. *The Savant of Australian Seas*. Hobart: Uniprint, for the Tasmanian Historical Research Association, 1997; TNA: PRO HO 45/6970.

59. Constance at the convent: a letter to John Wilmot reproduced in Summerscale, K. *The Suspicions of Mr Whicher*. London: Bloomsbury, 2008. pp 254–55. Other sources: *Annual Register*, 1865, pp 47–52; *The Bulwark or Reformational Journal*, 1 June 1865, pp 328–31; *Daily Telegraph*, 26 April 1860; TNA: PRO MEPO 3/61.

60. *The Times*, 6 May 1865; *Daily Telegraph*, 6 May 1865; *The Morning Advertiser*, 6 May 1865; TNA: PRO HO 144/20/49113; MEPO 3/61.

61. TNA: PRO HO 144/20/49113; MEPO 3/61; *The Morning Star*, 22 July 1865.

62. Trial details: *Morning Herald*, 21, 22 July 1860; *Daily Telegraph*, 21, 22 July 1865; *The Times*, 21, 22 July 1865; *The Morning Star*, 22 July 1865; Taylor, B. *Cruelly Murdered: Constance Kent and the Killing at Road Hill House*. London: Souvenir Press, 1979. pp 293–300; TNA: PRO HO 144/20/49113.

63. *Annual Register*, 1865, pp 229–31; *The Times*, 30 August 1865; *The Bulwark or Reformational Journal*, 1 June 1865, pp 328–31; TNA: PRO MEPO 3/61; HO 144/20/49113; Summerscale, K. *The Suspicions of Mr Whicher*. London: Bloomsbury, 2008. pp 254–55.

64. Griffiths, A. *Secrets of the Prison-house: or, Gaol Studies and Sketches*. London: Chapman & Hall, 1894. pp 10–11; Harrison, A. J. *The Savant of Australian Seas*. Hobart: Uniprint, for the Tasmanian Historical Research Association, 1997; TNA: PRO MEPO 3/61; HO 144/20/49113; Bridges, Y. *Saint – With Red Hands?* London: Arrow, 1958.

65. Griffiths, A. *Secrets of the Prison-house: or, Gaol Studies and Sketches*. London: Chapman & Hall, 1894. pp 10–11; Harrison, A. J. *The Savant of Australian Seas*. Hobart: Uniprint, for the Tasmanian Historical Research Association, 1997. Taylor, B. *Cruelly Murdered: Constance Kent and the Killing at Road Hill House*. London: Souvenir Press, 1979. pp 354–69; Rhode, J. *The Case of Constance Kent*. London: Geoffrey Bles, 1928; Simpson, H. *The Anatomy of Murder*. London: Macmillan, 1937; *Sunday Sun & Guardian*, 6 February 1944. The majority of the information concerning Constance Kent's later life in Australia was taken from Taylor, pp 355–69.

66. Confession to John Wilmot: see Summerscale, K. *The Suspicions of Mr Whicher*. London: Bloomsbury, 2008. pp 254–55.

67. For further examples see *Celebrated Trials and Remarkable Cases of Criminal Jurisprudence*. London: Knight & Lacey, 1825 (e.g. vol. 6, p. 470) and many editions of the *Annual Register*, which contain reports of murder. From these two sources alone I was able to find eleven cases where a razor had gone clean through the windpipe, muscles and arteries, leaving the head attached only by a thread of muscle and bone at the neck.

INDEX